MW00397227

Lorain Public Library System
351 W Sixth St
Lorain OH 44052

Honey

by C. Marina Marchese and
Howland Blackiston

for
dummies®
A Wiley Brand

Honey For Dummies®

Published by: **John Wiley & Sons, Inc.,** 111 River Street, Hoboken, NJ 07030-5774, www.wiley.com

Copyright © 2021 by John Wiley & Sons, Inc., Hoboken, New Jersey

Published simultaneously in Canada

No part of this publication may be reproduced, stored in a retrieval system or transmitted in any form or by any means, electronic, mechanical, photocopying, recording, scanning or otherwise, except as permitted under Sections 107 or 108 of the 1976 United States Copyright Act, without the prior written permission of the Publisher. Requests to the Publisher for permission should be addressed to the Permissions Department, John Wiley & Sons, Inc., 111 River Street, Hoboken, NJ 07030, (201) 748-6011, fax (201) 748-6008, or online at http://www.wiley.com/go/permissions.

Trademarks: Wiley, For Dummies, the Dummies Man logo, Dummies.com, Making Everything Easier, and related trade dress are trademarks or registered trademarks of John Wiley & Sons, Inc., and may not be used without written permission. All other trademarks are the property of their respective owners. John Wiley & Sons, Inc., is not associated with any product or vendor mentioned in this book.

LIMIT OF LIABILITY/DISCLAIMER OF WARRANTY: WHILE THE PUBLISHER AND AUTHOR HAVE USED THEIR BEST EFFORTS IN PREPARING THIS BOOK, THEY MAKE NO REPRESENTATIONS OR WARRANTIES WITH RESPECT TO THE ACCURACY OR COMPLETENESS OF THE CONTENTS OF THIS BOOK AND SPECIFICALLY DISCLAIM ANY IMPLIED WARRANTIES OF MERCHANTABILITY OR FITNESS FOR A PARTICULAR PURPOSE. NO WARRANTY MAY BE CREATED OR EXTENDED BY SALES REPRESENTATIVES OR WRITTEN SALES MATERIALS. THE ADVICE AND STRATEGIES CONTAINED HEREIN MAY NOT BE SUITABLE FOR YOUR SITUATION. YOU SHOULD CONSULT WITH A PROFESSIONAL WHERE APPROPRIATE. NEITHER THE PUBLISHER NOR THE AUTHOR SHALL BE LIABLE FOR DAMAGES ARISING HEREFROM.

For general information on our other products and services, please contact our Customer Care Department within the U.S. at 877-762-2974, outside the U.S. at 317-572-3993, or fax 317-572-4002. For technical support, please visit https://hub.wiley.com/community/support/dummies.

Wiley publishes in a variety of print and electronic formats and by print-on-demand. Some material included with standard print versions of this book may not be included in e-books or in print-on-demand. If this book refers to media such as a CD or DVD that is not included in the version you purchased, you may download this material at http://booksupport.wiley.com. For more information about Wiley products, visit www.wiley.com.

Library of Congress Control Number: 2021932806

ISBN 978-1-119-78093-9 (pbk); ISBN 978-1-119-78094-6 (ebk); ISBN 978-1-119-78095-3 (ebk)

Manufactured in the United States of America

SKY10025520_031221

Contents at a Glance

Recipes at a Glance

Table of Contents

Introduction

This is a handbook for serious honey lovers. After all, who doesn't love honey? If you don't, perhaps you haven't tasted the real thing! It's been treasured, coveted, idolized, and even revered by all of the world's major religions. It was hunted by primeval humans and was regarded as the food of Greek gods. Honey was so treasured by the early Romans, it was used to pay taxes. Through the ages honey has been the choice for ensuring good health, healing, and fertility. And honey has always been regarded as a natural, healthy ingredient for cooking, baking, beverages, and food accompaniments.

In recent years, honey has taken on even greater notice, with the ever-growing interest in beekeeping and the endless flavor profiles of each harvest, healthy eating, and the surge in social media and internet solely dedicated to epicurean delights. Today, honey has truly reached a celebrity food status, featured prominently on the menus of the world's finest restaurants. In fact, honey is becoming acknowledged with the same reverence offered to wine, coffee, cheese, and olive oil.

About This Book

This book is a reference, not a lecture. You certainly don't have to read it from beginning to end unless you want to. We organized the chapters in a logical fashion, each clustered under one of the book's seven different parts. We included lots of great photographs and illustrations (we hope each is worth a thousand words) and lots of practical information, advice, instructions, and suggestions.

Just take a look at the sorts of things we've included. This book

>> Travels back 10,000 years to share highlights of the role honey has played in cultures, religions, literature, and folklore

>> Explains why and how bees make honey and how it's harvested by honey gatherers and beekeepers

>> Provides a listing of 50 different honey varietals from around the world, along with their botanical sources, regions produced, color, aroma, flavor, terroir, suggested food pairings, and interesting notes

>> Describes honey's role as a natural source of good health, providing nutritional facts and sharing information about honey's use in apitherapy as a healing agent

>> Includes recipes for honey-inspired remedies in the form of soaps, lotions, salves, exfoliates, elixirs, and beauty baths

>> Helps you shop for honey by understanding the best places to buy, how to read and understand honey labels, and how to avoid honeys that may not be all that they claim

>> Teaches you how to become a "honey sommelier" by understanding the skills for properly tasting, evaluating, and describing a honey's sensory characteristics by using a subtle honey-centric vocabulary

>> Introduces the role "terroir" plays in determining the unique characteristics and flavors of honeys

>> Recognizes potential and avoidable defects in honey that are often the result of a beekeeper's poor management practices

>> Includes more than 50 delicious and tested recipes using honey in baking, cooking, cocktails and mocktails, and brewing honey wine (mead)

>> Celebrates honey with some fun ideas for hosting a honey tasting party

We also include some back-of-book materials, including helpful honey-related resources: websites, honey suppliers, where to buy rare and hard-to-find honeys, schools that certify professional honey sensory experts, and a list of great honey festivals worth attending. We've created a glossary of honey terms that you can use as a handy quick reference and some useful templates for tasting notes and other honey-related logs.

Note: You may have noticed that two authors are listed on the cover. And yet in all of the pages that follow this introduction, the text is written in first person. A lot of what we've written is anecdotal, opinionated, and based on lots of personal experience. So writing in a singular voice is much easier and less cumbersome than attributing each individually to Marina or Howland. And after all, we totally agree with each other on everything. Mostly.

Foolish Assumptions

We assume there must be something about you that's eager to know more about nature's most glorious food: honey.

Whether you're already quite knowledgeable about honey, or have just occasionally had honey on a slice of toast, we guarantee you will discover all sorts of new information. And it's likely all readers will be inspired to try out more of the many hundreds of varietals of honey available to consumers. After all, honey is much more than clover and orange blossom.

For beekeepers, this book has lots of betcha-didn't-know information about the treasured liquid gold that your bees produce. You will appreciate more than ever just how amazing and wonderful honey is. You will learn how to produce a better product and market it more effectively, through better beekeeping practices and effectively educating your customers about honey.

For consumers, chefs, cooks and foodies, this book will help you make informed choices about selecting and purchasing honey. You will understand the differences between a great honey and the ones to avoid. You will find out which honey varieties pair best with which foods. The book includes over 45 honey-inspired recipes for baking, cooking, and blending or brewing beverages with honey.

And for those with a yearning to become a honey sensory expert (honey sommelier), this book shows you the exact methods and detailed instructions for how to taste and evaluate honeys like a certified honey sensory professional.

Whichever of these categories you fit in, you'll appreciate the way the book has been organized for easy and ongoing reference. In short, this book is for just about anyone who's a fan of nature's most celebrated all-natural food: honey.

Icons Used in This Book

Peppered throughout this book are helpful icons that present special types of information to enhance your reading experience and make you a stellar beekeeper.

Think of these tips as words of wisdom that — when applied — will make your honey experience sweet!

WARNING

These warnings alert you to potential missteps that may make your experiences unpleasant and/or downright disappointing. Take them to heart!

REMEMBER

We use this icon to point out things that need to be so ingrained in your consciousness that they become habits. Keep these points at the forefront of your honey knowledge and experience.

Beyond the Book

Much more information is available from your authors, and from the *For Dummies* brand, for your learning pleasure. "Bee" sure to check out the online Cheat Sheet, which contains handy tools you can use as you fine-tune your honey tasting skills.

To access this Cheat Sheet, simply go to www.dummies.com and enter "Honey For Dummies Cheat Sheet" in the Search box.

Where to Go from Here

You can start anywhere with *For Dummies* books, but there's a logic to beginning at the beginning. However, if that's not in your personality, no problem. Consider starting with Chapter 17 and try one of the refreshing honey-infused cocktail or mocktail recipes. Then, while you're sipping, move over to Chapter 1 and read some historical information about honey's role in different cultures over the past 10,000 years. There's lots of trivia here that's sure to make you a honey superstar at your next party.

If you are keen on knowing how to professionally taste and evaluate honey, check out Chapter 9 to find out (scientifically) how your tasting apparatus actually works. Then try the tasting exercises to tune up your taste buds. Going on to Chapter 10, you can follow the same step-by-step methodologies used by certified honey sensory experts to taste, evaluate, identify, and describe different honeys' characteristics and flavors. And now that you are becoming a tasting guru, hop back to Chapter 7. It profiles 50 of the world's most famous varieties of honey. You can find detailed information, tasting notes, and food pairing suggestions for each of the honeys listed. We promise you'll appreciate honey as you never have before.

Hungry? Why not jump to Chapters 15 and 16 to savor different honey recipes for cooking and baking. Many of these recipes were provided by renowned executive chefs. Chapter 14 has recipes for making honey wine (mead). Waasail!

Or if you just want to have some yum fun, Chapter 19 is all about how to plan and host a honey tasting party. There are ideas for the invitation, the menu, and how to set up honey games, music, contests, and of course, the main event — honey tasting. Please don't forget to invite us authors!

Our advice is to not hurry through this book. There's a ton of information here, and all of it will help you appreciate, better understand, and find new ways to use and enjoy honey. So, whether you just want to discover how to cook with honey or you're planning to become certified as a honey sensory expert (sommelier), there's an abundance of sweet stuff here just for you.

And, although this book includes some info about bees and how and why they make honey, if you want to know more about honey bees and the art of beekeeping, check out *Beekeeping For Dummies*, by Howland Blackiston (Wiley), and *Honeybee, Lessons From an Accidental Beekeeper*, by C. Marina Marchese (Black Dog & Leventhal).

1

Honey, Give Me the Lowdown

IN THIS PART . . .

Journey back to the dawn of time and through the ages and discover how honey has been an influential contributor to our culture, spiritual beliefs, folklore, and culinary enjoyment.

Understand how and why honey bees make honey, as well as some other interesting facts about bees.

Gain knowledge about what's in honey and why it's considered such a beneficial and healthy food.

Find out how honey is harvested from the bees.

Get acquainted with the four basic styles of honey.

Chapter **1**

Dipping into Honey's History and Its Importance Today

The history of honey predates record keeping. But there are clues and documents that validate the significant role this remarkable and treasured food has played since the early days of life on earth. Honey is a celebrated food that has filled entire books. In this chapter I'll share some betcha-didn't-know information about honey's role throughout history. The information is sure to make you a trivia celebrity at your next party.

Introducing Discoscapa apicula — the World's Oldest Bee?

It may not be a catchy name, but *Discoscapa apicula* is the binominal nomenclature, or commonly, the genus and species, of one of the oldest known species of bees. A rare specimen of this bee was preserved in Burmese amber that was found in what is now Myanmar (Southeast Asia). This bee, shown in Figure 1-1, is believed to date from the Cretaceous period, which was about 100 million years ago. To put that timeline in perspective, this bee was buzzing around during the same period that T-Rex was hunting for prey. *Discoscapa apicula* certainly shows some resemblance to the modern honey bee. Pollen grains were found on its legs that showed the bee had recently visited one or more flowers before becoming stuck inside a drop of resin and preserved for millions of years. You've got to wonder whether this bee also collected nectar and made honey? Maybe?

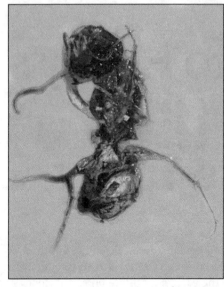

FIGURE 1-1: This little bee (entombed forever in amber) shared the earth with T-Rex, making it around 100 million years old. It's the oldest known species of bee.

Courtesy of George Poinar

Eight thousand years ago, long before humans "domesticated" honey bees and became beekeepers, our early ancestors enjoyed the wonderful sweet qualities of the honey that bees made. They would hunt the honey from wild hives. No doubt a dangerous pursuit, climbing tall trees and sheer rock cropping to hunt down the bees and steal the honeycombs from the defensive occupants. In this early cave painting discovered in Biscorp, Spain, circa 6000 BC, we see a figure harvesting wild honey (see Figure 1-2). These early honey hunters found nutrition and energy from eating the wild honey, as well as rich protein from the bee brood.

FIGURE 1-2:
Honey hunter
collecting
nourishment
from a wild
colony of bees.

Illustration by Howland Blackiston

Raising Bees in Ancient Egypt

The honey bee held great religious and spiritual significance in ancient Egypt. It was once thought that honey bees were the tears of the sun god Ra. Bees were regarded as a symbol of royalty and represented the lower Egyptian kingdom. There is no shortage of hieroglyphs documenting the significance of honey bees, the honey they produced, and the beekeepers who attended the hives. See Figure 1-3.

Honey was a treasured commodity for ancient Egyptians. They would float their beehives up and down the Nile following the bloom of the seasonal flowers. When the flowers stopped blooming in one region, the bees were moved further down the Nile to forage on other flowers, eventually traveling the entire length of Egypt. Honey was produced on a very large scale from a variety of floral sources. Surprisingly, the coveted Egyptian cotton is pollinated by honey bees.

The Egyptians loved their honey It was used as a sweetener in cooking and baking. It was used for paying taxes and preventing infection by being placed on wounds. An ancient Egyptian marriage vow stated, "I take thee as wife . . . and promise to deliver to thee twelve jars of honey each year." Honey was even presented as tribute to the Egyptians from the countries they conquered.

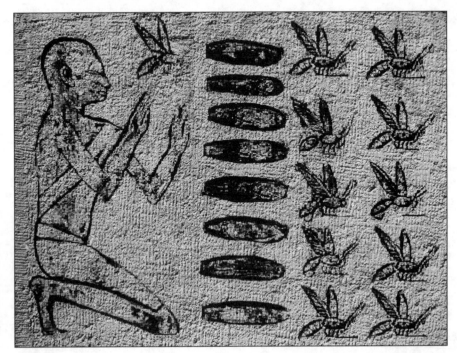

FIGURE 1-3:
Egyptian
beekeepers tend
to their clay hives
while helpers
smoke the
colonies to calm
the bees.

Illustration by Howland Blackiston

Honey was also used for religious purposes. Sacred animals were fed honey. Mummies were often embalmed in honey and propolis, and amphorae of honey were left in tombs, giving the deceased something to eat in the afterlife.

In short, the Egyptians revered honey as a very valued commodity.

As far back as the first dynasty, the Egyptians were known to value the quality and authenticity of their honey. The government assigned the title "Sealer of the Honey" to an esteemed individual who would witness all aspects of the production, insuring the best-quality honey for the Pharaohs and elite. Each vessel of prized honey was marked with an official seal insuring quality control.

Embalming with Honey and More

Spoiler alert. This section gets a little gross and may put you off honey for a while, but it's interesting to note that due to its high acidity and hygroscopic properties, honey acts by drying out the water necessary for microbes and bacteria to survive. And when combining that with the antiseptic qualities of the hydrogen peroxide produced by honey, you have a pretty effective embalming fluid. In fact, upon his death, it is said that Alexander the Great's body was preserved in a golden coffin filled with honey and taken back to Macedonia.

Now if that's not gruesome enough, here's a honey of a legend you may want to skip over. Have you ever heard of a mellified body? It is said that *Mellification* was a way for elderly people nearing the end of their lives to donate their body to become medicine that would be ingested by others to alleviate ailments. In short, turning the body into—yuck—a mummified human confection to be consumed for its healing properties. I'll skip over any further details.

Discovering the World's Oldest BeeHives

Archaeologists recently discovered ancient beehives dating back 3,000 years at the site of Tel Rehov in the Jordan valley in northern Israel (see Figure 1-4). This site appears to be the earliest physical evidence of beekeeping, around the time the prophet Elisha lived. Researchers estimate there were at least 180 hives made of clay cylinders, home to more than a million bees (shown in Figure 1-5). Archaeologists identified the remains of honey bees — including workers, drones, pupae, and larvae — inside about 30 clay hives. Each hive could have produced about 11 pounds of honey each year, making it a profitable business effort.

FIGURE 1-4:
The discovery of these beehives during the Tel Rehov Expedition suggests that beekeeping was already an elaborate agricultural practice in Israel 3,000 years ago.

Courtesy of Amihai Mazar and Amihai Mazar, The Hebrew University of Jerusalem

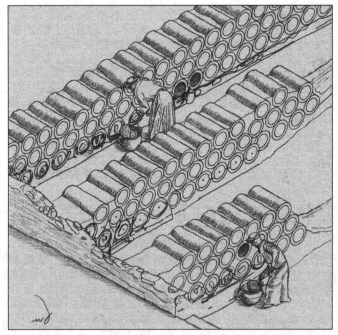

FIGURE 1-5: Artist rendering of this 3000-year-old apiary, which was estimated to have included over 180 clay hives.

Drawing by Ana Iamim. Courtesy of Amihai Mazar, The Hebrew University of Jerusalem

This is the earliest discovery of beekeeping from ancient times. Each hive had a small hole on one side for the bees to come and go, and on the other side was a lid for the beekeeper to access the honeycomb. The archeologists used carbon dating on grains (of pollen?) that had spilled from a broken storage jar next to the hives to estimate that they were about 3,000 years old.

"The location of such a large apiary in the middle of a dense urban area is puzzling because bees can become defensive, especially during routine beekeeping inspections or honey harvesting," the researchers wrote. They speculated that maybe the honey was so valuable it was worth placing in such a congested area where it could be watched and kept safe.

In Praise of Honey

Honey is referenced in all the world's most prominent religions. It always symbolizes richness and great wealth, usually provided through the goodness of God. Honey can be a reward or a gift, or simply a sign of prosperity and a sign of God's blessing. Following are some examples.

Islam

The religious text of Islam called the Qur'an has an entire chapter titled al-Nahl (the Honey Bee). According to the words and deeds of the Prophet Muhammad, honey is strongly recommended for healing purposes. The Qur'an also promotes honey as a nutritious and healthy food.

Hinduism

Honey is one of the five foods used in Hindu worship. It is widely mentioned as an offering to God. It is described as one of the five sacred elixirs of immortality. The sacred religious texts known as the Vedas mention the use of honey as a great medicinal and health food as the food of the gods. Honey's unique health attributes are common to all the major religions.

Judaism

The Torah describes the land of Israel as "flowing with milk and honey." In the Jewish tradition, honey is a symbol for Rosh Hashana. At the traditional meal during this New Year holiday, apple slices are dipped in honey (the apples represent life, and honey represents sweetness — grant us a good and sweet new year).

Buddhism

The festival of Madhu Purnima commemorates Buddha's making peace among his disciples by retreating into the wilderness. During this retreat, a monkey brought him honey to eat. On Madhu Purnima, Buddhists remember this act by giving honey to monks.

Christianity

The Bible contains 100 verses that reference honey. In the book of Judges, Samson found a swarm of bees and honey in the carcass of a lion (14:8). The book of Samuel includes, "See how my eyes have become bright because I tasted a little of this honey" (14:29). Plus, you can find 98 additional honey references!

Sikhism

There is a story of a prominent man who offered honey to the spiritual master, Guru Sahib. The guru refused the honey, stating that when he had needed it most, the man had refused to give it to him. When the man asked the guru for enlightenment, he pointed toward a poor Sikh who was hungry and had been denied honey by the same man. "Feeding the poor is feeding the guru," he proclaimed.

Finding Honey in Literature and Folklore

You don't have to look very hard to find honey referenced in popular culture. Throughout the ages, literature, folklore, mythology, and music have all praised honey in one way or another. The ancient Greeks considered honey sacred in addition to being nutritious. Greek artwork, poetry, and music celebrated honey and the bountiful honey bee.

The great Greek poet Homer referenced honey in several of his poems. The mythological Aristaios (son of Apollo) was a beekeeper, and he taught the Greeks how to maintain hives and harvest honey. For this reason, Aristaios became known as the patron god of beekeeping.

The ancient Romans valued honey, and like the Egyptians, used it to pay taxes. Because honey was rare and precious, it was a food only enjoyed by Romans who could afford it. Honey's culinary use is well documented in a cookbook by a Roman gourmand named Marcus Gavius Apicius. Thought to be written in the first century AD, his book is commonly referred to as "Apicius." Be sure to have a look at Chapters 15 and 16. Each contains an ancient Roman honey-inspired recipe. Hail Caesar!

Songs about honey (and honey bees) are plentiful. No big surprise, since "honey" has evolved into a term of endearment. In Chapter 19, I include a playlist of honey music you can groove to.

Hoodoo is an old spiritual practice — a mixture of African, Native American, and European Christian folklore. Honey plays an important role in some of the magic spells practiced by its followers. For example, here's one you can try at home. To sweeten up someone's feelings toward you, pour honey into a saucer and place it on a piece of paper containing the intended person's name. Place a candle (beeswax, I assume) in the saucer and let it burn until it goes out on its own. Now, just sit back and wait for the phone to ring.

And who can forget the adorable Winnie the Pooh? That loveable bear had an unwavering love for "hunny." And as Pooh said, "A day without a friend is like a pot without a single drop of honey left inside." Thank you, A. A. Milne.

Honey Bees Come to America

The European honey bee that we see on the flowers in our gardens is not native to the Americas. The first hives of honey bees came to Virginia aboard a ship in the spring of 1622 (see Figure 1-6). The early European settlers made good use of the honey and the beeswax that the colonies produced. The colonists also brought with them specific plants for the bees to pollinate. More bee colonies arrived on ships in the following years, and swarms from these original hives proliferated as feral bee colonies were established. But it was not until 1853 that the honey bees made their way to the west coast. Today, the estimated number of "managed" beehives in America is approaching 3 million colonies. (See Chapter 6 for the top ten honey-producing states in America.)

FIGURE 1-6: The honey bee, so familiar in the Americas today, is not native to this part of the world. The first honey bees were brought to Virginia by the early colonists in 1622.

Illustration by Howland Blackiston

Honey Today: Celebrity Status

Have you noticed? Honey seems to be everywhere these days. Honey varietals occupy more and more space on grocery shelves. It's the "all-natural" sweetener found in breakfast cereals and beverages; it's the miraculous ingredient in cosmetics; it's a featured "healing" product in health-food stores; it has found its way into the kitchens of the most elegant and refined restaurants. It's a star on many menus, spotlighted for its healthy and sophisticated taste profiles, distinct varieties, and pairing opportunities. There's no doubt that honey has gained the same "celebrity" status as fine cheeses, olive oils, and rare and expensive balsamic vinegars. Foodies and chefs alike realize that like great wine, honey can also be enjoyed by pairing it with fine foods and by bringing distinct flavors to many recipes.

This entire book is a celebration of honey's newfound celebrity status. In Chapter 7 you can find out about 50 different honey varietals and the foods they go well with. And in Chapters 9 and 10 you can discover how to taste, evaluate, and appreciate the nuances of different honey varietals. In Chapters 14–17 you will find fabulous recipes for making delicious wine from honey, baking with honey, cooking with honey, and even whipping up honey-based beverages and cocktails. To top it all off, Chapter 18 gives guidance in how to pair different honeys with food, and Chapter 19 shares ideas for planning and hosting a party where Honey is your featured guest.

Savor and enjoy!

Chapter **2**

Looking at How Honey Is Made and Harvested

oney bees are the only insects that produce a food that consumers eat. And we eat a lot of it. Here in the United States, the annual per capita consumption is around 1.7 pounds per person (eaten on its own, in cooking and baking, and as a sweetening ingredient in other food products).

Considering the U.S. population is around 328 million people, that's a whole lot of honey. But the bees don't do all that work just to feed us. It's their own sustenance.

In this chapter, you discover why and how bees make honey, the good stuff that honey contains, and how it's harvested. Plus, you find some interesting betcha-didn't-know info about the bees themselves.

Gathering Their Groceries

There are two raw ingredients that bees collect to convert into the foods they eat for nourishment: pollen and nectar.

The actual pollen-based food bees eat is called *beebread*. It's processed from the pollen that the field bees collect from flowering plants. This is the bees' source of protein. According to the USDA, pollen has between 2.5 percent to 61 percent protein content (depending upon its source). Visiting a flower, the foraging bee uses the pollen baskets on her rear legs to store and transport the pollen home (see Figure 2-1). Although pollen is not used by the bees to make honey, grains of pollen are found in all honeys and become part of the nutritional goodness of honey.

FIGURE 2-1: Photo of a worker field bee collecting pollen. Note the pollen baskets on her rear legs packed with pollen for the return trip to the hive.

Photo by Stephen Ausmus, USDA Agricultural Research Service

The field bees also forage flowering plants to collect nectar. This is what the bees use to make honey. Once they have chosen an attractive, sweet-smelling flower, they suck up nectar with their long, straw-like tongue (see Figure 2-2). Bees visit many flowers (about 40 per minute), eventually carrying the collected nectar back to their colony in a distension of the esophagus called a honey sac (also sometimes called the *honey stomach*). They can carry more than their own weight in nectar. Once back in the hive, the *house* worker bees take over (see the "Busy as a bee" sidebar).

FIGURE 2-2: Note the long tongue on this honey bee. It unrolls like a noisemaker on New Year's Eve.

USGS Native Bee Lab

"BUSY AS A BEE"

There's a reason the saying "busy as a bee" exists. In their relatively short life during the summer (six weeks), the all-female worker bees pack in a lot of job responsibilities. Worker honey bees spend the first few weeks of their lives carrying out very specific tasks *within* the hive. For this reason, they are referred to as *house bees*. The jobs they do are dependent on their age:

- **Housekeeping (Days 1 to 3):** A worker bee is born with the munchies. Immediately after she emerges from the cell and grooms herself, she engorges herself with bee bread (pollen) and honey. Following this binge, one of her first tasks is cleaning out the cell from which she just emerged. This cell and other empty cells are cleaned and polished and left immaculate to receive new eggs or to store nectar and pollen.

- **Undertaking (Days 3 to 16):** The honey beehive is one of the cleanest and most sterile environments found in nature. Preventing disease is an important early task for the worker bee. During the first couple weeks of her life, the worker bee removes any bees that have died and disposes of the corpses as far from the hive as possible. Similarly, diseased or dead brood are quickly removed before becoming a health threat to the colony.

(continued)

(continued)

- **Working in the nursery (Days 4 to 12):** The young worker bees tend to their baby sisters by feeding and caring for the developing larvae. On average, nurse bees check a single larva 1,300 times a day. The number of days spent tending brood depends on the number of brood in the hive and the urgency of other competing tasks.

- **Attending royalty (Days 7 to 12):** Because her royal highness is unable to tend to her most basic needs by herself, some of the workers do these tasks for her. They groom and feed the queen and even remove her excrement from the hive. These royal attendants also coax the queen to continue to lay eggs as she moves about the hive.

- **Stocking the pantry (Days 12 to 18):** In the hive, worker house bees take nectar or pollen from foraging field bees returning to the hive. These bees deposit the pollen and nectar into cells earmarked for this purpose.

  To the pollen, they add nectar and their saliva, which contains enzymes that inoculate the pollen with natural probiotic bacteria and the yeasts and sugars necessary to jumpstart the fermentation of pollen into the highly nutritious and protein rich beebread.

  To the nectar, they add saliva (enzymes) and set about fanning the nectar cells continuously to reduce the water content, eventually turning the watery nectar into thick, sweet, ripened honey with a moisture content of 17–18 percent.

- **Fanning (Days 12 to 18):** Worker bees also take a turn at controlling the temperature and humidity of the hive. During warm weather they fan furiously at the hive's entrance to draw air into the hive. Additional fanners are in position within the hives. In addition to cooling the hive, the fanning hastens the evaporation of excess moisture from the curing honey.

- **Becoming architects and master builders (Days 12 to 35):** Worker bees that are about 12 days old are mature enough to begin producing beeswax. These white flakes of wax are secreted from wax glands on the underside of the worker bee's abdomen. They help with the building of new *wax comb* and in the capping of ripened honey and brood cells containing developing pupae.

- **Guarding the home (Days 18 to 21):** The last task of a house bee before she ventures out is that of guarding the hive. At this stage of maturity, her sting glands have developed to contain an authoritative amount of venom. You can easily spot the guard bees at the hive's entrance. They are poised and alert, checking each bee that returns to the hive for a familiar scent. Only family members are allowed to pass.

- **Field bees (Days 21 till death):** When the worker bee is a few weeks old, she ventures outside the hive to perform her last and perhaps most important job — to collect the pollen and nectar that will sustain the colony. With her life half over, she joins the ranks of other field bees until she reaches the end of her life, some three weeks later.

Understanding the Composition of Honey

Honey is the sweet result of the bees magically transforming the nectar they gather from flowers. Honey is about 80 percent fructose and glucose, and between 17 and 18 percent water. Maintaining a balance between sugar and water is critical to the quality of honey. Excess water, for example from poor storage, can trigger yeast fermentation, causing the honey to spoil. The bees nail this balance instinctually, but we can upset the delicate ration by improper harvesting and storing of honey.

More than 20 other sugars can be found in honey, depending upon the original nectar source. There are also proteins in the form of enzymes, amino acids, minerals, trace elements, and waxes. The most important enzyme is *invertase,* which is an enzyme added by the worker bees. This is responsible for converting the nectar sugar sucrose into the main sugars found in honey: fructose and glucose. It is also instrumental in the ripening of the nectar into honey.

With an average pH of 3.9, honey is relatively acidic, but its sweetness hides the acidity.

The antibacterial qualities associated with honey come from hydrogen peroxide, which is a by-product of another enzyme (glucose oxidase) introduced by the bees.

The plants themselves and the soil they grow in contribute to the minerals and trace elements found in honey. See Figure 2-3 for a typical breakdown of honey content.

Composition*

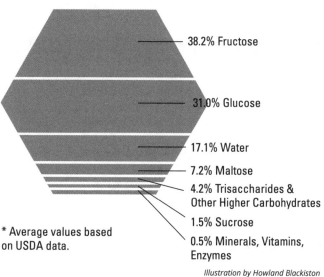

38.2% Fructose

31.0% Glucose

17.1% Water

7.2% Maltose

4.2% Trisaccharides & Other Higher Carbohydrates

1.5% Sucrose

0.5% Minerals, Vitamins, Enzymes

* Average values based on USDA data.

FIGURE 2-3: This chart illustrates the typical content of honey (based on data from the USDA).

Illustration by Howland Blackiston

WHAT IS HMF?

HMF (hydroxymethylfurfural) is an organic substance naturally found in all honeys. In the lab, it is used as a marker to prove the honey is raw, unheated, and it has not been stored for an excessive period of time. Freshly extracted honey displays HMF levels lower than 5 mg/kg. Levels higher than this indicate the honey may be old, overheated, or poorly stored. While the average customer may not necessarily taste the difference in honeys with high HMF levels, experienced honey tasters do.

In the European Union, non-tropical origins cannot exceed HMF limits of 40 mg/kg, and tropical origins must have a maximum HMF limit of 80 mg/kg. Honeys with HMF values above these limits are considered as "industrial honeys" and cannot be sold for direct consumption but as baker's honey (acceptable for use in baking and as an ingredient in commercial food processing) only.

There are no formal HMF limits legally established in the United States, although some beekeepers and commercial honey packers do follow the EU directive.

Honey owes its delicate aromas and flavors to the various volatile substances (similar to essential oils) that originate from the flower. As age and excess heat decompose the fructose, hydroxymethylfurfural (HMF) naturally found in all honeys increases, thus lowering the quality of the honey. (see sidebar, "What is HMF?"). Each of these components that make up honey is extremely fragile, and overheating honey or improper or long-term storage can compromise not only the healthful benefits but also honey flavors as well as darken the color.

Harvesting Honey: From Bee to Bottle

Whether you get your honey from a local beekeeper or a commercially available source, the process of harvesting honey is similar. Only the scale of operations differs.

Another difference in harvesting is the "style" of honey that's going to market. There are four major styles of honey, and the differences mostly have to do with how the honey is presented to the public:

>> Still in the wax comb

>> As a liquid extracted from the comb

>> As a combination of the preceding two

>> Whipped or creamed into a smooth, spreadable product

See Chapter 3 for more details.

How these styles of honey are harvested differ, but since here in the United States there is more extracted liquid honey sold than any other style, I use that as the example in the following sections.

It's all about timing

Generally speaking, beekeepers (whether hobbyist or commercial) harvest their honey at the conclusion of a substantial nectar flow and when the hive is filled with cured and *capped* honey (see Figure 2-4). Conditions and circumstances and timing vary greatly across the country.

FIGURE 2-4:
This frame is ready to harvest, as the bees have filled nearly every cell with cured honey and sealed each cell with a white capping of beeswax.

Photo by C. Marina Marchese

REMEMBER

The honey that is taken from the beehive is considered *surplus honey*. This term refers to the honey that's beyond what the bees need for their own consumption. This extra amount of honey is what the beekeeper can safely harvest from the hive without creating trouble for the colony (See Figure 2-5 for the components of a typical beehive).The bees may not have known at the time, but they made the surplus just for you and me! On average, a hive produces about 65 pounds of surplus honey each season. There is more in a really good season. Like farming, the yield all depends on the robustness of the bees, weather, rainfall, available forage, and other variable circumstances. Most are beyond the beekeeper's control.

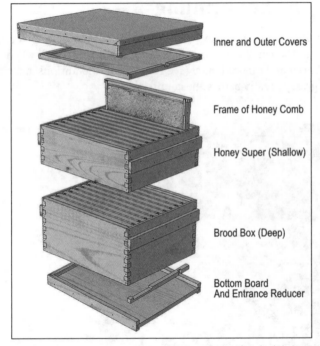

FIGURE 2-5: This illustration shows the anatomy of a typical beehive. The surplus honey that is harvested comes from the top boxes, called "honey supers."

Inner and Outer Covers

Frame of Honey Comb

Honey Super (Shallow)

Brood Box (Deep)

Bottom Board And Entrance Reducer

Courtesy of Howland Blackiston

HONEY IS HYGROSCOPIC

A substance is *hygroscopic* if it absorbs moisture from the air. Honey is one of those hygroscopic substances. On the positive side, this is why baked goods made with honey stay moist and fresh. It's also why honey is used in cosmetics as a moisturizer. On the negative side, being hygroscopic means you must keep your honey containers tightly sealed; otherwise, your honey will absorb moisture from the air, become diluted, and eventually ferment. That's why the bees seal the honeycomb cells with an airtight lid of beeswax.

Driving the bees out of the honey supers

Before beekeepers can extract the honey and bottle it, they must remove the bees from the frame's honeycomb. Beekeepers certainly don't need to bring thousands of bees into their extraction and bottling facility!

Removing bees from honeycomb can be accomplished in many different ways. But for commercial beekeepers (those with over 300 hives) and even for hobbyists with ten or more hives, the fastest and most practical way is to use a *fume board*. It looks like a hive cover, but it has an absorbent flannel inner lining. A liquid bee repellent is applied to the flannel lining, and the fume board is placed on top of the honey supers on a warm day. After just a few minutes, the bees are repelled out of the honey supers and down into the brood chamber. Instant success! The honey supers can then be safely removed and taken to the designated workspace for removing the honey from the comb.

Removing the honey from the comb

After collecting the frames of capped honeycomb (sans bees), beekeepers (large and small) follow the same process (illustrated in Figure 2-6) to get the honey out of the comb and bottle it. Only the scale of operations and size of equipment change. Here's how the process works for both:

1. After removing the bees and bringing the honey supers into a workspace, the beekeeper removes each frame of capped honey from the supers.

2. A handheld knife or uncapping machine is used to slice off the wax cappings and expose the cells of ripened honey.

   This process is called *uncapping*.

3. An uncapping fork (or similar device) is used to get any cells missed by the knife or uncapping machine.

4. Once the frames are uncapped, they are placed in a centrifugal extractor.

   As the frames spin, the honey is forced out of the cells and dribbles down the walls of the extractor into a holding area.

5. The honey is drained from the extractor, filtered, put into airtight containers, and labeled.

FIGURE 2-6:
These photos show the process for both a hobbyist beekeeper and a commercial operation. The steps are similar; only the scale of operations and size of equipment varies.

Photography by Howland Blackiston (top) and www.cooknbeals.com (bottom)

Chapter **3**

Appreciating the Different Styles of Honey

Honey comes in thousands of different varieties, really as many as there are different flowers. In Chapter 7 I profile 50 of the most popular varieties of honey. When you purchase honey, regardless of the variety, honey can be presented as one of several different *styles*. In this chapter we're talking about the different styles of honey. And there are only four style variations: comb honey, extracted honey, chunk honey and whipped honey. They are all worth a try and enjoyed in different ways.

TIP

In time, nearly all honeys form granulated crystals. There is nothing wrong with honey that has crystallized. It's perfectly okay to eat it in this form. However, if you want to get it back to the liquid state, crystallized honey can be easily liquefied by placing the jar in warm (not hot) water and stirred.

WARNING

Don't ever be tempted to heat *plastic* honey jars. The plastic can leech into the honey causing it to smell and taste like, you guessed it, like plastic. And besides, the chances are pretty good that you'll wind up with a deformed plastic bottle. For this reason, we recommend you always purchase your honey in glass containers.

Walkin' Talkin' Honeycomb

Comb honey (see Figure 3-1) is the jewel of the beehive — and carries a high retail price as a result. It's honey just as the bees made it, still in the comb. In many countries, honey in the comb is considered the only authentic honey untouched by humans while retaining all its pollen, propolis, and the natural health benefits associated with raw honey (never extracted, strained or touched by humans). When you uncap those tiny airtight beeswax cells, the honey inside is exposed to the air for the very first time since the bees stored it.

FIGURE 3-1:
This is beautiful, natural honeycomb, just as it comes from the hive.

Photo by Howland Blackiston

Encouraging bees to make large quantities of honeycomb is a bit tricky. The bees need a very strong nectar flow to get them going and controlled space arrangements inside the hive. There must be many warm, sunny days and just the right amount of rain to produce a bounty of flowering plants. The tricky part is controlling the bees' urge to swarm in tight conditions during a heavy nectar flow. Harvesting comb honey is less time-consuming for the beekeeper than harvesting extracted honey (but more labor for the bees); one simply removes the entire honeycomb and packages it. As a consumer, you eat the whole thing: both the honey and the beeswax. It's all edible!

Savoring Liquid Gold — Extracted Honey

Extracted honey (see Figure 3-2) is by far the most popular style of honey consumed in the United States. Wax cappings are sliced off the honeycomb, and liquid honey is removed (extracted) from the cells by centrifugal force. The honey is strained, left for a few days to rest, and then put in containers.

FIGURE 3-2: Extracted honey is the most common style of honey you see in grocery stores in the United States. These jars contain light and dark varieties of honey.

Photo by Howland Blackiston

The beekeeper needs an uncapping knife, extractor (spinner), and some kind of sieve to strain out the bits of wax and the occasional sticky bee. Chapter 2 has more information about how beekeepers harvest and extract honey.

Getting Chunky with Chunk Honey

Chunk honey (see Figure 3-3) is a piece of honeycomb that is placed in a wide-mouthed jar and then topped off with extracted liquid honey.

Photo by Howland Blackiston

FIGURE 3-3:
Chunk honey
makes for a very
appealing
presentation in
the bottle.

Chunk honey is a stunning sight; it resembles a stained glass window, especially when the honey is a light color. By offering two *styles* of honey in a single jar (comb and extracted), you get the best of these two worlds.

Whipping Your Honey

Whipped honey (see Figure 3-4) is also called *creamed honey, spun honey, churned honey, candied honey,* or *honey fondant.* Whipped honey is a semisolid style of honey that's very popular in Europe. In time, all honey naturally forms coarse granules or crystals. But by carefully controlling the crystallization process, you can produce extremely fine crystals and create a velvety-smooth, spreadable product. Sinful, like eating buttercream icing!

TIP

Granulated honey or *set honey* is liquid honey that has naturally crystallized. But *whipped* honey is carefully made by seeding one part of finely granulated (crystallized) honey into nine parts of extracted liquid honey and then placing it in a cool room until it completely crystallizes. The crystals are then ground into fine particles. The resulting consistency of whipped honey is thick and ultra-smooth. Making it takes a fair amount of work, but it's worth it! (See the sidebar on how to make it yourself.)

FIGURE 3-4:
Making
top-quality
whipped honey is
a craft, resulting
in a velvety-
smooth,
spreadable
delicacy.

Photo by Howland Blackiston

MAKE WHIPPED HONEY: THE DYCE METHOD

The Dyce Method is a process used to control the crystallization of honey. It was developed and patented by Elton J. Dyce in 1935. The process (described here) results in a nice, smooth whipped honey:

1. **Heat honey to 120 degrees Fahrenheit (use a candy thermometer — accuracy is important).**

   This kills yeast cells that are always present in honey. Yeast causes fermentation, and its presence can inhibit a successful result when making whipped honey. *Stir the honey gently and constantly to avoid overheating.* Be careful not to introduce air bubbles.

(continued)

(continued)

2. **Using a two-fold thickness of cheesecloth as a strainer, strain honey to remove foreign material and wax.**

3. **Heat honey again, this time to 150 degrees Fahrenheit.**

   Don't forget to stir continuously.

4. **Strain honey a second time to remove all visible particles.**

   Again, you can use a two-fold thickness of cheesecloth as a strainer.

5. **Cool honey as rapidly as possible until the temperature reaches 75 degrees Fahrenheit.**

   You can place honey in a container and "float" it in an ice water bath to speed the cooling process. Stir gently as honey cools.

6. **Add some finely crystallized honey to promote a controlled crystallization of your whipped honey.**

   It's kind of like adding a special *yeast culture* when making sourdough bread. Introduce these seed crystals by adding 10 percent (by weight) of processed granulated honey. *Granulated honey* is processed by breaking down any coarse crystals into finely granulated crystals. This can be accomplished by *fracturing* the crystallized honey in a meat grinder or a food processor.

7. **Place mixture in a cool room (57 degrees Fahrenheit).**

   Complete crystallization occurs in about a week.

8. **After a week, run mixture through the grinder (or food processor) one more time to break up any newly formed crystals.**

9. **Bottle and store in a cool dry room.**

(Information courtesy of National Honey Board)

What's the Story on Honey Straws?

You may have seen something on the market called "honey straws." Mostly these are sold as a healthy snack or a pick-me-up. They consist of clear plastic straws, pinched at both ends and filled with liquid, extracted honey (see Figure 3-5).

Courtesy of GloryBee (glorybee.com)

FIGURE 3-5: Honey straws are another way you may see honey marketed.

Some honey straws contain pure honey of some variety. But for others, the honey has been colored and flavored with the likes of root beer, caramel, mint, chocolate, lemonade, watermelon, and on and on. Kids seem to love them, but they are not intended for the honey connoisseur. Comparing honey straws to pure, raw honey is like comparing a fruit-infused wine to a vintage cabernet.

2

Nutrition, Health, and Honey

Read about apitherapy and how honey and other products of the hive are used worldwide to heal and improve health.

Discover honey's natural ability to kill bacteria.

Take a look at how honey is used in health, wellness, and personal care products.

Try your hand at making honey remedies and personal care products at home.

Chapter **4**

All About Apitherapy

Honey bees are sophisticated creatures, producing many substances (besides honey) that have proven health benefits for humans and some animals. The study and use of these products for healing and maintaining health is called *apitherapy* or "bee therapy" and include use of bee venom, pollen, royal jelly, propolis, beeswax, and honey.

Apitherapy gained national recognition through Charles Mraz, a beekeeper who founded the American Apitherapy Society (AAS) in the 1930s. During his lifetime he treated people with arthritis pain, multiple sclerosis, and other autoimmune diseases with bee stings and products of the hive. (He chronicles his personal journey as a pioneering healer along with case studies in his book *Health and the Honeybees* that was published in 1955.) The AAS continues to be dedicated to educating medical professionals, beekeepers, and the public about the benefits of bee medicine.

Well before the AAS was established, honey and bees were used as medicine for thousands of years. Evidence exists that the ancient Egyptians, Assyrians, Chinese, Greeks, and even Romans employed honey for various treatments, including wound care and diseases of the intestine. The oldest known medical text of Egypt dating back to 1553–1550 BC is known as *Papyrus Ebers.* There are passages about using honey along with herbal remedies as a natural antibiotic and to dress wounds. In 50 AD, Dioscorides the physician to the Roman army, wrote: "Honey is good for all rotten and hollow ulcers," alluding to treating the soldiers who suffered infected wounds during war time.

APITHERAPY COURSE

My first experience with apitherapy was at an American Apitherapy Society conference. I had always been interested in alternative medicine and wanted to learn more about how honey and bee venom were applied as a therapeutic treatment. So I signed myself up for the CMAC (Charles Mraz Apitherapy Course) certification course (see the following figure for a photo of Charles Mraz). It was three days of talks and workshops in the largely unknown world of honey-bee medicine. During one lecture we were told that after a short coffee break we would watch a live stinging demonstration by a trained apitherapist, Dr. Theo Cherbuliz, and a willing volunteer. I could not imagine how a bee could be forced to sting someone on purpose. Would the speaker release a handful of live honey bees into the room with hopes they would only sting the volunteer? I would quickly learn that bee stings are administered by a controlled procedure that requires specialized training and the use of a tool similar to a tweezer to direct the bee. A micro-sting would be given to the patient in a precise area on the body along a meridian similar to acupuncture points as a test. Later, I learned that the volunteer was not so random and had been receiving bee venom therapy (BVT) for pain. The conference ended with audience members sharing their personal stories about how they found relief in bee venom when traditional medicine had failed them. That's when I became teary eyed with a new appreciation of honey bees.

As early as 350 BC, Hippocrates, the Greek physician known as the "Father of Medicine," began using bee venom therapy to relieve joint pain and arthritis in his patients with some success. He also clearly understood the value of honey related to health and well–being and prescribed simple mixtures of honey and vinegar (oxymel) for pain and honey and water (hydromel) for fevers. He was a firm believer in the importance of honey's nutrition value to prevent or cure diseases and he is remembered for his famous quote "Our food should be our medicine and medicine be our food." During his work as a physician, he often prescribed honey internally and externally, as a contraceptive, laxative, or cough and sore throat reliever.

In this chapter, I discuss products of the beehive and how they have been used for health and healing.

Bee Venom

This ancient practice of stinging with live honey bees can be traced back to the second century BC in China where acupuncture was being used to promote health and healing by balancing the flow of energy within the body. By inserting fine needles at precise points along neurological trigger points, the theory is acupuncture opens up energy channels called *meridians* to release the body's natural supply of cortisone (cortisol). In turn, cortisone relieves inflammation and pain related to autoimmune diseases.

Bee venom is a white liquid released when a female worker honey bee stings in an attempt to protect her young, hive, and honey. Stinging is a defensive behavior that results in her losing her life when her stinger, venom sac, and the muscles and nerves surrounding it are ripped out of her abdomen as she pulls away from the point of her sting. BVT follows the same protocol as acupuncture by substituting a female honey-bee's stinger for a needle to prick the body in controlled doses by a trained apitherapist (see Figure 4-1). This practice has helped some people find relief from chronic pain associated with arthritis, multiple sclerosis, migraines, and lupus, in addition to simply boosting the immune system. Bee venom therapy has been used even to kill cancer cells. Today, BVT is used in hospitals around the world; the most famous is the bee therapy clinic Lianyungang Hospital of Traditional Chinese Medicine.

FIGURE 4-1:
Charles Mraz stinging a patient with a live honey bee to deliver bee venom offering relief from chronic arthritis pain.

Courtesy of Champlain Valley Apiaries

Generally, BVT is not recognized in the United States; however, the Winchester Hospital in Massachusetts has a BVT clinic if you are looking for alternative treatments.

ANAPHYLACTIC SHOCK

The greatest risk of using BVT as a medical treatment is anaphylactic shock, which is a severe allergic reaction that requires immediate medical attention. If you are stung by a bee for any reason and have trouble breathing, or feel faint or unwell, seek immediate medical attention at your nearest hospital. For this reason, patients who are considering BVT are carefully profiled before being administered bee venom. Most importantly they must cleanse their body of beta blockers, which suppress the immune system, and any anti-inflammatory drugs, including alcoholic beverages. Like any medical treatments, they are not a substitute for a healthy lifestyle, diet, exercise, and emotional balance or the care of a medical professional.

Bee Pollen

Most of us associate pollen with the unwelcome start of allergy season. Pollen is the male sex cells of a flowering plant, which is necessary to fertilize it so it can bear fruit and reproduce. If you are allergic to pollen, you are familiar with the typical symptoms, including headaches, sinus stuffiness, fatigue, and general aches and pains.

Honey bees are hairy creatures that naturally attract pollen while gathering nectar for honey making. They use their feet to comb the tiny pollen granules off their hairy bodies and mix it with nectar and their own enzymes to form it into tiny balls now called *bee* pollen. Bees will carry the bee pollen balls back to the hive on their hind legs in their *pollen baskets.* Beekeepers can collect pollen by placing a piece of equipment at the entrance of the hive called a pollen trap. As the bees return back to the hive with pollen in their pollen baskets, they are encouraged to crawl through a narrow hole in the pollen trap, which separates the pollen from their legs. Pollen comes in a rainbow of colors, like honey, depending upon the type of flower it was gathered from. The granules are commonly sold in jars in health-food shops or farmers' markets.

Bee pollen is said to be nature's most complete food, containing every nutrient needed to sustain human life. It is a complete source of protein that contains all the basic elements in the human body, including 22 amino acids, 18 vitamins, 25 minerals, 59 trace elements, 11 enzymes or co-enzymes, fatty acids, and carbohydrates. Chock-full of B-complex vitamins and C, D and E, many people consume bee pollen orally for nutrition value similar to a daily vitamin.

Athletes swear that bee pollen increases energy and endurance during competitions. However, the most common reason people consume bee pollen is to build up a natural immunity, especially to seasonal pollen allergies. After all, allergy shots are injections of pollen and other allergens to build your body's own natural immunity to what you are allergic to, so why not eat your medicine? Sprinkle some bee pollen on salads, or mix it into power smoothies, yogurt, or oatmeal. Since bee pollen is considered a raw superfood, it should be kept refrigerated and consumed within a few months of harvest.

Royal Jelly

Probably the most mysterious substance produced by honey bees is a milky white liquid called royal jelly. You may have seen royal jelly as an ingredient in power drinks, facial creams, or even supplements at your natural food shop and had no idea what it was. Secreted by the hypopharynx glands of young nurse bees to feed young growing larvae inside their cells, royal jelly is best known as the magical food of the queen. It is what gives her fertility and the supernatural ability to lay up to 2,000 eggs a day. It is also why she lives three to five years longer than any other bees, essentially increasing her longevity.

To gather one ounce of royal jelly, you would have to visit 120 queen cells, and in fact it is not always present in every hive unless the colony is actively rearing a new queen. For this reason royal jelly is extremely rare, labor intensive to harvest, and costly.

Royal jelly is another superfood chock-full of amino acids; vitamins A, C, D, E, and B-complex; and trace minerals, as well as calcium, copper, iron, potassium, phosphorus, silicon, and sulfur, essential fatty acids, sugars, sterols, and acetylcholine, a neuronal transmitter. These elements are necessary for human survival and maintaining a healthy the immune system.

Royal jelly also contains collagen that benefits the skin, hair, and nails, making it a popular ingredient in personal care products. A potent antimicrobial protein called *royalisin* has also been found in royal jelly. In addition, royal jelly has been touted to aid in mood disorders and insomnia, repair nerve cells, strengthen liver function, and aid in digestive disorders. Considering all the benefits that royal jelly offers, I can tell you from experience that royal jelly is extremely sour and tastes like a seriously stinky cheese, but many things that are good for you do not always taste good.

Propolis

Beekeepers curse propolis because it sticks to their hands, hive tools, and the frames inside the hive while they are inspecting their colonies. For this reason, it is often called "bee glue," and it leaves a permanent stain on everything it comes into contact with. A type of tree resin similar to myrrh and frankincense, propolis is produced when honey bees gather the sticky sap from conifer trees like spruce, pine, or fir. They mix the sap with their own enzymes and beeswax to produce one of the most powerful antibacterial, antifungal and antiviral substances in the natural world.

Propolis resembles sticky taffy when it's warm, and it shatters like glass when it's cold. Beekeepers scrape chunks of propolis from the woodenware inside their hives and save it to make tinctures, dissolving it with grain alcohol. Personal care items like topical salves, throat sprays, lozenges, and toothpaste found in most health-food stores tout the benefits of propolis. If you have infected gums, a toothache, or a sore throat, try sucking on a small piece of propolis; it will relieve pain pretty quickly by numbing the area. Because propolis contains essential minerals, iron, calcium, aluminum, manganese, and all the vitamins known to man except vitamin K, it is known to stimulate the body's own immune system.

The name *propolis* was dubbed by Aristotle when the ancient Greeks observed bees calking the crevasses in their hives to fortify against bacteria in preparation for the oncoming winter. Propolis translates to *pro* (before) and *polis* (city) referring to a bee colony's ability to defend its own city. It is a well-known fact that the ancient Egyptians used propolis and honey to embalm the mummies, and for this reason they have survived for thousands of years. Stradivarius polished his violins with beeswax and propolis, which acted as a preservative for the wood. Today, beekeepers often mix tinctures of propolis with paint to preserve the woodenware of their beehives.

Beeswax

After honey, beeswax is the most commercially valuable and labor-intensive product made by honey bees. Beeswax is secreted by glands on the bottom of the female workers' abdomens as tiny white flakes. Then they form it into hexagonal cells, creating a repeating pattern that becomes honeycomb. These beeswax cells are where the bees store their honey, pollen, propolis, and beebread. The beeswax cells also serve as the nest where the bees live and the queen will lay her eggs. An interesting fact is that while bees are constructing their honeycomb with beeswax, they can be seen linking themselves together by their feet, creating a single chain. There does not seem to be any explanation for this behavior. Some say they are re-creating scaffolding or they are simply using their own bodies to measure the size of each hexagon they build. Either way, we can all agree that honey bees are master builders and mathematicians.

Producing beeswax and building honeycomb are not only labor intensive for bees, but harvesting beeswax and honeycomb is also labor intensive for the beekeeper. Over time beeswax becomes visibly old, turning black and stinky from overuse by the bees. Beekeepers know it is time to swap it out and replace it with new frames of beeswax foundation for the bees to build new honeycomb.

Thrifty beekeepers harvest their beeswax and clean it by boiling it in water then straining out the excess honey and any residual particles a few times until the beeswax is clean and bright yellow again. This can take hours, mostly because of the time needed to boil and cool down the beeswax in between straining.

Beeswax can be used to make candles and mixed with oils, butters, and scents to make personal care products or even wood polish. Beeswax candles are highly desirable because they burn two to three times longer and cleaner than paraffin wax. Beeswax candles are also an ecologically safe choice for the environment because they do not emit toxic smoke or messy drips. It is said that the light from a burning beeswax candle is identical to sunlight.

When used as an ingredient in skin care or hair products, beeswax has a warm, nostalgic, honey scent. It is emollient, allowing oils and butters to absorb completely into the skin to moisturize, while offering antibacterial properties and a certain amount of protection from the sun.

Enjoying the Many Benefits of Honey

And now to the star of this little book: honey. It's a truly magical substance that cannot be replicated by humans. Although some have successfully made a sweet, syrupy substance that tastes very similar, it is impossible to mimic honey's chemical composition or its unparalleled health benefits. Beginning with its low pH, honey is an acidic environment, inhibiting the growth of most bacteria, fungi, and viruses, which prefer to thrive in a more alkaline state. Honey registers at 3.2–4.5 on the pH scale, much lower than most pathogens can survive.

Next, honey is *hygroscopic*, meaning that when it is openly exposed to moisture or humid conditions, it will absorb water. This is because honey is a supersaturated solution and honey bees are able to dissolve much more sugar in water than normal using heat. This hygroscopic behavior comes in handy when honey comes in contact with bacteria. Honey will absorb any moisture surrounding bacteria, which will dehydrate and kill the cell. So be sure to put the lid back on your honey jar, especially when it is humid.

The last amazing thing that honey bees do is add their own enzymes to honey, and one in particular, called *glucose oxidase*, is added during the ripening process. Glucose oxidase prevents the honey from fermenting and is what breaks down the glucose sugar in honey to gluconic acid. This action produces hydrogen peroxide and is another major factor in why honey is said to have antibacterial properties. Hydrogen peroxide occurs in small quantities for a short time, and this happens only when the honey has *not* been heat treated and is in the presence of water. The pH of hydrogen peroxide is 6.2 (ideal for contact with blood and tissue), so consuming a spoonful of honey or applying it to an open wound will activate these unique properties.

Honey is good for your insides and also for your outsides. Try honey on skin irritations, scratchy throats, or a mask to make your face glow. Here we recommend some other not so common uses of honey.

Cuts, burns, and scratches

It is a fact that when new skin grows as a result of open wounds, it heals faster if it is kept clean, warm, and moist. This is why honey is ideal for soothing cuts, burns, scratches. It acts as a sealant to keep skin abrasions moist and clean while new skin is growing. Honey has been known to reduce blistering burns and speeds up the regeneration of new tissue with less scarring. A medical grade honey has been developed for use as a wound dressing in hospitals by doctors called Medihoney. It is available only by prescription, and I can bet that most beekeepers would claim their own honey is the best medicine.

Fixing sore throats and coughs

I think we can all agree that there is something comforting about swallowing a spoonful of honey. The sweet, syrupy liquid just feels good slowly slipping down the back of your throat. Honey gives instant comfort to the scratchiness associated with sore throats and seasonal allergies, and suppresses coughs better than some over-the-counter drugs without the side effects. It is common to find honey as an ingredient in cough suppressants and lozenges because it works. If you have not tried honey when you're under the weather, you may be pleasantly surprised that honey is your best (and most natural) medicine.

Getting the honey glow

Honey may be great on toast, but have you tried honey on your face? More and more personal care products are touting the benefits of honey in their ingredients. No doubt you've seen honey in facial cleansers, shampoos, and moisturizers.

Honey can be used as a moisturizing face wash to reduce dryness. Honey is an excellent humectant that seals in the moisture in your skin, making it soft and supple. Honey's antibacterial properties can help with acne on the surface of your skin by soothing and reducing inflammation.

Dry or damaged hair can use a honey treatment to return it to a healthy and shiny mane.

Honey also has varying amounts of polyphenols, which are powerful antioxidants that help protect your body from cell damage, are anti-aging and are known to fight against heart disease and cancer. As we find out more about the benefits of honey inside and out, it begins to make sense that honey has a place in your medicine cabinet as well as your kitchen.

TIP

Be sure to see Chapter 5 for honey-inspired health and beauty recipes you can make at home.

AVOIDING HONEY NO-NO'S

Honey is safe for adults to consume; however, infants and children under two years of age risk exposure to a bacterium called *Clostridium botulinum.* These spores are often found in soil, air, dust, and agricultural products. Infantile botulism is a bacterial infection that occurs in the large intestine of young children who ingest raw or uncooked foods, including honey. A toxin found in this bacterium can make children sick and even cause them to become paralyzed. In the United States, all honey sold is required to include a warning on the label about feeding honey to children under two years of age.

Chapter **5**

Making Honey Remedies at Home

S*pecial thanks to my friend and fellow beekeeper Patty Pulliam for her help in preparing this chapter.*

Honey is nice on toast. But did you know it can also relieve a multitude of medical issues — from taming a cough and alleviating allergies to healing cuts or burns? Because of honey's low pH and hygroscopic properties, bacteria cannot survive in it. The pollen in the honey contains various minerals as well as enzymes and B vitamins, which impart immune-boosting properties that help the body fight infection. This is all good stuff.

TIP

Generally speaking, the darker the honey, the greater the minerals and antibacterial qualities.

REMEMBER

The recipes that follow are all natural and contain no preservatives. That's great, of course. But it also means these products have a limited shelf life, so be sure to keep unused product in the fridge to extend its useful life. Or just make what you need in the short term.

Although most of the ingredients are easy to find and you may already have them, I include some resources in Appendix B for obtaining the harder-to-find ingredients.

When selecting a honey to use in these recipes, be sure to use a honey that's just as it came from the hive. That is, not having been heated nor pasteurized, nor ultra-filtered. These processes remove many of honey's nutritional and health benefits. Unfortunately, product labelling will not reliably tell you this information. So I recommend avoiding the national brands found in supermarkets. Get your honey from local farmers' markets or a neighboring beekeeper. See Chapter 13 for how and where to shop for the good stuff.

Mixing Up Some Honey-Based Hair and Skincare Products

In this section you'll find some of my favorite recipes for honey-inspired personal care products. They are all natural, healthy, and work great. I know, when you think of honey, *sticky* is probably one of the first adjectives that comes to mind. But for many of the honey remedies in this section, the honey is not at all sticky. It's silky smooth.

Honey's hygroscopic quality means it absorbs moisture from the air. This is one of the many reasons why honey is such a desirable ingredient in cosmetics. It's a star at moisturizing and preventing dryness. This is why honey is considered a natural *humectant* — it retains moisture.

TIP

The simplest and most effective use of honey is to directly apply it! Rub a drop or two of honey on chapped lips before bed. For super-dry skin, add a tablespoon or two of honey to your warm bathwater.

Honey Sugar Body Scrub

A basic, invigorating body scrub to gently exfoliate the skin.

PREP TIME: 5 MIN	YIELD: 1½ CUPS

INGREDIENTS

1 cup white granulated sugar

1 lemon, juiced

½ cup honey

DIRECTIONS

1 Mix all the ingredients and blend well.

2 Take a handful of scrub and rub all over your body; you can use a washcloth or just the palm of your hand.

3 Rinse and then follow your usual bathing routine.

NOTE: A few additional ingredients make this scrub rejuvenating and leave your skin silky soft. For extra moisturizing properties, omit the lemon juice and add 2 tablespoons of coconut oil. Add 4 drops of an essential oil of your choice to smell divine.

Honey Facial Cleanse

Try this exfoliating polish once a week and watch your skin glow!

INGREDIENTS

½ cup baking soda (sodium bicarbonate)

¼ cup honey

DIRECTIONS

1 Mix the ingredients together and rub on face or dry, flaky skin.

2 Rinse and pat dry.

Honey Facial Wash/Mask

Honey is so hydrating and emollient that you can massage this into your face as a quick pick-me-up facial.

PREP TIME: 5 MIN	YIELD: 4 TREATMENTS

INGREDIENTS

¼ cup honey

1 drop tea tree oil

2 drops lavender essential oil

DIRECTIONS

1 In a small bowl, mix together the honey and oils.

2 Tie back your hair; then apply 1 tablespoon to wet skin and massage in.

3 Allow to remain on skin 1–2 minutes, or longer if using as a mask.

4 Rinse and pat dry.

Honey Body Wash

This soap is gentle on your skin and perfect for the shower.

PREP TIME: 10 MIN

YIELD: ¾ CUP

INGREDIENTS

¼ cup liquid castile soap

¼ cup sweet almond oil

¼ cup honey

Your choice of essential oil, if desired

Squeeze bottle

DIRECTIONS

1 Mix all the ingredients with a whisk in a bowl.

2 Pour into squeeze bottle.

Honey Mineral Bath

The honey will scent the bath and soothe your skin. The Epsom salts relax tired muscles. The baking soda helps release the magnesium in the salts for total relaxation, making for a very alkaline soak. Honey take me away!

PREP TIME: 5 MIN	YIELD: 1 BATH

INGREDIENTS

1 cup honey

1 cup Epsom salts

½ cup baking soda

Lavender essential oil, optional

DIRECTIONS

1 Add all the ingredients to a warm bath.

2 Now, soak away and relax.

Honey Bath Bomb

Bath bombs are easy and fun to prepare. They also make great gifts. I use a 2-ounce ice cream scoop to form and place the balls in colorful muffin papers. Or, you can form the balls by hand or even use silicone molds. Then I wrap in clear cellophane bags tied with natural brown twine or colorful ribbons.

TIP

Citric acid is easily found at home brewing stores. You can find some suggested resources in Appendix B as well.

PREP TIME: 20 MIN	YIELD: 2¼ CUPS

INGREDIENTS

1 cup baking soda

½ cup citric acid

½ cup cornstarch

¼ cup Epsom salt

2 tablespoons coconut oil

1 tablespoon honey

1 teaspoon essential oil of your choice

DIRECTIONS

1 Mix all the ingredients in a non-reactive bowl. The mixture should hold together when squeezed but will have a dry consistency. If the mixture is too dry, you can spritz it with some water, but be conservative as it is supposed to be dry but hold together under pressure.

2 Divide the mixture and form it into small balls.

3 Let air-dry for 1 hour before packaging.

Hair Rinse

This rinse will make your hair silky soft and shiny. Use it once a week after you wash and condition your hair.

PREP TIME: 5 MIN	YIELD: 3 CUPS (1 APPLICATION)

INGREDIENTS

5 tablespoons honey

1 cup white vinegar

2 cups water

DIRECTIONS

1 Mix all the ingredients together.

2 Rub the mixture into hair and scalp; leave on for 5 minutes.

3 Rinse with warm water.

Shaving Lotion

This luxurious lotion gives you a close shave while making your skin as smooth as silk.

INGREDIENTS

½ cup coconut oil

½ cup liquid castile soap

¼ cup honey

6–8 drops essential oil of your choice; a very herbal lavender or rosemary is nice

A squeeze or pump style bottle

DIRECTIONS

1 Combine all the ingredients in a bowl.

2 Whisk until all the ingredients are incorporated and the mixture looks creamy.

3 Put into a squeeze or pump style bottle. The honey may separate, so shake well before applying. Put a generous amount into the palm of your hand and apply to the area to be shaved. Enjoy your velvety skin.

TIP: If using Dr. Bronner's essential oil–infused castile soap, omit the essential oil.

Honey Whipped Hand and Body Cream

The honey is whipped into the oil and butter base after cooling. You're going to absolutely love this very rich and hydrating cream. You'll feel like you are putting whipped cream on your skin.

PREP TIME: 15 MIN PLUS COOLING TIME	YIELD: 10 OUNCES

INGREDIENTS

4 ounces organic extra-virgin coconut oil

4 ounces organic unrefined shea butter

¼ cup honey

DIRECTIONS

1 In a double boiler, melt the coconut oil and shea butter. Remove from heat and let cool.

2 Using a stand or a hand mixer, beat the cooled, solidified oil mixture until fluffy, like whipped cream. Slowly add in the honey until the mixture is emulsified.

3 Put into a container, date, and use within 6 months.

Sunburn Skin Soother

If you forgot to use your sunscreen and got too much sun exposure, this quick remedy will help calm the burn down. *Note:* This is not a sun*screen*. It's a soothing gel to relieve sunburn.

PREP TIME: 5 MIN	YIELD: 1 APPLICATION

INGREDIENTS

⅛ cup honey

⅛ cup aloe vera gel

DIRECTIONS

1 Whisk together the honey and aloe vera gel until well blended.

2 Apply on clean, dry sunburned area.

Honey-Based Elixirs

The previous recipes in this chapter are meant to apply, not to ingest. But here are a few honey remedies you consume to relieve the discomfort of various ailments and to naturally improve your overall health.

EATING HEALTHY WITH HONEY AND CINNAMON

If you eat honey and cinnamon daily on your toast, in your oatmeal, or on your griddle cakes, you will boost your immune system, regulate cholesterol, and even relieve pain from arthritis. Cinnamon is a spice that is made from grating the twigs of a cinnamon tree. This winning combination should be in every kitchen. Ceylon cinnamon is considered the real cinnamon, and it comes from the inner bark of the Cinnamomun verum tree in India or Sri Lanka. The other, more common cinnamon is Cassia, which is less expensive. If you get it at the supermarket, it may not be the real deal. Try online or at a specialty spice store.

By the way, cinnamon is great, but it should be used in moderation as it contains coumarin, which in high doses can cause liver damage. I suggest that you speak with your doctor to determine the appropriate amount of cinnamon you should consume.

Honey Lemon Ginger Cough Drops

These drops are soothing to the throat and delicious. This recipe uses honey to make a soft crack stage candy, which means bringing the syrup to 275 degrees Fahrenheit, so you need to be vigilant about monitoring the temperature of the syrup. I like to use a candy/deep-fry thermometer that hooks on the side of the pan. I also recommend that you use a high-sided saucepan because the mixture will foam up as the temperature rises. When working with hot syrup — or hot anything — always take care not to burn yourself.

PREP TIME: 10 MIN	COOK TIME: 25 MIN	YIELD: 24 LOZENGES

INGREDIENTS

One 2-inch knob of ginger

1 cup water

½ cup honey

1 lemon, juiced (about 2 tablespoons)

Cornstarch to coat cooled lozenges (optional)

SPECIAL TOOLS

Candy/deep-fry thermometer

Silicon candy molds or parchment paper

Silicon spatula

DIRECTIONS

1 Prepare silicon candy molds (if using) or, to make lozenges without molds, line a baking tray with parchment paper and have ready a large soup spoon.

2 Wash the ginger (no need to peel), slice thinly, and add to 1 cup of water. Heat until reduced to ¼ cup; then strain out the ginger, keeping the reduced tea.

3 With the reduced ginger tea returned to the tall-sided saucepan, add the honey and lemon juice, insert the candy/deep-fry thermometer, and cook over medium heat. Constantly monitor the temperature of the syrup, as it can rise quickly. The mixture should be stirred constantly with a silicon spatula (as silicon does not conduct heat like a metal spoon or burn like a wooden spoon).

4 When the syrup reaches 275 degrees Fahrenheit, remove from heat and either pour into silicon candy molds or use a large soup spoon to ladle out small dollops onto the parchment paper–lined baking sheet.

5 When cool, place in an airtight container with wax paper separating layers. The lozenges can be lightly dusted with cornstarch to help keep them from sticking together.

Honey & Propolis Throat Spray

Propolis is a natural resin mixture honey bees produce from resins collected from plants and trees. Propolis extract can be found online or at any health-food store in the supplements section. The addition of honey and water makes the propolis go down easier and is one of the quickest reliefs for sore throats.

PREP TIME: 10 MIN | **YIELD: 2-OUNCE SPRAY BOTTLE**

INGREDIENTS

2 tablespoons distilled water

2 tablespoons honey

2 dropperfuls (0.14 milliliter) propolis liquid extract

2-ounce spray bottle

DIRECTIONS

1 Warm distilled water and honey over low heat until blended.

2 Stir in the propolis extract.

3 Pour into the spray bottle.

Honey & Lemon Throat Gargle

During cold and flu season, this is a tried-and-true go-to remedy to relieve scratchy sore throats. Did you know opera singers and vocalists swear by honey before performing?

PREP TIME: 5 MIN	YIELD: 1 DOSE

INGREDIENTS

½ teaspoon salt

½ cup hot water

2 tablespoons honey

½ lemon, juiced

DIRECTIONS

1 In a glass, dissolve salt into hot water, add honey and dissolve; then add lemon juice. Stir until mixed.

2 While still warm, gargle with the mixture (do not drink). Repeat as necessary.

Honey Lemon Water

One of the easiest elixirs to prepare, honey and lemon water is best to drink on an empty stomach to perk up your morning routine.

| PREP TIME: 5 MIN | YIELD: 1 DOSE |

INGREDIENTS

1 cup water

1 tablespoon honey

½ lemon

DIRECTIONS

1 Bring 1 cup of water to a boil and remove from heat.

2 Add 1 tablespoon of honey and the juice from half a lemon. Stir to blend.

3 Drink up!

BENEFITS: Promotes better digestion (because honey lemon water increases stomach acids); improves bowel movements; eliminates excess fluids in the body that can cause inflammation; and is known to detox the liver (which improves skin tone). These benefits may also help with weight loss.

Oxymel: Honey and Apple Cider Vinegar Shot

Apple cider vinegar (ACV) is basically fermented apple juice where yeast turns the sugars to alcohol, and then bacteria turns the alcohol into acetic acid. It has been used as a home remedy for many ailments because of its antioxidant properties, which are known to slow damage to cells. Now pair that up with honey's antibacterial properties and you have an elixir the ancient people called *oxymel*. This drink is best as a small shot rather than a heaping full glass. Taken once a day or before each meal, it helps everything go down easier.

PREP TIME: 5 MIN	YIELD: 1 DOSE

INGREDIENTS

1 tablespoon honey

1 tablespoon apple cider vinegar

DIRECTIONS

1 Combine 1 tablespoon of honey and 1 tablespoon of apple cider vinegar. We suggest using organic vinegar if possible.

2 Mix well until the honey is dissolved; then drink.

BENEFITS: Oxymel has antioxidant properties, which are known to slow damage to cells. It also balances blood sugar, relieves acid reflux, and aids in weight loss. You'll sleep better too.

Golden Milk: Honey and Turmeric

A traditional hot Indian drink named after its brilliant golden color, golden milk is used in Ayurvedic medicine to heal a multitude of ailments.

PREP TIME: 15 MIN	YIELD: 1 DOSE

INGREDIENTS

1 teaspoon turmeric paste (prepare using a mortar and pestle to crush fresh, peeled turmeric root into a fine, smooth paste)

1 cup of milk (you may substitute almond or coconut milk)

3 teaspoons honey

DIRECTIONS

1 In a small saucepan, combine the turmeric paste and milk. Heat gently for 3–5 minutes (do not let boil).

2 Turn off flame. Add 3 teaspoons of honey and stir until melted. Enjoy!

BENEFITS: Golden milk is a natural drink that detoxes your body; improves heart functions; is good for your skin; relieves colds and coughs; and fights digestive disorders.

Honey and Ginger Tea

Whether you consume it as a hot tea or a cold drink, ginger and honey are a winning combination for health. Believe it or not, ginger is a flowering plant and its roots or rhizomes, called ginger root, are a spice in the turmeric family. It was the very first spice exported from Asia by the ancient Greeks and Romans.

PREP TIME: 10 MIN	YIELD: 1 DOSE

INGREDIENTS

1-inch knob of fresh ginger

3 teaspoons honey

1½ cups water

DIRECTIONS

1 Add water to a small saucepan and place on the stove.

2 Wash the ginger (no need to peel), slice it thinly, and add it to the water.

3 Bring the water to a boil to release the ginger's oils.

4 Remove the saucepan from heat and strain out the ginger, keeping the tea.

5 Add the honey to the hot tea and stir to dissolve completely.

6 Drink either hot or cold. It's beneficial either way.

BENEFITS: Helps control cholesterol; assists in weight loss; aids regulation of blood pressure; and is an anti-inflammatory, which helps relieve joint pain.

3 Honey Varietals

IN THIS PART . . .

Honey is made in every corner of the world. Find out which countries are the top ten honey producers, and which states are the top ten in the United States.

There are thousands of different varietals of honey, depending upon the floral source. Become acquainted with 50 fantastic varieties worth trying.

Honey is one of the most adulterated foods. Find out how you can avoid becoming a victim to these greedy practices.

Chapter **6**

Discovering the World's Top Honey Producers

H oney is produced in every state in the United States and in every country around the world (see Figure 6-1 for a visual of where the top producers are located). So it's inconceivable to realize that there's still not enough honey produced to meet the growing demand. Beekeepers can never be sure how much their bees will produce, yet the demand increases each year.

In this chapter we explore who's making the honey, where it's produced, and some other interesting details about the beekeepers, the floral sources, and the varieties of honeys they produce. This data clearly shows the importance of a honey crop to agriculture, international trade, and ultimately honey consumption by consumers. *Note:* Although these are ranked in order, data changes from year to year and can vary depending upon who is doing the reporting.

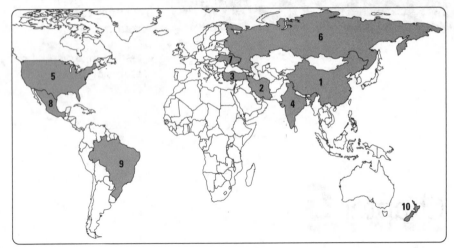

FIGURE 6-1:
The world's top ten honey producers. Number 1, China, produces more honey than any other country.

© John Wiley & Sons, Inc.

1. China (500,000 tons)

The People's Republic of China is the fourth largest country in the world, yet it ranks number one in the world for honey production and consumption. And it shows no sign of slowing down anytime soon. Covering 3,705,406 square miles with 7 million managed bee colonies, beekeepers in the land of the red dragon produced a whopping 500,000 tons of honey, out-producing any other country in 2019. Because of its vast landscapes and climatic regions between the north and south, there are nectar-bearing plants in bloom almost year-round. The locals enjoy honey produced from a wide range of floral sources like rapeseed, milk vetch, lichee, longan, jujube, linden, acacia, sweet clovers, buckwheat, sunflower, and ivy. A good part of this honey is exported to Japan, Germany, the United Kingdom, and various countries in the European Union. The Chinese love their honey and consume three times more than they produce, so they rely on New Zealand's highly regarded Manuka honey to keep them sweetened up. Presently, honey from China is banned from being imported into the United States. However, sources say that a lot of Chinese honey is still coming (being laundered through third countries).

2. Iran (112,000 tons)

Beekeeping in Iran dates back some 2,000–3,000 years, and the tradition of producing honey has not changed much over the years. Iranian beekeepers swear the modern honey we taste today has the same high-quality flavors the Shahs once consumed. Beekeeping is a family tradition, and hives have been handed down to the next generation. There are close to 138,000 beekeepers in Iran and 98 percent are working with modern beehives and the other 2 percent work with traditional wild hives. Iran produces nearly 112,000 tons of honey annually from 10.6 million bee colonies. West Azerbaijan, East Azerbaijan and Ardabil top the list of Iranian provinces where honey is produced. Iran exports 1,400–1,500 tons of honey every year. Because of the country's wide floral diversity and four seasons in arid, semi-arid, and cold climates, Iran is well suited to produce a wide range of varietal honeys. Milk vetch, thyme, jujube, orange blossom, eucalyptus, coriander, sunflower, alfalfa, dill, honeydew, cotton, barberry, camelthorn, and acanthus are produced throughout the seasons.

3. Turkey (110,000 tons)

Turkey is a major player in the world of honey production with more than 110,000 tons produced annually. They produce 92 percent of the world's most sought after pine honey or honeydew, called *Basra*, which is produced by honey bees who sip up the sweet droppings of the *Marchalina hellenica* aphids that live on the pine trees.

Seventy-five percent of the country's beekeepers are migratory, moving their bee colonies to follow the bloom in order to produce mono-floral honey. Beekeeping is a traditional activity among every region of Turkey. However, due to erratic and unpredictable climate, beekeepers can never be sure of their actual production each year. Nearly all the honey produced in Turkey is consumed domestically, and there are high tariffs on any honey imports. In 2014, Turkey did export honey to Germany, the United States, Jordan, Hungary, and other Middle Eastern countries. Honeys produced are orange blossom, chestnut, Anzer, and of course, mad honey and Elvish honey.

4. India (85,000 tons)

Beekeeping is not a new practice in India. Honey was mentioned in ancient Vedas and Buddhist sacred writings, specifically in their traditional Ayurvedic medicine. There are 20,000 different bee species in India, and only 7 are honey bees. Apiculture is practiced by poor, landless farmers who live in the forest to provide employment to support their families. Beekeepers produce 85,000 tons of honey. In 2019 the market for honey in India was worth 233,843,338 U.S. dollars. Per capita consumption is only 50 grams per year. Of the honey produced in India, 85 percent is exported to the United States, the European Union, and the Middle East. Common honeys produced are acacia, lychee, sunflower, rapeseed, and eucalyptus. However, beekeeping is not a sweet business, as pesticides have been found in honey produced in India. And honey is largely unregulated by the government. India is known as the land of spices because it produces an unparalleled diversity of spice. Many of these spices are pollinated by honey bees.

5. United States (81,000 tons)

In 2016, the United States produced 81,000 tons of honey. There were 2.78 million colonies producing all that sweet stuff. Below is the breakdown of the ten states (shown in Figure 6-2) that are doing most of the heavy (and sticky) lifting.

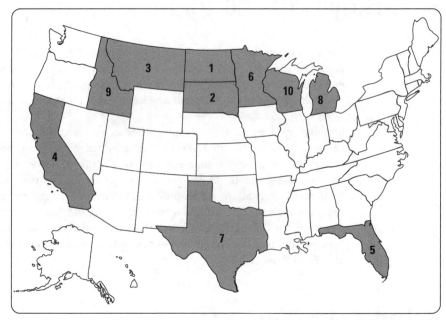

FIGURE 6-2:
The top ten honey-producing states in the U.S. Number one and number two are tied for first place.

© John Wiley & Sons, Inc.

1. North Dakota (19,000 tons)

This state wins as the state that produces the most honey in the United States. There are more than 246 registered beekeepers with somewhere between 1,000 and 1,500 colonies of honey bees. Each colony can produce approximately 78 pounds of honey, totaling over 38 million pounds. At $1.80 per pound, that's a whopping $71 million dollars in value.

A good number of these beekeepers move their bees to warmer climates during the harsh, cold winters of North Dakota, allowing them to produce honey all year long. The honeys produced in North and South Dakota are highly prized for their mild, pleasant flavors. This is where the truest white sweet clover is produced, as well as delicate alfalfa honey. One beekeeper sells a 2-pound jar of clover honey for $54! If you've never tasted pure white sweet clover honey, then you're missing out on one of our national treasures. When this honey crystallizes it becomes a delightful spreadable cream, and there is no other honey in the world that has its unparalleled cinnamon spice flavor.

2. South Dakota (19,000 tons)

South Dakota may only have 270 beekeepers, but 30 percent of them are considered commercial and manage 280,000 colonies. The climate of South Dakota is perfect for nectar production, as the flatlands offer four distinct seasons ranging from cold, dry winters to warm and semi-humid summers. For this reason, the flowers secrete nectar best on the prairies during warm days and cool nights. The primary honeys produced are alfalfa and sweet clover, which are light and highly sought after for their delicate flavors. South Dakota crops that benefit from honey bee pollination include alfalfa, buckwheat, canola, legumes, and sunflowers and are worth over 15 billion dollars of agricultural production.

3. Montana (7,000 tons)

Big Sky Country is a prime habitat for honey bees. After working the almond orchards in California and then pears, apples, and apricots in the Pacific Northwest, bees find the diverse landscape and long, warm summer days a welcome retreat. Currently there are around 230 registered beekeepers in Montana with 160,000 colonies, many of these being commercial beekeepers. They produce 7,000 tons of honey. In the last 40 years, production has doubled.

4. California (6,850 tons)

California is the world's largest producer of almonds and supplies nearly 80 percent of the world's supply. All those almond trees require honey-bee pollination in February and March just to produce the little nut we are so dependent upon. This type of mass production requires more than half of all honey-bee colonies in the U.S. to be shipped into California for pollination. Most of the resulting almond honey is fed back to the bees as they will be moved to the next farm to continue the pollination trail. Beekeepers in The Golden State produce very little honey — just about 12 pounds per colony — because of ongoing drought, fire, mudslides, and the wine industry. But the 6,850 tons of honey that California does produce are exquisite; sage, avocado, eucalyptus, and orange blossom. In 1976, Ormond R. Aebi of Santa Cruz extracted 404 pounds from a single hive, setting a Guinness World Record.

5. Florida (5,950 tons)

The Sunshine State boasts more than 4,000 registered beekeepers who produce 5,950 tons of honey. Domesticated honey bees are the state's most valuable agricultural asset because they pollinate all the major crops throughout the state, including strawberries, citrus, squash, avocado, and blueberries.

The Florida panhandle is known for its tupelo honey production. It was made famous by the film *Ulee's Gold* starring Peter Fonda as a beekeeper, which is most likely how honey came to be dubbed "liquid gold." Between beekeepers in southeastern Georgia and those in Florida, only 200 beekeepers are allowed to float their bees into the swamps of the Apalachicola River basin in Gulf County, Florida, where the tupelo trees bloom. Don't blink your eyes, because the delicate pom-pom-shaped tupelo flowers only bloom for a short two weeks, and if the weather doesn't cooperate, bees can completely miss the nectar flow. If you miss out on this green-colored honey, there are always orange blossom, various citrus, saw palmetto, black mangrove, and gallberry honeys to spread on your morning toast.

6. Minnesota (3,905 tons)

Minnesota may be the land of 11,842 lakes, but that doesn't stop its 126,000 bee colonies from producing honey. In 2017, honey production from beekeepers with five or more colonies in Minnesota totaled 3,905 tons, up 18 percent from the previous year. The honey crop was valued at $14.5 million — a good reason to argue that Minnesota's nickname should be changed from the bread and butter state to the bread and honey state. The state's 86,943 square miles enjoy a humid continental climate, with hot summers and cold winters allowing beekeepers to produce some interesting and rare honeys you just won't find on the shelves of mass grocers. One beekeeper sells limited harvest of buckthorn, Joe Pye weed, and purple loosestrife honey. More common honeys produced around the state are basswood, dandelion, alfalfa, sweet clover, and black locust — all delicious in their own right.

7. Texas (3,700 tons)

As the saying goes, everything is bigger in Texas, and the Lone Star state is perfectly suited for honey making because it is the state with the most farmland in the entire United States. In 2019 Texas reported 132,000 honey-producing colonies, which made 3,700 tons of honey. Most of this honey is produced in the eastern part of Texas because the climate is nearly perfect.

The western side is drier, and fewer sources of nectar flow. Central Texas has a decent spring flow, but it freezes in the panhandle, so very little honey is produced there.

Texas has another big secret: The historical city of Uvalde, in the Texas Hill Country, is known as the honey capital of the world. During the 1905 World's Fair held in Paris, France, their famous guajillo honey won first prize. Guajillo is a native plant that is also known as huajillo in Spanish because it is also produced just south of the border in Mexico. Slow Food's *Ark of Taste* has designated guajillo honey as one of the endangered honey plants. Next time you're in Texas, you must taste this warm, fruity honey. Texas also produces citrus honeys, especially ruby red grapefruit and orange blossom. You'll also find some clover and mesquite honey.

8. Michigan (2,650 tons)

Not only do Michigan's beekeepers lead in honey production, but the state is also widely recognized as having the most meaderies. Michigan produced a total of 2,650 tons of honey from beekeepers with 76,000 colonies. About 50 percent of the Michigan fruit and vegetable industry depends on the honey bee, second only to California in crop diversity, and making for great sources of fruit for mead making. Leading crops are apples, sweet cherries, blueberries, strawberries, pears, plums, and peaches, all perfect for sweetening up mead.

The top honeys produced in Michigan are star thistle and buckwheat, but you can always find blueberry blossom, red bamboo, basswood, and all kinds of clovers. We think it's safe to say that honey and mead are always in season.

9. Idaho (1,650 tons)

Honey is a sweet business in Idaho; however, it trails second to Idaho's nationally loved potatoes. But on a national level, Idaho is considered a major honey-producing hub. In fact, its 124,000 registered beekeepers manage 143,000 colonies of honey bees and produce a whopping 1,650 tons of honey. These lucky honey bees get to enjoy a diverse range of floral sources as forage: sweet clover, alfalfa, rapeseed, safflower, sunflower, mustard, and flax. The other major commodity produced in Idaho is mint oil. Honey bees are needed to pollinate the 17,000 acres of mint and are essential to the 2 million pounds of oil produced each year. If that's not enough, Idaho's nickname is the Gem State because every type of gemstone can be mined in Idaho. In fact, the largest diamond ever found in the United States was unearthed there, and it was the size of a tennis ball. But we can all agree that the true gems of Idaho are definitely its honeys.

10. Wisconsin (1,500 tons)

Honey bees settled in Wisconsin in the 1820s by way of naturally migrating across the continent from the east coast. The open prairies and forest provided places for bees to settle into hollow trees and take advantage of long bloom seasons.

Wisconsin quickly became the land of milk and honey, touting the most wild honey outside of New England. Eventually, bees were domesticated, and in 2018 there were some 51,000 colonies producing more than 1,500 tons each year. The most important types of honey plants in Wisconsin are dandelion, clover, basswood, sweet clover, fireweed, buckwheat, goldenrod, Spanish needle, and asters.

6. Russian Federation (70,000 tons)

Russia is by far the largest country on the planet, spanning 6.6 million square miles with seven time zones, yet it is home to only 2 percent of the world's inhabitants, just 1.3 billion people. There are only 300,000 beekeepers with a total of 5 million colonies of honey bees. The country is the home of the Russian honey bee, a species that was brought to the United States in 1997 because of its ability to manage Varroa mites and overwinter better than most other bee species. Annual production of honey in Russia is 70,000 tons (considered very little for such a huge country). The average volume of consumption of honey in Russia is about 500 grams per person per year — almost nothing in comparison to the annual consumption level in Germany and Japan of between 2 and 3 kilograms. Beekeepers combat fake honey imported from China, which is largely unregulated and sells at prices the locals can't compete with. Due to a decline in bee populations from pesticides, lack of forage, and monoculture, 20 percent less honey is being produced and prices for Russian honey have risen. Russian honey varietals include linden, sainfoin, chestnut, alfalfa, dandelion, sunflower mountain, and forest honeydew.

7. Ukraine (66,500 tons)

In 1814 a Ukrainian beekeeper named Petro Prokopovych was credited for designing the first beehive with detachable movable frames, paving the way for modern beekeeping. Today, bees are kept in boxes that look like treasure chests with frames inside. Ukraine is the home of The Ukraine Beekeeping Museum, one of the largest in the world. Beekeeping is a skill handed down from one generation to the next and is a large part of the Ukrainian culture. Honey has always been an important part of the Ukrainian economy, with 700,000 beekeepers tending 4 million beehives that produce close to 66,500 tons of honey a year. It's one of the largest honey producers in Europe. Nearly 36,000 tons of honey are exported to the European Union, focusing on Germany, and some 40,000 tons are consumed domestically. Kyiv, the capital city of Ukraine, produces some very desirable honeys. Look for acacia honey, forest (honeydew), rapeseed, linden, and sunflower. The Ukrainians inscribe geometric designs on eggs using their beeswax to create the traditional Ukrainian Easter eggs; this traditional craft is called *pysanka*.

8. Mexico (57,000 tons)

Before the European honey bees were introduced in the West, honey was produced by the native stingless bee *(meliponini)*.Today, Mexican beekeepers have learned to manage the Africanized honey bee, a mutation of inbred Western honey bees. These bees are defensive and somewhat difficult to work with, but they have natural defenses against diseases. Also, they forage longer days and travel farther from their hives, producing more honey than the typical Western honey bees.

Because of Mexico's high diversity of ecosystems and floral sources, it is an excellent region for organic honey production. In 2015 Mexico produced 57,000 tons of honey, exporting 25,000 tons to Germany, the United States, the United Kingdom, Saudi Arabia, and Belgium. Mexico produces 1,150 tons of organic honey from 20 organic-certified beekeepers. This organic honey is mainly produced in the states of Yucatan, Campeche, Quintana Roo, Chiapas, Oaxaca, Morelos, and Jalisco. Some of Mexico's noted honey varieties include avocado, orange blossom, mesquite, mimosa and thyme.

9. Brazil (42,400 tons)

Bee-lieve it or not, beekeeping in Brazil revolves around managing Africanized honey bees (AHB). In 1956, a scientist named Dr. Warwick Kerr traveled to South Africa to study the AHB hoping to learn the secrets of their resistance to diseases and ability to make larger quantities of honey than European honey bees. Dr. Kerr brought back to Brazil 26 swarms that accidentally escaped and slowly began interbreeding and hybridizing with the European honey bees, earning them the name "killer bees." Forty years later, Brazilian beekeepers have learned to successfully work with these bees despite their well-known defensive behavior.

A major producer of organic honey, Brazil has captured the market's attention and the awards to support this unique claim. The honey from Santa Catarina has won four gold medals in Australia (2007), Ukraine (2013), South Korea (2015) and Turkey (2017) for the best honey in the world, at the International Apicultural Congress known to beekeepers around the world as Apimondia.

The United States and the European Union are lucky to be on the receiving end of Brazil's 42,400 tons of honey production, sharing 90 percent of it. Beekeeping is a family tradition with 2.5 million beehives passed down to generations who learn from their grandparents. The beekeepers do not use antibiotics or pesticides, nor do they feed their bees, which allows for clean honey harvest. It's increasingly difficult to find forage for bees away from industrial farms, but the rainforest is a perfect hideaway. You can find Brazil's eucalyptus, orange blossom, and clover honeys with the USDA organic seal of approval.

10. New Zealand (23,000 tons)

Apiculture is a 5 billion dollar industry in New Zealand, and the value is distributed among honey, other bee products, and critical pollination services. You can't talk about New Zealand without mentioning its world-renowned Manuka honey production. In 2018–2019, New Zealand produced 23,000 tons of honey, coming from 36,841 managed hives. Seventeen thousand tons were identified as Manuka. New Zealand exported 4,587 tons of honey, of which 52 percent were Manuka, and the craze is growing. The United States is the top market for mono-floral Manuka honey, followed by China and Japan. The average price for a 1-pound jar of UMF/MGO Manuka honey is $85 USD. In 2019, the value of natural honey exported from New Zealand was nearly 241 million U.S. dollars. Beware — Manuka fraud is a huge business; there's a lot more honey sold that is labeled as Manuka than is actually produced. Believe it or not, the Western honey bee was not introduced to New Zealand until 1893 by an English beekeeper named Mary Bumby, who brought two colonies of *apis mellifera* in woven skep on a six-month journey from England. She settled those two colonies in the eastern shore of the north island, where Manuka was native. It wasn't until 1980 that New Zealand biochemist Dr. Peter Molan confirmed the antibacterial properties unique to the nectar produced from this particular plant. If you can't get your hands on Manuka, other unique honeys produced on the island are well worth trying. Check out the clover, Kamahi, Bush, Kanuka, or Rata honeys.

Chapter **7**

Getting to Know 50 Varietals of Honey

There are literally thousands of different nectar-bearing flowers blooming in the United States and around the world that honey bees visit to produce honey. Surprisingly, some honeys are produced from the sweet droppings of various aphids (read about honeydew honey in Chapter 6). A honey produced primarily from one single floral source is called a *varietal*, and each one has distinctive sensory characteristics.

In this chapter, I profile 50 varietal honeys that are produced from important nectar sources. In addition to all kinds of facts about each honey, I include tasting notes describing what you can expect. These notes can come in handy while you tune up your taste buds and practice your tasting skills. For you chefs, home cooks, and foodies, you can use these notes to match the flavors in each honey to specific ingredients, which is very helpful when developing recipes for foods and drinks. And for you beekeepers, this chapter gives you some insight into the many nectar sources your bees may be visiting.

Note: For each honey in this chapter, I provide valuable information about its bloom time or when the bees would generally be visiting each floral source, its botanical and common names, plus, where in the world this honey is produced, or its provenance, and the environmental variables, terroir, that will affect this plant's ability to thrive and produce nectar for honey making. I hope you'll especially enjoy the tasting notes for each honey and try some of my pairing suggestions. The more you read, the more you'll be inspired to try each honey varietal. (Appendix B has a list of places to purchase some of these honeys.)

Learning about Varietal Honeys

The honeys in this list were chosen based upon their popularity, availability or unique characteristics on a global scale. Following is my list of the 50 most important honey varietals to become familiar with. I've listed them alphabetically for you to easily navigate each one.

1. Acacia

Acacia is a hardwood tree that can reach up to 100 feet tall. Its flowers are pea-shaped and hang in bundles like grapes on a vine. They are creamy white or yellow colored and emit a soft, fragrant floral scent. Acacia flowers produce copious amounts of nectar but not consistently each year. The pollen is gray-colored.

Blooms: May through June for seven to ten days.

Botanical name: *Robinia pseudoacacia.*

Common names: False acacia or black locust.

Provenance: Native to the U.S. Appalachian Mountains and the Ozark Mountains. It can also be found in the European Union, specifically France, Italy, Hungary, also the United Kingdom, Canada, and China.

Terroir: Prefers well-drained soil types and tolerates shady areas.

Honey color: Palest straw, almost transparent with a shiny, glasslike appearance.

Tasting notes: A sweet, delicate, and flowery honey. Primary notes of dried pineapple, vanilla, and almond often with strong ale notes. Slightly acidic. A fairly high fructose content that prevents this honey from crystallizing quickly.

Pairings: Acacia is light enough to be considered an everyday honey that goes well with everything. Perfect for all types of tea, fruit, or cheeses. Drizzle it over a Pecorino Romano cheese or any salty cheeses to balance its sweetness. Use this honey to infuse your favorite herbs, truffles, or nuts, as acacia will not change the flavor. Perfect to enjoy with light beer, chardonnay, or prosecco.

2. Ailanthus

Ailanthus, or tree of heaven, is a medium-sized tree with smooth bark and is often confused with sumac (*Rhus glabra*) because of the similarities of the leaves. The flowers are small and yellowish green with five petals. Both trees have long, swordlike leaves but sumacs are serrated with a single leaf at the end of each branch. On the other hand, tree of heaven's leaves are smooth and have a very pungent odor when crushed. Tree of heaven produces seed pods called samaras that hang in clusters and are orange-brown in color. Sumacs have a spiky panicle of flowers that produces a deep red cluster of fuzzy fruits, which can easily persist into winter.

Blooms: June through July.

Botanical name: *Ailanthus altissima.*

Common names: Tree of heaven, varnish tree, or Chouchun.

Provenance: Native to China and Taiwan. Found in the European Union, specifically Germany, Austria, Italy, and the northeast United States as well as California, Iowa, Texas, Pennsylvania, New Mexico, and Washington.

Terroir: A very rapidly growing invasive tree that needs full sun and is tolerant of dry soil. Dense urban areas.

Honey color: Bright red-amber.

Tasting notes: Bold character; tropical fruit, litchi, cassis, muscat grapes, very persistent with a peach tea finish. Savory and astringent.

Pairings: Try ailanthus honey, if you can find it, on a medley of tropical fruit salad, custard, or rice pudding.

3. Alfalfa

A perennial flowering herb, alfalfa is an important honey plant that resembles the clover with white, greenish-yellow, or violet flowers and lemon yellow pollen. Alfalfa yields abundant amounts of honey when fields are left uncut and grown for seed. In an ironic event in nature, visiting bees are smacked in the head as they try to collect pollen when the alfalfa flower trips. Tripping is a necessary action that releases the pollen from the flower sheath in order for pollination to take place. Older bees learn to avoid tripping the alfalfa flower by drawing nectar from the side of the flowers. It takes younger, inexperienced bees to pollinate alfalfa, as they have not learned to avoid being smacked.

Blooms: April to October.

Botanical name: *Medicago sativa.*

Common names: Lucerne grass, Spanish trefoil, or purple medick.

Provenance: Native to Europe and China; the alfalfa belt of the United States is found in the midwestern part of the country along the corn belt.

Terroir: Prefers well-drained, fertile lime soils. Grows in a wide range of climates, from cold northern plains to mountains to deserts.

Honey color: Light amber with a warm orange tint.

Tasting notes: A smooth, buttery honey with delicate overtones of dry grass and hay. Beeswax flavors. Granulates quickly; high in protein.

Pairings: Drizzle over toasted and generously buttered cornbread or Irish oatmeal. Perfect for all types of teas and baking.

4. Avocado

The avocado tree is a subtropical fruit tree with small greenish-yellow flowers and deep yellow to brown, heavy, and sticky pollen. Avocado trees bear an egg-shaped fruit, which is technically a berry. The blooms are unusual in that each flower begins as a female or male and then changes to the opposite sex throughout the day. The leaves are glossy and leathery, staying green most of the year.

Blooms: Spring and again in summer.

Botanical name: *Persea americana*

Common names: Midshipman's butter, vegetable butter, butter pear, or alligator pear.

Provenance: Native to California, Florida, Mexico, the Caribbean, Israel, Chile, Argentina, and many African countries.

Terroir: Survives in diverse soils, red clay, sand, volcanic loam, lateritic soils, and limestone. Requires humidity and a tropical or near-tropical climate, especially during flowering and fruit setting.

Honey color: Very dark amber often with red-orange hues.

Tasting notes: Avocado blossom honey has a creamy rich, heavy body and texture and is slow to granulate. Look for robust, smoky flavors, baked plums, blackstrap molasses, and warm notes of caramelized sugar and licorice. This honey is full of minerals, antioxidants, and vitamins.

Pairings: Avocado honey makes a perfect ingredient in a BBQ sauce for ribs; drizzle on bacon cheeseburgers or pulled pork.

5. Basswood

Basswood is a fast-growing, softwood tree that produces an abundance of honey called linden or lime tree in the European Union. Small, yellowish-white, fragrant flowers are heart-shaped in drooping clusters and yield large quantities of nectar very quickly. The leaves are heart-shaped with jagged edges.

Blooms: Late June and July.

Botanical name: *Tilia Americana.*

Common names: American linden, lime tree, linden tree, or American basswood. Also bee tree because of its attractiveness to bees.

Provenance: Native to northeast and central United States and Central America.

Terroir: Prefers deep, moist soils in limestone regions, and cold winters and warm summers. Humid air promotes nectar secretion.

Honey color: Pale straw yellow.

Tasting notes: Vegetal and green unripen fruit notes with a strong menthol finish. Astringent.

Pairings: Chardonnay, Fromage blanc; drizzle on green apples then roll into finely chopped walnuts, vanilla ice cream, honey mustards, green melon with fresh mint.

6. Bell Heather

Bell heather is a low-growing, brushy evergreen shrub with flowers that are white to bright fuchsia and also include a wide range of purples and reds. Bell heather is part of the heath family known throughout the Scottish Highlands and becomes a spectacular sight when these attractive bell-shaped flowers are in bloom.

Blooms: Late July to November.

Botanical name: *Erica cinerea.*

Common names: Heather bell, erica, erica cinerea or twisted heath.

Provenance: Scotland and Western and Central Europe. Iceland and Siberia.

Terroir: Drought tolerant. Prefers well-drained soil and full sun.

Honey color: Very dark amber with a tinge of red.

Tasting notes: One of the most well-loved honeys of the world. A strong-flavored and dark-colored honey. Slightly bitter with an earthy aftertaste of burnt caramel, fudge, licorice, rum, and plums.

Pairings: Drizzle over Stilton or cheddar cheeses, and serve with cabernet sauvignon. The Scottish Highlands' famous heather-honey cake is made with bell heather honey.

7. Blackberry

The blackberry is a prickly shrub with pale pink or white-lavender flowers with five starlike petals and clear, dull, greenish-white pollen. In some parts of the country, blackberries are considered invasive and compete with native plants. It requires several visits by honey bees to fully pollinate each nodule, which increases the value and flavors of the blackberry.

Blooms: April to June.

Botanical name: *Rubus fruticosus.*

Common names: Bramble, blackberry, dewberry, and goutberry.

Provenance: Native to Europe, Asia, and Africa, as well as Oregon, Washington, and Mexico.

Terroir: Tolerates poor-soil wastelands, woods, and hillsides.

Honey color: Light amber with a reddish tinge.

Tasting notes: Warm stewed jamlike fruit, deep dark berry flavor. Sour and slow to granulate.

Pairings: Drizzle over a berry cobbler with clotted cream, vanilla ice cream, mix with cardamom to fill Linzer torte.

8. Black mangrove

The black mangrove is an evergreen shrub with tiny clustered white flowers with yellow centers. The oval leaves are green with a gray underside and often covered with salt from the seaside where it is commonly found growing. Black mangroves thrive in salty waters and provide shelter and food sources to marine life, making them key to the local ecosystem.

Blooms: May to July.

Botanical name: *Avicennia germinans.*

Common names: Blacktree, blackwood, mangrove, mangle negro.

Provenance: Native to Belize and Ambergris Caye. Cuba. Found on the banks of the forested Indian River Lagoon and on the salty oceanside of the Gulf Coast of Florida, Louisiana, Mississippi, and Texas.

Terroir: Thrives in the shallow, muddy, brackish wetlands of tropical regions. Requires full sun.

Honey color: Very light amber with a greenish tint.

Tasting notes: Thin bodied, swampy aroma, with mild, sweet but salty notes. Granulates rapidly.

Pairings: Drizzle over Camembert and sliced fresh pineapple, and serve with chardonnay. Mix with brines for pickles and sauerkraut.

9. Blueberry Blossom

The blueberry plant is a native flowering shrub with bell-shaped, white or pinkish flowers. The fruits are edible when they change from pale green to deep blue at their peak in July. Blueberries need to be "buzz" pollinated to produce the fruit; this is best accomplished by bumblebees which can easily hang upside down from the flowers and flap their wings to shake the pollen out of the flower. However, it is the honey bee that gathers nectar to produce blueberry blossom honey.

Blooms: June to September.

Botanical name: *Vaccinium cyanococcus – high bush (cultivated),*

Vaccinium angustifolium – low bush (wild).

Common name: Highbush blueberry lowbush blueberry.

Provenance: Primarily Maine, Michigan, Oregon, Washington, and Canada.

Terroir: Lowbush blueberries prefer an acidic soil and are cold tolerant; on the other hand, highbush blueberries prefer sandy or loamy soil.

Honey color: Light golden amber with a red tinge.

Tasting notes: Buttery and smooth texture. Lactic, fruity with hints of dark berries and tomato paste. Granulates fairly quickly into large crystals.

Pairings: Mix into vanilla bean yogurt with chopped almonds and sliced fresh bananas. Drizzle over sour cream coffee cake or crumb cake.

10. Borage

Borage is a hardy herb with vibrant blue star-shaped flowers with 5 petals and gray pollen. Often grown as an ornamental, borage blooms profusely for weeks at a time providing nectar and pollen for pollinators. Its leaves are silvery, fuzzy, coarse, and edible.

Blooms: June to October in North America and November to March in New Zealand.

Botanical name: *Borago officinalis.*

Common names: Viper bugloss, starflower, or British borage tailwort.

Provenance: Native to the Mediterranean, Germany, Spain, United Kingdom, and New Zealand.

Terroir: Dry wasteland; grows wild in arid areas. Prefers rich soil and full sun.

Honey color: Very pale amber to light lemon yellow, often with a gray tinge.

Tasting notes: Light, delicate, herbal, and floral bouquet with hints of cucumber and orange pekoe tea. Sugary aftertaste. Delicate and silky texture. Slow to crystallize.

Pairings: Add to tea, scones, biscuits, and salad and fruit dressings. Borage flowers are used to garnish the traditional gin-based drink called Pimms.

11. Buckwheat

Buckwheat is an annual herb that is cultivated for flour and is also an important honey plant. The small, fragrant, pink buds mature into clustered white flowers. They secrete nectar early in the morning; the bees work it intensely and then become very cross in the afternoon when nectar flow ceases.

Buckwheat honey is known to be high in minerals, antioxidants, and iron.

Blooms: Spring until summer.

Botanical name: *Fagopyrum esculentum.*

Common name: Common buckwheat.

Provenance: Mainly grown in New York, Pennsylvania, California, Minnesota, Virginia, Michigan, Washington, Ohio, Wisconsin, and eastern Canada. Native to Asia.

Terroir: Grows best in cool, moist climates, preferring light and well-drained soils, although it can thrive in highly acidic, low fertility soils as well.

Honey color: Dark almost black in some cases with red highlights; opaque.

Tasting notes: The smell is intense and pungent with strong notes of leather, horse stalls, or cat pee. The flavor is complex malty with notes of cocoa, coffee and red cherries.

Pairings: Drizzle over blue and other strong cheeses; serve with cabernet sauvignon, port, or Madeira. A perfect replacement for maple syrup on pancakes, waffles, buttered rye bread, and gingerbreads. Good for mixing in barbecue sauces and for brewing dark ales.

12. Chestnut

The chestnut tree or shrub is valued for its large edible nuts and for its wood. The flowers are burr-like and yellowish green and give way to two or three egg-shaped nuts in late autumn. Billions of American chestnut (Castanae denata) trees were devasted by a blight at the turn of the century and the few remaining are listed as an endangered species.

Blooms: May to July.

Botanical name: *Castanea sativa* (Castanea from the name of the town of Kastania in Thessaly, Greece).

Common names: Spanish chestnut, Sweet chestnut, chinquapin.

Provenance: Native to southern Europe, growing in Turkey, Portugal, France (particularly in Corsica), Hungary, Italy, Croatia, Spain, and Bosnia.

Terroir: Requires a mild climate and adequate moisture for good growth. Is sensitive to late spring and early autumn frosts, and is intolerant of lime.

Honey color: Reddish amber.

Tasting notes: Intense, aromatic and pungent. Distinct fruity, dry woody flavors reminiscent of nut shells. Persistent and bitter aftertaste.

Pairings: Drizzle over Gorgonzola or stinky blue cheeses and walnuts, and serve with cabernet sauvignon. Pour over poached pears.

13. Coriander

Coriander is a strong scented annual herb. Its flowers are white or very pale pink and grow in small, spiky clusters. The bright green stems are erect and the leaves have jagged edges. Coriander refers to the seeds of this plant and cilantro is the stalk and its leaves.

Blooms: September and October.

Botanical name: *Coriandrum sativum L.*

Common names: Chinese parsley, dhania, or cilantro.

Provenance: Native to the Mediterranean region. Found especially in Italy, the Pacific northwest of the United States, and the Middle East.

Terroir: Coriander prefers well-drained loamy soil, an acidic soil. Full sun in the morning and partial shade in the afternoon.

Honey color: Light amber; beige when crystallized.

Tasting notes: Aromatic, vegetal, spicy, lime rind, white chocolate, coconut. Crystallizes quickly into a chewy granular texture.

Pairings: A delightful and surprisingly flavored honey, it is best eaten straight off the spoon.

14. Cranberry Blossom

Cranberry blossom is a semievergreen shrub producing dark pink flowers that resemble the neck and head of a crane — hence, the original name "craneberry." The fruits are shiny scarlet berries that are very sour. Its flowers require honey bees to pollinate them.

Blooms: May to June.

Botanical name: *Vaccinium macrocarpon.*

Common names: American cranberry, bounceberry, large cranberry.

Provenance: Native to the United States: Cape Cod, Massachusetts; Wisconsin; New Jersey; Oregon; and Washington. In Canada: Quebec.

Terroir: Acidic, sandy bogs and swamps in cooler regions of the northern hemisphere. Requires full sun.

Honey color: Medium amber with a rich reddish tint.

Tasting notes: Warm, fruity flavors with strong, pungent hints of tart berries and deep, tangy plum notes. Crystallizes very quickly.

Pairings: Drizzle over Brie and walnuts, and serve with zinfandel. A Thanksgiving favorite spread for turkey. Mix into apple butter and vinaigrettes. Enjoy with dark chocolate and over spice breads.

15. Dandelion

Known to most people as a weed, the perennial dandelion is an important flower for honey bees, producing an abundance of pollen and nectar. The flower, a single, golden yellow blossom, is known as a *wishie.* When the seeds mature they form snowy white puffballs that are blown off by the wind.

Blooms: One of the first spring nectar sources.

Botanical name: Taraxacum officinale

Common names: Lion's tooth, blowball, yellow gowan, swine's snout, telltime, priest's crown, bitterwort, wild endive, Irish daisy. (The English name "dandelion" is a corruption of the French *dent de lion,* meaning "lion's tooth," referring to the coarsely toothed leaves.)

Provenance: Found worldwide. Native to Europe and Asia.

Terroir: Northern temperate regions. Grows in pastures, meadows, and wastelands.

Honey color: Deep golden yellow to amber.

Tasting notes: Very intense. Strong, pungent, sharp ammonia flavor. Hints of marsala wine, dirty socks, and dried dandelion flowers. Granulates quickly; creamy.

Pairings: Drizzle over goat cheeses, figs, and pine nuts, and serve with sauvignon blanc. Used to make lemon vinaigrette, herbal jelly, and wine.

16. Eucalyptus

Eucalyptus is an aromatic evergreen tree or shrub with distinctively fragrant flowers that can be cream, pink, or red. The leaves and bark are covered with a blue-gray, waxy bloom that gives this plant the common name "red gum." It's known as the fastest-growing tree in the world.

Blooms: Beginning in spring and flowers all season.

Botanical name: *Eucalyptus camaldulensis.*

Common names: Red river gum, Murray red gum.

Provenance: Native to Australia, Tasmania, and New Guinea. Also found in Italy, Spain, Portugal and Greece. Grown in Arizona, Texas, California.

Terroir: Temperate rain forest or wet regions but drought tolerant. Requires full sun to partial shade.

Honey color: Pale amber to beige, grayish.

Tasting notes: This honey can be described as intense, savory and salty, animal with strong brothy notes. Look for toffee, licorice, and a persistent aftertaste.

Pairings: Salty cheeses, savory meats, cold cuts, olives, or brazil nuts.

17. Fireweed

Fireweed is a tall perennial herb with magenta-purple flowers that grow in large, spiky clusters. Its pollen is deep green-blue to purple. After a forest fire, fireweed is one of the first plants to grow on land that was scorched.

Blooms: June to late September.

Botanical name: formerly known as *Epilobium angustifolium* or *Chamerion angustifolium*, and is now *Chamaenerion angustifolium*.

Common names: Great willow herb, blooming Sally, rosebay willow herb, St. Anthony's laurel.

Provenance: In the United States: Washington, Oregon's Cascade Mountains, southern Michigan, Alaska, and Minnesota. Also found in Canada.

Terroir: Thrives in moist, clay-rich humus, yet tolerates sandy or rocky soils and cool temperatures. Cool nights and warm days produce the best nectar flow.

Honey color: Transparent, palest straw.

Tasting notes: Known as the champagne of honeys. Delicate, fruity, sweet, and smooth. Subtle, tea-like notes with hints of spice and butter. Granulates quickly.

Pairings: Drizzle over fresh ricotta cheese with fresh berries and pine nuts, serve with champagne or prosecco. Fireweed jelly is made from the whole flower.

18. Gallberry

Gallberry is a tall, evergreen shrub with white flowers that produce so much nectar it can be seen shining on the leaves. Black berries hang on to the tree throughout the winter. It's an important native honey plant in Georgia.

Blooms: May to June.

Botanical name: *Ilex glabra*.

Common names: Inkberry, evergreen winterberry, holly, Appalachian tea, dye-leaves.

Provenance: Georgia and Florida.

Terroir: Moist to wet, swampy, sandy, acidic soil found along coastal regions. Ideal production, according to beekeepers, occurs when the gallberry bush has "feet in water, head in sunshine."

Honey color: Light to medium amber with a reddish cast.

Tasting notes: Warm stewed fruity notes, aromatic pine needle finish. Viscous with a glassy texture. Slow to granulate.

Pairings: Drizzle over warm Brie or Camembert and pecans; serve with sauvignon blanc.

19. Goldenrod

Goldenrod is a perennial with long beautiful branches and clusters of bushy golden flowers that produce large quantities of nectar. Goldenrod is an important late summer nectar source for honey bees and must be cross-pollinated by insects and honey bees.

Blooms: August through October. Many people think they are allergic to goldenrod, but in fact it's ragweed that is usually responsible for causing reactions.

Botanical name: *Solidago.*

Common names: Rigid goldenrod, solidago. Solidago comes from the Latin *solidare,* meaning "to make whole."

Provenance: Native to North America, especially New England and eastern Canada, and Mexico. Also found in Hawaii.

Terroir: Tolerates poor, dry soil. Thrives in full sun or shade. Found in meadows, fields, and open woods, and along highways and train tracks.

Honey color: Brilliant golden amber to a warm sunny yellow.

Tasting notes: Intense, bright floral flavor with sharp ale notes and a butterscotch finish. Granulates coarsely.

Pairings: Drizzle over freshly sliced strawberries and toasted pine nuts with cottage cheese; serve with chardonnay or pale beer. Spread on cinnamon raisin toast or challah bread.

20. Honeydew

Honeydew is produced when honey bees sip up the sweet droppings from various plant sucking aphids. There are many plants that host aphids; most often they are types of conifer evergreens like fir, spruce or oak trees. For this reason honeydews are named after the particular type of aphid and not necessarily the plant.

Blooms: Produced in late summer.

Honeydew and insect names:

Metcalfa honeydew: *Metcalfa pruiniosa*

Fir honeydew: *Dreyfusia nordmannianae*

Spruce honeydew: *Chermes viridis*

Common names: Honeydew, forest honey, or mountain honey.

Provenance: Italy, France, Turkey, Eastern Europe, Russia.

Terroir: Honeydew is generally produced from aphids who prefer evergreens which are hardy and prefer colder climates especially mountain forest.

Honey color: Dark brown amber, red or green tint.

Tasting notes: Balsamic, condensed milk, dates, pine needles, medicine, resinous, ash.

Pairings: Sugar substitute for coffee, drizzle over pancakes, waffles, or French toast.

21. Honeysuckle

A bushy, herbaceous perennial, honeysuckle has bright red flowers that resemble a common clover but grows to three feet tall. Its leaves are oval shaped. It's grown for animal forage and hay.

Blooms: May to June.

Botanical name: *Hedysarum coronarium.*

Common names: French honeysuckle, Soola, cock's head, Italian sainfoin, Sulla.

Provenance: Italy, Spain, and France; Northern Africa and the Mediterranean.

Terroir: Honeysuckle prefers fertile, well-drained alkaline soil. Drought resistant because of its deep root system.

Honey color: White, transparent, yellow cream.

Tasting notes: Delicate, crystallizes moderately quick, green vegetal notes; also hay, walnuts, fruity dates, lactic milky.

Pairings: Light and delicate, everyday honey. Drizzle over warm focaccia bread, cheese cake or struffoli.

22. Huajillo (pronounced wa-HE-yo)

A small- to medium-sized desert shrub, huajillo is not to be confused with the Guajillo chili pepper. The blooms are fragrant, small, round, and creamy white to yellow in color, with globular heads. It's one of Slow Food's Ark of Taste honeys.

Blooms: March to early May.

Botanical name: *Acacia berlandieri.*

Common names: Cat's claw, mimosa cat's claw, huajillo.

Provenance: Native to southwest United States and Mexico. Unique to the Edwards Plateau of Texas and to southwestern Texas, including Uvalde County; and northern Mexico.

Terroir: Chaparral or brush country. Sandy, rocky soil in dry desert and uplands. Prefers intense sun.

Honey color: Mild, light golden amber-colored; crystal white when crystallized with a pearly reflection, like new milk.

Tasting notes: Extremely delicate and distinctive taste that is described as very light, smooth, and tangy. Hints of apricot, prune, and cranberry.

Pairings: Drizzle over grilled pork chops rolled in pecans. Use in pineapple-tamarind glaze for pork chops and lamb.

23. Japanese Knotweed

Japanese knotweed is an invasive, perennial plant that has hollow stems with raised nodes that resemble the bamboo plant. It has small, creamy white flowers that are clustered and lace-like. They are an important source of nectar in late summer when little else is in bloom. Japanese knotweed honey is sometimes referred to as red bamboo honey by old-school beekeepers.

Blooms: August to October.

Botanical name: *Fallopla japonica.*

Common names: Japanese knotweed, Japanese bamboo, Asian knotweed or red bamboo.

Provenance: Native to eastern Asia (Japan, China, and Korea), the northeastern United States (Pennsylvania and New York), and Europe.

Terroir: Moist soil, wetlands. Disturbed areas.

Honey color: Very dark amber with reddish tones.

Tasting notes: Warm, confectionary, hints of caramel, brown sugar, and maple syrup flavors.

Pairings: Drizzle over Norwegian gjetost cheese, raisin bread or pears and walnuts. Spread over waffles, pancakes, gingerbreads, banana muffins, and rum cakes. Use in salted caramel recipes.

24. Kāmahi (pronounced car-MY)

Kāmahi is a slow-growing evergreen shrub with small, creamy white flowers resembling a bottle brush and producing white pollen.

Blooms: October to December (New Zealand spring).

Botanical name: *Weinmannia racemosa.*

Common name: Red birch.

Provenance: Produced in both the North and South islands of New Zealand.

Terroir: Rugged subalpine native rainforests or shrublands of New Zealand. Kāmahi prefers full sun and a temperate climate.

Honey color: Golden yellow to light amber to green.

Tasting notes: Strong-flavored honey with hints of caramel, toffee, and molasses, balanced by nutty, bitter flavors. Full-bodied, with very fine crystallization giving it a buttery texture.

Pairings: Perfect for honey fudge, drizzle over granola or spread over tea cakes. Use as a glaze to fish and meats.

25. Kiawe (pronounced kee-AH-vay)

An invasive thorny tropical bush in the same family as mesquite, white kiawe has small flowers in pale yellow–green spikes that bear light yellow bean pods. Kiawe is an excellent honey tree.

Blooms: When three to four years old, frequently flowers twice a year in March and September.

Botanical name: *Prosopis pallida*.

Common names: Huarango, American carob, algarroba, bayahonda.

Provenance: Native to Colombia, Ecuador, and Peru. Naturalized in Hawaii, the honey comes from only the Puako Forest of Hawaii's Big Island, where it has been harvested for 100 years. The Kiawe forest in Hawaii is isolated, making it possible to produce organic honey.

Terroir: Grows in the arid, tropical volcanic lava of an isolated oasis in the coastal forest.

Honey color: Pearly water white with waxy, golden overtones.

Tasting notes: Rich tropical fruit and menthol flavors. A smooth, creamy consistency and extremely fine crystals that produce an effervescent sensation on the tongue. This honey crystallizes very, very rapidly, right in the comb, which gives it the lovely texture.

Pairings: Complements ginger, lemon curd, chocolate, lavender, bee pollen or matcha.

26. Kudzu

Kudzu is referred to as "the vine that ate the south" because of its highly aggressive nature enabling it to literally swallow up entire buildings, cars, and high wires. This trailing, woody perennial vine has trifolate leaves and spiky, purple-violet flowers with a highly fragrant aroma of grape jelly. Kudzu is a copious nectar producer, and honey bees are highly attracted to the flowers.

Blooms: Late summer.

Botanical name: *Pueraria montana.*

Common names: Known as foot-a-night vine, mile-a-minute vine, porch vine, telephone vine, and wonder vine because kudzu can grow aggressively.

Provenance: Native to China and Japan. Found in Alabama's Choccolocco Valley, as well as in Georgia and Mississippi.

Terroir: Prefers open, sunny, abandoned fields and roadsides where winters are mild and summer temperatures rise above 80 degrees Fahrenheit. Deep, loamy soils. Resistant to low-nitrogen soils.

Honey color: Bluish to very dark purple.

Tasting notes: A unusually sweet honey with a candy-like flavor. Fruity notes of grapes and bubblegum.

Pairings: Drizzle over roasted carrots. Mix into whiskey lemonade garnished with sprigs of fresh mint. The blossoms are used to make famous kudzu blossom jelly.

27. Lavender

A small, shrubby herb, lavender is an aromatic plant with a camphor scent; slender leaves; deep bluish, thin stalks; and purple flowers. Lavender honey from Southern France is highly desirable and commands premium prices.

Blooms: From July to August.

Botanical name: *Lavendula L.*

Common names: Lavender, Lavandan, Javanda, lavendel espliego.

Provenance: Native to Southern Europe, especially Provence, France; Bulgaria; Spain; and Portugal. Also Asia and India.

Terroir: Thrives in dry, well-drained, gravelly soils and full sun.

Honey color: Golden amber.

Tasting notes: Delicate notes of dry hay and fresh peaches.

Pairings: Use in lavender ice cream, shortbreads, lavender mint julep. Stir into chamomile tea.

28. Leatherwood

An evergreen tree and one of the largest flowering trees, leatherwood attains maturity at around 250 years old. It is so-named because of the leathery texture of its glossy leaves. Its blooms are delicate, white, rose-like flowers with a honey scent. Leatherwood honey of Tasmania has a reputation throughout the world.

Blooms: Mid-January until early March (Tasmanian summer).

Botanical name: *Eucryphia lucida.*

Common names: Swamp gum, mountain ash.

Provenance: Western Tasmania.

Terroir: The cool, damp rainforest regions throughout the western portion of Tasmania where the soil is rich. The leatherwood tree is part of Tasmania's World Heritage Zone of protected forest, a botanically unique area of rainforest and acidic soils.

Honey color: Golden to medium amber.

Tasting notes: A savory and spicy honey that has a creamy texture. It has persistent floral notes of rose, violet, and caraway seeds.

Pairings: Drizzle over Tasmanian smoked cheddar or Australian cheeses; serve with sourdough bread and cabernet sauvignon. Used to make ginger beers and ales.

29. Ling Heather

Ling heather is a low-growing, perennial shrub with evergreen leaves and purple stems bearing pink-lilac flowers that produce brown to golden red-brown pollen. Ling heather honey is highly respected, commanding high prices.

Blooms: August to September. Beehives are moved to the moorland and heathland regions each summer.

Botanical name: *Calluna vulgaris* (*Calluna* is derived from a Greek word meaning "to sweep," and the plant was used to make brooms.)

Common names: Ling heather, Scotch heather, or calluna.

Provenance: Scottish Highlands.

Terroir: The dominant plant of the Highlands, it covers moors, heaths, and open woods, thriving in the damp, rocky, acidic soil, and in both sunny and shaded locations.

Honey color: Dark amber with a reddish hue.

Tasting notes: Aromatic. Strong, slightly bitter, smoky, toffee-like flavor with plum tones. Known as "the port wine of honeys," ling heather honey has an unusually thick, jellylike consistency. It is too thick to extract from the comb, so it must be gently pressed out. The honey can be stirred until it becomes liquid but will return back to its original jellylike state.

Pairings: Drizzle over Stilton or cheddar cheeses, and serve with cabernet sauvignon. Use in relish and chutney. Makes a nice honey beer.

30. Litchee

Litchee is a tall evergreen tree with gray/black-colored bark and oblong leaves. The panicles grow in clusters of ten or more and bear hundreds of tiny white, green, or yellow flowers that are highly scented. The fleshy fruits are edible and surrounded by a brown rind and inside a seed.

Blooms: June.

Botanical name: *Litchi chinensis.*

Common name: Lychee or litchi.

Provenance: Southeastern Madagascar, Mexico, Australia, and Southern China; tropical Asia; Florida.

Terroir: Subtropic regions, full sun with generous rainfall and humidity. Acidic well-drained soil.

Honey color: Golden amber with red highlights.

Tasting notes: A delicate honey that is both sweet and savory. Fruity and floral flavors of rose and jasmine; crystallizes quickly.

Pairings: Perfect for honey ginger litchee mojitos, smoothies or cantaloupe popsicles.

31. Macadamia

Macadamia nut blossom honey is produced by an evergreen tree with shiny broad leaves and sweetly scented flowers of creamy white, pink, or purple that grow in clusters on long stalks. Each flower bears a round, edible nut that is highly nutritious.

Blooms: February to April (Australian summer).

Botanical name: Macadamia integrifolia.

Common names: Queensland nut, bush nut, maroochi nut, bauple nut; indigenous Australian names include gyndl, jindilli, and boombera.

Provenance: Native to New South Wales and Queensland in Australia. Found in the United States in Hawaii, Arizona, and San Diego, California.

Terroir: Plantations in tropical, mild, high-rainfall, and frost-free climates. Fertile, well-drained soils.

Honey color: Medium amber to dark, deep amber.

Tasting notes: Exotic, savory, not too sweet, with delicious tangy, musky floral undertones. Hints of velvety butterscotch and nuts.

Pairings: Drizzle over ricotta or goat cheese with sliced fresh pineapples or passion fruits, and serve with sauvignon blanc or zinfandel. Enjoy with dark or white chocolate and coconut desserts. Drizzle over banana cakes, vanilla ice cream, fruit salads, and waffles. Used to make honey butter.

32. Manuka

Manuka is an evergreen tree or shrub with dark-colored branches and prickly leaves dotted with oil glands. When bruised, these leaves give off a gingery, peppery smell. Its white or pink fragrant flowers have white pollen.

Blooms: September to June (Australian spring/summer).

Botanical name: *Leptospermum scoparium*.

Common names: Mānuka, manuka myrtle, New Zealand tea tree, broom tea tree, or just tea tree.

Provenance: New Zealand and southern Australia.

Terroir: Found in various habitats from sandy coastal woodlands to sunny wetlands and forests. Tolerant of frost, strong winds, and acidic soils.

Honey color: Medium to dark mocha colored with an orange or red tint.

Tasting notes: Intense medicinal flavors with overtones of burnt sugar. Pleasant gingery, peppery, earthy, woody flavors. Heavy body with a chewy texture. Commonly sold crystallized.

Pairings: Manuka honey is known around the world for its supernatural healing properties and is taken mostly internally as a health remedy for digestive issues and applied topically for Methicillin-resistant Staphylococcus aureus (MRSA).

33. Meadowfoam

Meadowfoam is an annual herb bearing white flowers with yellow centers that are self-seeding. The name "meadowfoam" is a reference to the white foam that accumulates from the ocean waves. Meadowfoam is grown for its seeds, which are pressed into oil and seedcakes to feed cattle.

Blooms: February to April.

Botanical name: *Limnanthes douglasii.*

Common name: Poached egg plant or Douglas meadow foam.

Terroir: Native to Oregon and California where it grows in wet, poorly drained soils, grassy habitats and spring meadows. It survives on moderate sunshine and is cold tolerant.

Honey color: Brilliant golden-reddish amber.

Tasting notes: Vanilla, roasted marshmallows, caramelized custard, burnt sugar.

Pairings: Perfect for mead making, smores or sweet potatoes.

34. Mesquite

Mesquite is a small, deciduous, thorny shrub or scraggly tree with droopy branches of feathery foliage bearing spikes of yellow beans or pods. It has long clusters of fragrant yellow-orange flowers.

Blooms: April and again in June.

Botanical name: *Prosopis glandulosa.*

Common names: Honey mesquite, honey pod, glandular mesquite and algarroba.

Provenance: Native only to California, Arizona, New Mexico, Texas, and the Chihuahuan Desert of Mexico.

Terroir: Shallow, loamy, sandy, desert prairies. Prefers well-drained soil and full sun; tolerates heat and is drought resistant. Abundant rain and then hot periods are ideal for nectar flow.

Honey color: Light to medium amber often with a red or brown tint.

Tasting notes: Sweet yet warm caramel, woody, smoky and nutty flavors. Light, delicate, floral and aromatic. Granulates quickly into a dense paste.

Pairings: Drizzle over goat cheese with sliced fresh mango, and serve with champagne or Sauternes. Mix with lime for barbecue sauces and rubs for smoked ham or ribs. Spread on blue-corn pancakes, whole-grain breads, and corn muffins.

35. Ōhi'a Lehua

Ōhi'a Lehua is the official flower of the big island of Hawaii. It is a widespread evergreen tree on the island of Hawaii, with fiery red, pink, orange, or yellow pom-pom flowers, which are very popular with bees. The flowers are the symbols of erotic love and are sacred to Pele, the goddess of fire and volcanoes, and to Laka, the goddess of hula. The honey is rare and highly sought after.

Blooms: May to July.

Botanical name: *Metrosideros polymorpha.*

Common name: Lehua tree.

Provenance: Native to the forests of the volcano Mauna Loa in the remote Ka'u district on the big island of Hawaii.

Terroir: Found in moist rainforest and shrublands on the north side of the volcanoes. Requires full sun.

Honey color: Water white to light golden amber.

Tasting notes: Fragrant and savory with a buttery flavor. Overtones of butterscotch, salted caramel, English toffee, and lilies. Lehua crystallizes extremely fine, making it naturally creamy and spreadable.

Pairings: Complements roasted almond butter, curried coconut sauce, or oatmeal with cinnamon.

36. Orange Blossom

A small flowering tree, orange blossom bears the citrus fruit that is actually considered a berry. This evergreen tree has oval leaves and white blossoms that are highly fragrant. If you've ever spent time in an orange grove, you will remember the hypnotic, sweet-smelling aroma of the flowers. Honey that is harvested from grapefruit, lemon, tangelo, tangerine, and orange blossoms are usually marketed in the United States as simply orange-blossom honey, with no distinction between the sources.

Blooms: March to April.

Botanical name: *Citrus sinensis.*

Common name: Citrus.

Provenance: Native to Asia. Citrus groves flourish in Spain, Mexico, and Israel, and in the United States in California, Florida, Arizona, and parts of Texas around the Gulf of Mexico.

Terroir: Tropical to subtropical climate; regions free of frost. Light, loamy, moist soils. Secretes abundant nectar when the climate is very warm with no fog.

Honey color: Palest amber with a bright orange tint.

Tasting notes: Delicate floral notes of jasmine, gardinia, and freesia flowers. Fruity with hints of beeswax, lactic and orange lollipops or marmalade.

Pairings: Drizzle over goat cheese and fresh rosemary leaves, and serve with sauvignon blanc. Use in glazes for pork chops, ham, or chicken wings. Ideal for use in marmalades, cranberry sauces and frosting for carrot cakes.

37. Rapeseed

Rapeseed or Oilseed Rape (OSR) is an annual/biennial stalky plant that grows up to 4 feet tall with bright yellow, four-petal flowers. It is one of the oldest cultivated plants on the planet, dating back 10,000 years ago. It's used as a wintertime cover crop because it prevents soil erosion. It serves as an early spring source of both nectar and pollen for honey bees. Rapeseed is primarily grown for animal feed and cultivated for canola and vegetable oils.

Blooms: Early spring

Botanical name: *Brassica Napus* L.

Common names: Oilseed rape, rape, or Siberian kale. Canola is a cultivar.

Provenance: The United Kingdom, Canada, the United States, China, and other European countries.

Terroir: Well-drained soils with a moderate pH; tolerates salty soil.

Honey color: Light yellow, pasty.

Tasting notes: Intense, savory, and sweet. Notes of green vegetal stalks, pigsty, and sauerkraut. Texture can be described as oily at times. Crystallizes very rapidly into large coarse granules.

Pairings: Drizzle over roasted Brussels sprouts, avocado and cheddar cheese sandwiches or use to glaze bacon, pork, or ribs.

38. Raspberry

The name refers to the edible, sweet-tart fruit of the thorny American red raspberry shrub. Usually, the cane growth is attained the first year; then the fruit is produced the second year. The flowers are pink to white and bloom in the late spring through summer. Raspberry is an excellent honey plant.

Blooms: Late spring.

Botanical name: *Rubus strigosus.*

Common names: American red raspberry, lampone, framboisier, frambueso.

Provenance: Native to North America. A leading honey plant in parts of Maine, New Hampshire, Vermont, Washington, and Wisconsin.

Terroir: Typically found in acidic, sandy forest soils. Prefers full sun.

Honey color: Extra light amber with reddish yellow hues.

Tasting notes: Smooth and floral, warm notes of stewed fruit. A distinctive raspberry flavor that has a tart finish. Crystallizes rapidly.

Pairings: Drizzle over goat or Brie cheeses and walnuts, and serve with dessert wines or champagne. Stir into Earl Grey tea or lemonade. Use to make vinaigrettes and mint jams.

39. Rhododendron

The Rhododendron family is divided into two groups: azaleas, funnel-shaped flowers, and Rhododendrons, a large evergreen shrub with oval leaves. Rhododendrons have showy bell-shaped flowers that have tight clusters of large, pink, five-petal flowers.

Blooms: Late June to July.

Botanical name: *Rhododendron spp.*

Common names: Hairy alpen rose or alpenrose, snow-rose, or rusty-leaved alpenrose.

Provenance: Native to the mountains of Europe especially Turkey, including the Italian Alps, Austria, Switzerland, and France.

Terroir: High altitudes, full sun, neutral to acidic soil.

Honey color: Colorless straw; creamy when crystallized.

Tasting notes: Delicate, sugary, beeswax, vegetal, berry jam, watermelon, musky, cosmetic, and propolis notes. Short finish.

Pairings: Drizzle over Val d'Aosta cheese and sliced fresh pears or figs, and serve with vin santo; mix with cinnamon to season winter squash.

40. Rosemary

Rosemary is a woody, perennial herb with grey-green needlelike evergreen leaves that are strongly scented. The flowers are white, pink, purple, or blue clusters and are attractive to honey bees.

Blooms: April to June.

Botanical name: Salvia rosmarinus, previously known as *Rosmarinus officinalis.*

Common names: Rosmarino, romarin, romero.

Provenance: Native to the Mediterranean regions of Spain, Italy, and France.

Terrior: Dry, sandy, rocky soils. Full sun. Warm summers and dry winters.

Honey color: Light yellow to straw.

Tasting notes: Intense herbal and floral flavors. Delicate and aromatic herbal flavors, bitter almond and fruity. Granulates quickly.

Pairings: Glaze roasted lamb or lemon chicken, drizzle over rosemary roasted potatoes.

41. Sage

Sage is a woody shrub with blue-gray aromatic leaves and blue-purple flowers. The foliage secretes a highly pungent, sticky oil. It's an attractive nectar plant for honey bees. The Romans called it the "holy herb" and used it in sacred rituals.

Blooms: April to July.

Botanical name: *Salvia mellifera* (from the Latin word *salveo,* meaning "to save because of its medicinal value").

Common names: Ball sage; black button sage; purple, black, and white sage.

Provenance: Native to the Mediterranean and the California desert coast.

Terroir: Sandy, dry soil; prefers full sun and low humidity. Not cold tolerant.

Honey color: Water white, light amber with a green tinge.

Tasting notes: Elegant with a mild, sweet flavor. A bit of pepper and anise with a floral essence. Heavy bodied. Slow to granulate.

Pairings: Drizzle over butter and sage pasta, sauteed mushrooms with lemon or drizzle on pumpkin soup.

42. Saw Palmetto

Saw palmetto is a slow-growing, dwarf palm tree or shrub with yellow-green sword-shaped leaves that form a fan. The yellow-white flowers have large, reddish black berries that are edible and used as a homeopathic remedy for some types of cancer.

Blooms: April to May.

Botanical name: *Serenoa repens.*

Common name: Saw palmetto, dwarf palm plant.

Provenance: Native to the southeastern United States, most commonly along the Atlantic and Gulf Coast plains of North Carolina, Georgia, Alabama, Texas, and Florida.

Terroir: Sand coastal dunes, flatwood forests, and islands near marshes. Cold hardy. Hurricane and wind resistant. Prefers loamy, sandy soil.

Honey color: Light amber to deep amber.

Tasting notes: Salty and citrusy with anise, prune, and herbal, woody overtones. Often a runny honey as a result of humid climates where it is produced.

Pairings: Drizzle over hard cheeses and serve with ham or prosciutto. Mix as dressings for tart greens or citrus salads. Stir into black teas.

43. Star thistle/Knapweed

There are a few different star thistle species. Some are yellow such as the yellow star thistle, and others are of the purple spotted knapweed variety. Both are tall, thorny weeds with a bushy flower surrounded by sharp spikes that protect its nectar and yellow pollen. They are important honey plants.

Blooms: Summer to late Autumn.

Botanical name: *Centaurea sp.*

Common names: Yellow star thistle, golden star thistle, yellow cockspur, St. Barnaby's thistle, spotted knapweed.

Provenance: Native to the Mediterranean region. In the United States, star thistles are generally found on the west coast and knapweed on the east coast.

Terroir: Dry, drought-tolerant soil. Poor soil on hedgerows, on barren hills, and in neglected fields.

Honey color: Light yellow amber with a greenish cast.

Tasting notes: Vegetal, green banana peel, tropical fruit, pineapple, spice, baby wipes. Granulates quickly. Buttery texture and somewhat astringent.

Pairings: Drizzle over salty cheeses or kiwi and mango fruits. Pairs well with green melon with fresh mint or banana bread; glaze a grilled salmon and serve with sparkling wine or beer.

44. Strawberry tree

The strawberry tree is an evergreen shrub with dark green, shiny leaves and fragrant pinkish-white, bell-shaped flowers. The showy edible fruit is round, prickly, and bright red, and despite the plant's common name, is not the same strawberry as the garden variety *fragaria*.

Blooms: October to December into January.

Botanical name: *Arbutus unedo.*

Common names: Strawberry tree, cain tree, cane apple, Killarney, bitter honey Irish strawberry tree.

Provenance: Native to the Mediterranean region, especially Sardinia, France, Greece and Northern Africa; and Ireland.

Terroir: Grows in lime soils. Prefers dry, hot summers. Drought resistant.

Honey color: Medium to dark coffee.

Tasting notes: Strong, intense bitter, flavors of caramel, licorice, fresh green peppers, herbaceous, and slightly smoky and savory.

Pairings: Drizzle over traditional seadas, goat and alpine cheeses.

45. Sunflower

Sunflowers are tall, annual herbs with hairy stalks and bold-faced, daisy-like flowers. The leaves are hairy, rough like sandpaper, and somewhat oval shaped. The face of the flower is brown, and the petals are supple and golden yellow. These flower heads follow the direction of the sun, rotating from east to west during the day, thus giving them the genus name *helios*, meaning sun. Sunflowers are grown for edible oils and their seeds.

Blooms: June and August or September.

Botanical name: *Helianthus annuus* L.

Common names: Marigold of Peru, corona solis, sola indianus, chrysanthemum peruvianum.

Provenance: Grows in Georgia, Delaware, Minnesota, North and South Dakota, Nebraska, Wisconsin, and Utah as well as Italy, Austria, France, and Spain.

Terroir: Prefers dry plains, prairies, meadows with dry soil and full sun. Fast growing.

Honey color: Bright yolk yellow.

Tasting notes: Vegetal, fresh pollen, dry hay, fresh apricots, and tomato paste. Crystallizes rapidly and usually into a very compact mass.

Pairings: Drizzle over yogurt and serve with sliced fresh peaches or nectarines. Spread on biscuits or sesame bread. Used in making candy nougat.

46. Thyme

An aromatic perennial herb, thyme grows in small clusters close to the ground. Its tiny flowers are white, pink, or purple and grow in long clusters at the end of its woody stems. The leaves are evergreen in most species and filled with oil glands that show off its strong aroma.

Blooms: July through September.

Botanical name: *Thymus capitatus.*

Common names: Common or garden thyme, Persian hyssop, or Spanish oregano.

Provenance: Greece, Italy, Spain, Croatia, and Mediterranean islands.

Terroir: Hot, sunny locations with well-drained soil, although it is drought tolerant.

Honey color: Caramel, beige to amber.

Tasting notes: Intense, reminiscent of dried magnolia flowers, aromatic, cloves, cedar or pencil wood, burnt plastic.

Pairings: Drizzle over Greek salad with feta, tomatoes, red onions, and cucumbers. Mix into Greek yogurt with granola. Use to make lemon-pepper glaze for lamb, fish, and poultry.

47. Tulip poplar

The tulip poplar is an ornamental tree with stunning, fragrant, cup-shaped flowers that have two rows of six petals. These flowers are pale yellow with a brilliant yellow and orange stripe on the inside. Unfortunately, since the tulip tree often towers well above 100 feet high, you may not notice the flowers until they drop to the ground. The tree has four-lobed leaves that turn a blaze of gold each autumn.

Blooms: April to June.

Botanical name: *Liriodendron tulipifera.*

Common names: Tulip tree, white wood, yellow poplar, tulip magnolia, American tulip tree.

Provenance: Native to the middle eastern seaboard of North America. An important honey plant in Virginia, Tennessee, Kentucky, Georgia, and North and South Carolina.

Terroir: Moist, well-drained, acidic soil; full sun. Sensitive to heat waves and drought.

Honey color: Dark amber with a very deep reddish amber tinge.

Tasting notes: Rich, savory notes of dried fruits, dates, and prunes.

Pairings: Pour over maple walnut ice cream or pecan pie. Spread on cinnamon toast, cornmeal and bacon waffles or warm bran muffins.

48. Tupelo

The tupelo is a gum tree with clusters of yellow-greenish flowers that develop into soft, red, berrylike fruits. Tupelo honey is rare and is considered one of the most delicious honeys. In order to harvest the honey, honey-beehives are placed on platforms in the swamps where the tupelo gum grows. The process is expensive and labor intensive, making this honey sought after and highly respected.

Blooms: March to May.

Botanical name: *Nyssa ogeche.* (The name of the genus is derived from Nysseides, the name of a Greek water nymph.)

Common names: Tupelo, nisa, Ogeechee tupelo, river lime. (Tupelo comes from two Cree words that mean "tree of the swamp.")

Provenance: Native along the Apalachicola, Choctahatchee, and Ochlockonee rivers of Georgia and along the Chipola and Apalachicola rivers of northwest Florida.

Terroir: Prefers moist, well-drained, acidic soils of the pineland swamps. Likes full sun, but tolerates light shade.

Honey color: White or extra light amber with a greenish cast.

Tasting notes: Rich buttery texture. Floral aroma with herbal notes and hints of cinnamon, melon, and pears. Because of its high fructose levels, the honey is very sweet and crystallizes slowly.

Pairings: Drizzle over blue, aged pecorino, and other robust cheeses, and serve with cabernet sauvignon or Syrah. Mix as a glaze for pork chops.

49. Ulmo

A slow-growing evergreen shrub, Ulmo has large white, camellia-like flowers with four petals. The leaves are dark green and oblong shaped. Honey bees are attracted to its aromatic nectar. Ulmo trees are threatened by logging because the wood makes excellent firewood.

Blooms: January to March (Chilean spring).

Botanical name: *Eucryphia cordifolia.*

Common names: Gnulgu, muermo, roble de Chile.

Provenance: Native to Patagonia, Chile, and the Cocham Valley in Argentina. It is also found in Araucania and Chiloe in Chile. Ulmo grows well in Scotland too and has been introduced in the north Pacific coast of the United States.

Terroir: Every year the coastal evergreen forest is covered with the white Ulmo flowers. In the temperate rainforests along the Andes Mountains. This land is rich in humus, and the climate is humid. Full sun.

Honey color: Light amber with pink tones.

Tasting notes: Silky, buttery, with exotic perfume of aniseed, jasmine, vanilla, violet, and cloves. Touches of tea and caramel.

Pairings: Drizzle over traditional Chilean chanco, panquehue, and quesillo cheeses. Pour over vanilla ice cream, dulce de leche, rice pudding, flan, and corn cakes.

50. Yellow Sweet Clover

The small yellow flowers are clustered on long, spiky stems. Yellow sweet clover is grown for hay or to improve the soil. The oval shaped green leaves have jagged edges and grouped in three's. This clover honey is the honey all other honeys are compared to because it is thought to be the most pleasing to the widest variety of consumers.

Blooms: Spring to summer.

Botanical name: *Melilotus officinalis.*

Common names: Clover, trifoglio, trefle, trebol.

Provenance: Native to Europe and Nebraska, North and South Dakota, Canada, and New England.

Terroir: Prairies, disturbed areas. Prefers moist, temperate climates with lime soils and sufficient rain.

Honey color: Water white to straw yellow.

Tasting notes: Sweet, delicate flavor. Notes of vegetal, dry hay with a distinctive cinnamon and spice finish. Crystallizes quickly into a creamy paste with very fine, smooth granules.

Pairings: Best honey to eat on toast with butter. Perfect for herbal teas and spreading on tea cakes, scones or warm biscuits.

A Word about Wildflower Honey

Wildflower honey is produced when bees forage for nectar in a region that has a wide variety of floral sources throughout any given season. The various nectars are naturally blended inside the hive by the bees, and the honey will take on its own unique characteristics from the type of flowers and the region it was produced. Much of the honey produced in the United States is a unique combination of the local plants and can be just as delicious or complex as any honey produced from a single floral source. For example, a wildflower honey produced in Tennessee will look, smell, and taste different from one produced in Nebraska or Croatia because each environment has its own local floral sources and terroir. No two harvests of wildflower honey will taste the same. An experienced honey taster often can pick out specific floral sources in a batch of wildflower honey if they are familiar with the floral sources and the sensory qualities of the honey produced in the region. For example, a particular wildflower honey produced in the Northeast can have intense ale and butterscotch notes mixed with caramel.

Take note that when honey bees blend honey it is a natural process of the local nectar sources of that region; however, when humans intervene and blend honeys from different floral sources or regions that would never naturally grow together, the flavor profile can end up tasting unnaturally muddy.

Chapter **8**

All That Glistens Is Not Liquid Gold

Did you know that more than half of the honey sold in the United States can be funny honey, and some of it may not even be produced by bees? When humans become greedy and intervene in the wholesome qualities of honey for the sake of making profits, it damages honey's reputation and hurts beekeepers. Unfortunately, honey is the third most adulterated food after olive oil and milk, making it subject to widespread fraud. In this chapter, we introduce the common types of honey fraud found in the marketplace.

According to the National Honey Board, the United States consumed 596 million pounds of honey in 2017, yet if we gathered up every drop of honey produced by U.S. beekeepers, we would only come up with 148 million pounds. Something doesn't add up! Where does all that extra honey come from? Anyone involved in the honey industry knows quite well that it is extremely labor intensive and expensive to produce. So, in order to meet the growing demand, honey is imported from other countries by U.S.–based honey importers and packers — a whopping 75 percent of it. Much of this honey is used as an ingredient to sweeten packaged foods like cereals, power bars, and baked goods. Honey adds perceived value and health benefits, so it makes perfect sense for marketers to use it to their advantage to sell more food. This chapter reveals the dark side of the honey industry so you can be aware of the types of honey fraud that exist in the marketplace and become a honey detective to make informed choices.

Laundering Honey

Have you ever considered that much of the honey you purchase may be a blend of various honeys from different countries? Some of it may have traveled 15,000 miles, stopping at a few different countries before arriving at your local grocery store. More often than not, this honey from several countries is blended together and then filtered at high temperatures to remove pollen and slow down the natural crystallization process. Sometimes the color of a honey is intentionally lightened to make it more visually appealing, and other times honey is mislabeled as to the country of origin. In fact, you may come across honey that has been cut with cheap sweeteners or wasn't made by honey bees at all. These shady practices are called *honey laundering* and are, unfortunately, what happens when greed meets profits and humans try to deceive customers just to avoid the law.

Why on earth would anyone corrupt nature's oldest and most perfect sweetener? In truth, honey's popularity is growing, so no doubt these nefarious practices are economically driven. Honey consumption is up, and yet honey prices are down. To meet the ever-growing demand for honey, the United States imports honey from Argentina, Brazil, India, and Vietnam. It is also common to see Canadian and Mexican honey in the marketplace. Argentina and Brazil are attractive because they produce honey that can be labeled USDA organic, and if customers do not read the fine print, they often believe this organic honey is produced in the United States. Some of this imported honey is legitimate and fairly good quality; however, misleading consumers as to authenticity and country of origin is illegal and considered fraud.

WARNING

The sad truth is that adulterated honey can be an unhealthy combination of processed sugars, very old and possibly fermented, or just have off flavors. These imports often sell at lower prices than beekeepers can sell their own honey for, and they damage honey's virtuous reputation.

Presently, there are very few regulations and standards regarding honey quality; however, the USDA has a honey grading system for liquid, also referred to as *extracted*, honey. The system is similar to the one for maple syrup, and it was instituted in 1951 and last amended in 1985. The system is confusing and complicated because it is based upon a point system that rates each honey by its moisture content and the presence of defects and foreign particles, but aroma and flavor receive little consideration. The system also allows for honey to be heated to slow down crystallization. Beekeepers and honey producers are encouraged on a volunteer basis to use this grading system and slap the seal with the appropriate grade on their labels. The ratings are Grade A for the best-quality honey, then B and C for honeys of lower quality, and D for the lowest or substandard quality used for baker's honey and not intended for human consumption. In fact, I have never seen any honey sold in retail stores with a grade lower than A, for obvious reasons. Sadly, there is very little enforcement of this system, and basically it only works when the government receives complaints from consumers.

Honey is graded based on certain standards. They are based on a technical point system using water content, flavor and aroma, clarity, and absence of defects as a ruler. You find these grades mostly on commercially produced or imported honeys. Here are the four grades of honey and their standards:

>> U.S. Grade A honeys appear clear, have good flavor and aromas, and are free from caramelization, air bubbles, pollen, propolis, and wax particles.

>> U.S. Grade B honeys are considered reasonably clear, have reasonably good flavor and aromas, and may have few air bubbles and pollen, propolis, and wax particles.

>> U.S. Grade C honeys are fairly clear, have fairly good flavor and aromas, and are fairly clear of air bubbles and pollen, propolis, and wax particles.

>> Substandard is the quality of extracted honey that fails to meet the requirements of U.S. Grade C.

The American Beekeepers Federation and other honey associations want a legal definition and federal standard for honey and have petitioned the FDA to establish one, yet the FDA has continually refused. There is an international standard for defining honey used by Codex Alimentarius (a collection of internationally recognized guidelines, standards, codes of practice, and other recommendations relating to foods, food production, and food safety that is voluntary.) The FDA states that honey is "a thick, sweet, syrupy substance that bees make as food from the nectar of plants or secretions of living parts of plants and store in honeycombs." This definition sounds fair; however, there is very little oversight in the United States.

REMEMBER

Because honey has a complex supply chain, it can be adulterated at many points along the way. Any qualified lab that specializes in honey adulteration has developed a different test for each type of fraud. The most commonly requested test is to identify added sugars, heat treatments, pollen analysis, and botanical origin. It isn't possible for consumers to test every jar of honey, so we recommend purchasing your honey closest to the source or beekeeper. This way you are supporting beekeepers and consuming a healthy product.

Transshipping Honey

At one time, China was our biggest supplier of honey. It dominates the world in honey production, and in 2016, China produced 700 million tons, exported 128,000 tons to the United States and sold it well below what domestic beekeepers can sell their own honey for. In 2001 the United States placed anti-dumping duties or tariffs on Chinese honey imports to reduce competition with domestic producers. That's when the Chinese got clever and began *transshipping*, or rerouting honey to third-party countries to bypass these tariffs. Shipping documents were falsified to change the country of origin from China to Taiwan, Malaysia, Indonesia, or the Philippines to dodge U.S. customs and deceive consumers.

WARNING

Chinese honey and beeswax were also found to have traces of a veterinarian-approved antibiotic, *chloramphenicol*, which is a treatment beekeepers use to control a devastating bacterial disease called *foulbrood* in their colonies. American foulbrood can wipe out a colony of bees unless the beekeeper takes action to treat them with this antibiotic. Unfortunately, some beekeepers did not follow the instructions and overtreated their colonies or applied the treatment during a nectar flow when bees are producing honey that is intended to be harvested. In high doses, chloramphenicol can kill an otherwise thriving colony and, in the least cases, it ends up in the beeswax and honey. Consuming honey with high levels of chloramphenicol can induce a rare blood disease in humans called aplastic anemia where your body stops producing new blood cells and leaves you fatigued and open to other infections. Other honey samples that were traced back to China were tested in the lab and found to have heavy metals, which are banned in the United States because of their links to cancer.

HONEYGATE

Your favorite honey brand just may not be what you think it is.

International honey laundering is a problem for the global honey industry as well as consumers. In 2013 U.S. Immigration and Customs Enforcement and Homeland Security uncovered the largest food fraud sting in history. Two of the largest U.S. honey suppliers and 14 others, including executives from a German-owned food company, were charged with purchasing honey from China, faking documents, and illegally importing more than 3,000 drums of mislabeled honey, some containing high levels of antibiotics. Driven by deep profits, illegal honey can be sold well below the cost beekeepers can charge, and more importantly, it is a public health issue.

Honey laundering is considered a federal crime, and any company that takes advantage of the law can be fined and those involved can even be sent to prison. It is estimated that 180 million dollars have been uncollected in duties from imports of counterfeit honey.

Removing Pollen to Conceal the Honey's Origin

Removing pollen from honey to prevent crystallization may sound like an innocent practice; however, there's more to it than meets the eye. Pollen finds its way into every step of the honey-making process. It falls from the flowers into its own nectar. Then the hundreds of foraging bees return back to the hive covered with pollen from the various floral sources they each have visited. It's a given that every drop of honey produced by bees contains a wide range of pollen granules from various floral sources. Each tiny pollen granule is as unique as a snowflake in size, shape, and texture and reveals valuable information about the geographic and botanical origin of each honey sample.

The study of pollen in honey is called *melissopalynology,* and specially trained pollen experts or *palynologists* are employed by honey-testing labs to investigate honey adulteration and fraud in the marketplace. By studying each grain of pollen in a honey sample, they are able to learn about the history of it. They begin by isolating the pollen from the liquid honey using centrifugal force and then view it under the microscope. This work is quite laborious, and very few people in the United States are trained experts in this field (see one expert in Figure 8-1). A palynologist must be knowledgeable about pollen and flower morphology and take into account that some flowers deposit unequal amounts of pollen into their nectar.

FIGURE 8-1: Palynologist Dr. Vaughn M. Bryant at his microscope.

Courtesy of Vaughn M. Bryant

Consideration must also be given to the fact that when bees sip up nectar, it is deposited inside their honey stomach, where the transformation to honey begins. During this process, pollen is separated from the nectar by an organ called the *proventriculus* and passed through the bees' digestive system. To further complicate this process, a coefficient factor to accurately measure the pollen in each honey sample must be considered for each specific floral source.

Once all the types of pollen in a honey sample have been identified and counted, a pollen profile is created, which is matched to the floral sources of the region or country where the honey was allegedly produced. This profile must be consistent with the floral sources of the country of origin that is listed on the honey label. If not, the honey is considered mislabeled and fraudulent.

WARNING

Unfortunately, the practice of intentionally removing pollen from honey is used by some larger producers and importers to conceal the country of origin to avoid importation taxes. Some unscrupulous companies remove the pollen through a process called *ultra-filtering,* which requires applying extremely high heat to the honey to thin it out. This allows the honey to be easily forced through tiny filters to remove all traces of pollen and other flavor faults. If you thought that was bad enough, some importers take the process one step further by carefully adding pollen granules back into the honey that match the floral sources of the country they want listed on their honey label. Thus, it's nearly impossible to accurately trace the honey to its true floral sources and country of origin.

Blending Honeys

As the demand for honey increases, some beekeepers quickly realize that they are unable to produce enough to meet their customers' expectations. When the pressure is on to keep the shelves stocked and customers happy, beekeepers are forced to take action or lose business. After all, honey is a product of nature, and a beekeeper can never know for sure how much they will produce each year. In an attempt to keep up with increasing honey orders, it makes perfect sense to purchase honey from other beekeepers not only to keep your customers well supplied but also to increase your own offerings. Some may think that there is nothing wrong with this practice as long as the honey purchased is good quality. Some customers insist on locally produced honey, and that may not always be an option. In truth, most consumers who purchase honey are not expecting a single origin flavor profile; they just want something sweet to put in their tea or on toast. Most importantly, is the honey a beekeeper purchases to resell as his own a product that he would proudly put his own business name on?

The most common form of honey fraud is mixing honey to bulk up supply without changing the flavor enough for the unsuspecting consumer to notice. This can take on a few different forms. In one scenario, producers may blend their premium unifloral honey with 10 percent of another floral source or a low-quality honey. One common honey used for cutting prime honeys is soybean honey because it is light in color and nearly odorless and flavorless and barely changes the flavor when added to a larger batch of premium honey. Soybeans are grown in several states such as Illinois, Iowa, and Minnesota, and they are quite attractive to honey bees because of their high sugar content and abundance of nectar. In the United States, there are over 90 million acres of soybean crops!

Another common practice of commercial producers with a familiar brand name is to blend honeys from various sources to come up with a consistent flavor that is tasty and will be popular with their customer base. Each bottle of their honey is always a medium amber–colored honey that is a bit too sweet and tastes exactly like generic honey. This is successful because some consumers expect their honey to have a consistent flavor just like their favorite soft drinks. It takes an experienced taster to understand consumer preferences and come up with a pleasing flavor profile, but once the recipe is determined, it works like a charm.

Blending honey from different floral sources or regions is more common than you may think, and there is nothing illegal with this practice as long as everything inside the jar is 100 percent honey. But what if some honey is a blend with honeys from different countries? You would have to read the fine print on the back of the label or the side seam of the jar to find out. For some consumers the country of origin is important, especially if foreign honeys are blended with domestically produced honeys. You may ask what's wrong with that — it's all honey, right? In theory, all honey is honey regardless of where it was produced. But honey that is commercially imported in bulk is often shipped in large metal drums inside containers. They are required to be pasteurized to kill botulism spores and slow down the crystallization process. When honeys from different regions and floral sources are intentionally blended by humans and are not a result of the bees' natural foraging, the flavors tend to taste like a muddy mess to experienced tasters. This is because some of these floral sources do not naturally bloom at the same time of year or even in the same region and would never be blended in nature by bees.

Cutting Honey

Another common form of honey adulteration is cutting honey with cheaper sugars or artificially feeding bee colonies sugars like rice fructose syrup, high fructose corn syrup, or cane or beet sugar in various combinations. Even just 10 percent added to your liquid gold can easily bulk up inventory and income without the customer noticing a difference in flavor. Anything that is added to a bottle of honey, whether it is sugars, nuts, or herb or spice infusions, must be clearly listed somewhere on the label or it is considered adulteration.

Intervention of Humans

If honey laundering isn't enough to convince you to check your honey label twice, here are a few more ways humans devalue honey, creating sickly, sweet syrups, most of which are difficult to identify in laboratory tests.

In an attempt to produce more honey faster, some beekeepers have been known to artificially feed their bees liquid sucrose, high fructose corn syrup, or other sweet liquids rather than letting bees forage for blossom nectar. Bees happily sip up sweet liquids when readily available to them rather than expend energy foraging for nectar to turn into honey. This not only artificially speeds up the honey-making process, but also produces a honey that is flavorless and unnaturally sweet with no health benefits whatsoever. Unfortunately, some of these sugars are difficult to identify in the lab because they have a similar chemical composition to honey.

Another scheme is to harvest immature or unripe honey before the bees have fully finished transforming and capping it with beeswax. This honey has a high water content, appears runny, and most likely will ferment prematurely because the bees did not have time to finish the job. To counter this, industrial-sized drying machines that act as dehumidifiers are used in the honey house to dry out the honey and reduce the water content to 17 percent to keep the honey stable. Another tactic is to add plain white granulated sugar to absorb excess moisture to bring the water content down.

Again, this honey lacks any flavor and tastes just sweet because the nectar was removed from the hive before the bees were able to completely transform the nectar into honey.

TIP

Despite all the opportunities to cheapen and undervalue honey, there is a bright side, and that is to make it a point to meet and support your local beekeepers. You may even consider taking up beekeeping yourself to make your own liquid gold.

4

Becoming a Honey Tasting Expert

IN THIS PART . . .

Develop the skills needed to become a honey tasting expert.

Become familiar with the differences between flavor and taste, and between odor and aroma.

Understand how to refine your taste buds and improve your sense of smell.

Take a test to find out if you are a *supertaster*.

Use our aroma and flavor wheel to communicate what you are tasting.

Use our color wheel to define and describe the color of honey being sampled.

Find out about the different grades of honey.

Get the story on things that can go wrong with honey and how to recognize and avoid these defects.

Take a look at the role that soil, climate, and geology play in influencing the honey harvest.

Chapter **9**

Thinking Like a Honey Sommelier

'll bet if you are reading this book, you have eaten honey on many occasions. Perhaps spread it on your breakfast toast? Maybe drizzled it into a nice cup of tea? But here's a question . . . have you ever really and truly *tasted* honey? Can you detect the subtle flavor nuances that differentiate one honey from another? Can you identify the floral source the honey came from? Can you tell where in the world it came from? Discovering how to taste and truly appreciate honey is a fine art similar to tasting wine or olive oil. All honey does not taste the same. And there are so many amazing varietals, each just begging to be savored and appreciated (see Chapter 8 for profiles of the world's most famous varieties of honey).

Trained wine sommeliers understand the many flavor nuances of wine — which grapes the wine is made from, where it likely came from — and they know the perfect pairing of a particular wine with a particular food. Now it's honey's turn, as it's the next artisan food obsession.

In this chapter (and the three that follow), you'll uncover the basic skills and techniques to become a honey sommelier. Now that's something you can really brag about! But first, you need to understand a few things about your tongue and nose and a bit of science before you dive into honey tasting. I will also give you some hints and fun exercises on how to describe what you are tasting, smelling, and observing.

WHAT'S A HONEY SOMMELIER?

I actually coined the term *honey sommelier* years ago in my first book. After completing my training in Italy to become an officially Certified Honey Sensory Expert, I realized that the skills I cultivated are not that different from a trained wine sommelier. A *honey* sommelier is someone who is a professional trained in the sensory analysis of honey, specific to tasting, evaluating, and pairing honey with foods.

Differentiating Taste and Flavor

Did you know there's a difference between taste and flavor? We tend to use the two words interchangeably. But scientists know better. These two are not the same. *Taste* refers to what we experience on our tongues. *Flavor* is something we experience in our noses.

Taste sensations

When you put food in your mouth, it comes in contact with your taste buds. You have thousands of taste buds on your tongue. There are also taste buds on your upper palate, the side of your mouth, and even down your throat. All of these tiny taste buds have receptors that are able to distinguish between just five basic taste sensations: sweet, sour, salty, bitter and something called *umami* — a Japanese word that describes that nom–nom sensation we associate with "savory." For example, think about the taste sensation associated with mushrooms, tomato paste, or soy sauce. See Figure 9-1.

Flavor sensations

While food is in your mouth and you are breathing, the food molecules move up the back of your throat toward your *olfactory bulb* (it's behind your nose). Here the molecules are translated into *flavors*. Think of flavors as things like cinnamon, lemon, green asparagus, or lactic cheese.

REMEMBER

In fact, often when we say that something tastes delicious, we really mean it smells delicious.

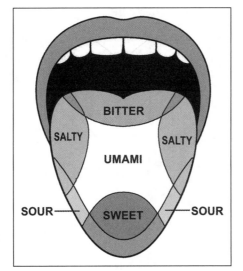

FIGURE 9-1:
This illustration maps the five different tasting zones of the tongue.

BITTER

SALTY   SALTY

UMAMI

SOUR   SWEET   SOUR

Illustration by Howland Blackiston

TIP

Here's an easy way to appreciate the difference between taste and flavor. Remember as a kid when you had a bad cold and maybe Mom made you chicken soup. At first, you could only appreciate the *taste* of the warm, salty broth because your taste buds on your tongue were working, but your stuffed-up nose put your olfactory bulb out of commission. Once you started feeling better, you could actually begin to *recognize* the distinct *flavors* of the carrots, celery, onion, and chicken bits.

Other taste sensations

You experience other sensations through the nerves around your mouth and face when you have honey in your mouth. They are physical and chemical reactions that are separate from taste and flavor. Some honeys can be described as having qualities of astringency, spiciness, refreshing, or warmth. Tannins in honey make your mouth pucker, and you feel like you need a drink of water. And have you ever chomped into a habanero pepper? Zowie! Those are wicked hot. In contrast, there's the refreshing cool sensation of powdered sugar versus the comforting warmth of malt sugar. All these hot and cold sensations are not related to the actual temperature of the food, but to a sensation that's triggered by the trigeminal nerves in your head. These sensations add to the overall mouthfeel experience of tasting honey. See Figure 9-2.

Now you're starting to think like a sommelier!

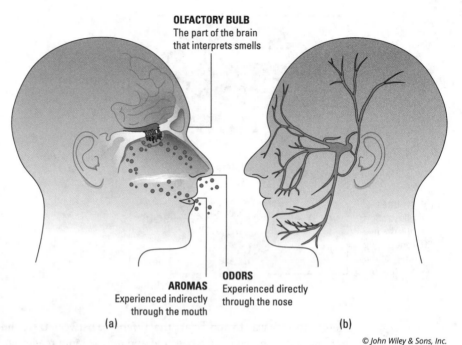

OLFACTORY BULB
The part of the brain that interprets smells

AROMAS
Experienced indirectly through the mouth

ODORS
Experienced directly through the nose

(a)

(b)

© John Wiley & Sons, Inc.

FIGURE 9-2:
Honey *flavors* are actually aromas that vaporize in the mouth and are then perceived by the olfactory bulb (a) and your trigeminal nerves (b).

Are You a Supertaster?

Does a cup of bitter espresso make your toes curl? Or does radicchio salad over-power your palate? Then you just may be a supertaster. Sensory scientists define supertasters as those who are very sensitive specifically to the bitter sensation in certain foods. Also, the flavor of certain foods is perceived as much stronger for supertasters. This is attributed to the gene TAS2R38 and a dense configuration of taste buds *(papillae).*

TIP

By the way, women are far more likely than men to be *supertasters.*

If you're wondering whether *you* are a supertaster, try this test at home. You'll need the following items:

>> Paper hole punch

>> Small sheet of white paper

>> Blue food coloring

>> Mirror

>> Magnifying glass

When you have what you need, follow these steps:

1. **Using the punch, make a hole in the piece of paper.**

   You need a piece of paper that's just about an inch larger than the hole itself.

2. **Dab a little blue food coloring on your tongue.**

   You only need to stain the front third, center of your tongue. This will highlight your taste buds.

3. **Now place the paper with the hole on your tongue. See Figure 9-3.**

4. **Using the magnifying glass, look into the mirror and count the taste buds inside the hole.**

If you can count more than 35 taste buds within the hole, congratulations! You are considered a supertaster! I'll bet you can't wait to tell your friends!

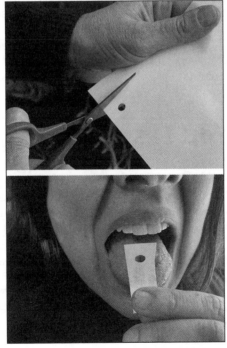

FIGURE 9-3:
A simple test for counting the number of taste buds within the area created by a paper hole punch.

Photo by Howland Blackiston

The Nose Remembers

Our sense of smell may be the most underutilized of our five senses. While you can taste only five basic sensations on your tongue, you can likely recognize thousands of flavors by smell. Smells are powerful memory makers, and we all associate smells with people, places, and things we've experienced during our lives. Smells also can alter your moods and emotions without your full awareness.

Smells are also used by savvy marketers to tempt consumers into spending more money. Did you know that in many grocery stores they introduce the sweet odor of cinnamon rolls to make our mouths water so we buy more groceries?

Have you eaten food or smelled something that has left a distinctive mark on your memory? For me, it's that amazing pumpkin pie my Aunt Jennie always baked at Thanksgiving. And it's the nostalgic smell of granddaddy's aftershave lotion. These are known as *scent memories,* and they can take each of us back to a unique experience in our lives. In fact, it is the repetition of specific scent memories that helps us identify everyday objects. For example, if you rode horses as a youth, you would no doubt immediately recognize the smell of hay if you were blindfolded. The more diverse scent memories you consciously remember, the better you become at picking out flavors in honey. So, by all means, keep sniffing and remembering those scents!

Describing What You Taste

I often hear people describe honey as sweet, yummy, or unique. Unfortunately, these words don't really tell us what the honey actually tastes like. Describing the nuances and individual flavors of a honey and then putting it into words takes a bit of practice and experience. You need to develop a large vocabulary of descriptors.

How do honey sommeliers describe all those complex flavors and sensations as they taste honey? They begin by understanding the basic flavor families. These are broad categories to describe the aromas and flavors of honey. Table 9-1 lists the nine major flavor families and a few examples of foods and items that can help you increase your ability to describe what you taste.

The more varieties of honey you sample, the more likely you are to come across some that have surprising and unexpected smells and flavors. I'm sure you will eventually come across a honey you will describe as cat pee or a gym bag. These are not necessarily negative adjectives. If the honey reminds you of cat pee, it most likely also has additional smells, some good and others not so much. When you describe the flavors of a honey, these are objective observations. Everyone has different perceptions. Some love cilantro, and others think it tastes like soap. To each their own.

TABLE 9-1

Honey Flavor Families

Flavor Family	Samples of This Flavor Family
Fruity	Stone fruits, berries, citrus, melon
Floral	Violet, rose, honeysuckle, dried flowers
Warm	Confection, chocolate, coconut, dairy, nuts, marshmallow
Refreshing	Peppermint, aromatic
Vegetal	Green stalks, freshly cut grass, hay
Chemical	Pharmacy, cosmetic, detergent, turpentine
Animal	Sweat, cat pee, gym bag, leather
Woody	Sawdust, old trunk, attic, clove
Spoiled	Beer, fermented, vinegar, mold, basement

Cat pee adjectives never stopped anyone from buying a high-priced bottle of sauvignon blanc.

REMEMBER

Tuning Up Your Taste Buds and Sharpening Your Sniffer

Before you get into the next chapter and start actually tasting, evaluating, and describing honeys, here are ways you can train and appreciate your own sense of taste and flavor.

Training your sense of taste

Here's a fun tasting exercise (shown in Figure 9-4) you can do at home, or better yet, with a friend or family member. It helps you identify the five basic categories of taste. You'll need a few things from your kitchen to stage the challenge.

1. **Gather a few small containers.**

Small shot glasses, demitasse cups, or mini bowls will do the trick.

2. **Label each container 1–6, as follows: Salt–1, Sweet–2, Sour–3, Bitter–4, Umami–5, and Plain Water–6 (that's the control).**

3. **Gather the makings for the five actual taste categories.**

   You can use table salt for the salt sensation, granulated sugar for sweet, lemon juice or white vinegar for sour, powdered espresso coffee for bitter, and soy sauce for umami. For the control, just use plain water.

4. **Mix a pinch of each of the dry ingredients or a few drops of liquid ingredients with 4 ounces of plain water.**

   Mix well until completely dissolved. Use a clean spoon for each.

5. **Now have someone line up the five containers in a random order.**

   Make sure the labels are hidden from your view (assuming you are doing the exercise).

6. **Take a sip from each container and swoosh it around your mouth where it can touch all the taste-bud zones.**

   Try to identify each taste category. Record your choices on the notepad. Do this for all six samples. How did you do?

FIGURE 9-4:
Ready for the tasting exercise. You can tell from looking closely at the notepad that this was a tasting session in Italy.

Photo by C. Marina Marchese

TIP

For a Tasting Sheet that you can copy and print for your own use, be sure to visit the *Honey For Dummies* online Cheat Sheet at dummies.com.

Refining your sense of flavor

Maybe you're not so sure what "fruity," "vegetal," or "animal" smells like. You may have trouble describing the flavor of these and the other nine members of the flavor family. Anyone can improve their skills and become a better honey taster simply with a bit of practice using simple everyday items found right in your own kitchen, garden, or garage. This exercise can help.

1. **Begin with our list of nine flavor families (see Table 9-1) and gather up sample items for three to five of the flavor families.**

   It may be a piece of chocolate or fruit, fresh sawdust from your workshop, herbs or fresh flowers from your garden.

2. **Place each sample in a small, clean glass container.**

3. **Find a quiet place to sit and start sniffing. Sniff the first item by inhaling through your nose with your mouth closed. Move it away from your nose and try again.**

   The first sniff is the most accurate, but a few will reinforce the scent. Covering the lid with one hand holds the aroma inside the glass until you're ready to sniff again.

4. **Concentrate as you inhale each and try to describe in words what you smell. If you are unable to describe it, think about what memories you associate with that object.**

   Does it remind you of familiar foods, places you've vacationed, or even a special person? Does it make you feel a certain way?

5. **Locate the object in the list in its appropriate family. Take notes as you work; this reinforces the experience and keeps your thoughts organized.**

6. **Move on to the next object and do the same.**

You may try this exercise with a friend and share your notes and learn together. Often one person smells something that another doesn't until it is mentioned. This is a great way to increase your "smell vocabulary."

Continue practicing using new objects each time. It doesn't hurt to revisit old ones as well to keep your senses sharp.

TIP

You can fatigue your olfactory bulb by over-smelling during this exercise. We suggest sampling only five to eight items at a sitting. Take a break in between and smell your sleeve or your skin. This refreshes your nose by neutralizing your senses so you can begin to use your nose fresh again.

Chapter **10**

Knowing How to Taste Honey

nlike other sweeteners, honey is not just sweet, it has *flavor!* Most people don't take the time to really *taste* honey side by side to appreciate the interesting nuances of the smells and flavors of different types of honeys.

I first became fascinated with the honey my own bees make and its ever-changing flavors, year after year. It became clear to me that honey production paralleled wine production in respect to *terroir*, a French term to describe the variables of environmental conditions like the soil, climate, and geography (see Chapter 11 for more on terroir), which are responsible for the unique characteristics of any food produced in nature. In regards to honey, we also have to take into account the work of the bee and the many floral sources from which they gather nectar. As a beekeeper, I figured there must be a way to match all those complex flavors in honey to the specific flowers from which the bees were producing it.

On a trip to Montalcino, Italy, I stumbled upon a honey festival where honey experts were presenting a honey tasting by passing around samples of unifloral honeys. The honey was beautifully presented in wine glasses. They described the color, smells, and flavors of each honey in detail, much like a wine sommelier. My passion and enthusiasm earned me an invitation to attend an introductory course in the sensory analysis of honey in the remote town of Guspini, Sardinia. It was four eye-opening days of smelling and tasting dozens of honeys under the guidance of Italian honey experts. It was everything I dreamt it could be. Italy is the world leader in the sensory analysis of honey — like wine and olive oil, honey holds a noble place in their food culture. Over the following year, I completed my formal training in Bologna, Italy as a honey sensory expert. And in 2015, I was honored to become the first American to be accepted into the Italian National Register of Honey Sensory Experts. This chapter brings to you much of what I learned in honey school.

Tasting honey is as much an art as it is a science. And it is a bit different than just eating honey. In this chapter, you discover the step-by-step methods used by professional honey sensory experts to evaluate any honey sample. You find out what to look for and expect as you are guided through the tasting process. The methods are easy to grasp, but they can take years to master. But it's a great way to learn and challenge yourself, and along the way you gain more experience and discover new ways to taste honey in a conscious and organized manner. The more honey you taste, the quicker you learn. And when you taste honeys side by side, you create reference points and memories that sharpen your tasting skills. It's a delicious adventure.

Looking, Smelling, and Tasting: Sensory Analysis

Looking, smelling, and tasting are the three basic steps for understanding how to taste honey using the methods of *sensory analysis.* Now, what's sensory analysis? It is a method originally developed to taste and evaluate wine and it's also used to evaluate chocolate, olive oil, tea and other artisan foods. Now it's being applied to honey. When you train to be a honey sensory expert, you discover how to objectively look and evaluate the characteristics of a honey sample including its color, smell, taste, flavor, and texture. In effect, you are using the same methods and skills as a "wine sommelier."

REMEMBER

As you work your way through the process, remember that your evaluations shouldn't express your personal opinions. So, when you say a honey is bitter, you are not expressing negativity; you are simply stating that it has a bitter quality or note. It's important to remember that an expert taster may not particularly like a bitter note in a honey, but he can objectively identify it and still appreciate this characteristic. And some people actually enjoy bitter foods and honeys.

TIP

Some of the more unusual and unexpected qualities of some honeys begin to grow on you. When you're ready and brave enough, check out Corbezzolo honey to find out how much bitter in a honey you are able to tolerate (see Chapter 22 for a list of ten honeys to put on your bucket list).

You are encouraged to use your own personal references or scent memories while taking notes. For example, you may note that a certain honey reminds you of a horse stall or perhaps a particular brand of soap. These personal references are familiar to you and can help you to remember each honey you taste. Use them!

Sensory analysis is not the only tool to evaluate honey and identify its floral source, but it is something almost everyone can use and learn. You can do it right in your own home. You don't need to hire a lab or buy special equipment.

Sensory analysis complements *chemical and pollen analyses,* which are performed in a lab, require an expert, and cost you plenty. The chemical analysis of honey can identify adulteration, overheating, and even freshness of a honey. Pollen analysis can determine the region in which the honey was produced by identifying the pollen of a specific geographic area, and in some instances, its actual botanical source.

Sensory analysis gives you the tools to describe and identify a honey by its characteristics and identify off flavors and defects. All three evaluations (sensory, chemical, and pollen) are part of painting the entire portrait of a honey.

In Chapter 12, we discuss some defects of honey that can only be identified through a trained honey sensory expert, as a lab test cannot always detect some of them.

Creating the Right Environment for Tasting

The environment in which you decide to taste and evaluate your honey is almost as important as the honey itself. You will be utilizing your senses in a deliberate and conscious way that can become emotionally exhausting. Choose a quiet space away from distractions where you can spread out and enjoy the process.

Making certain you are fresh and rested

Be sure to get some rest before you begin a session. Find a quiet room with natural lighting and a comfy chair at a table, so you can spread out your honey samples and tools. Avoid an area where there are cooking or other foreign odors that can interfere with your ability to smell and taste. You may find that places with loud music or distracting sounds can also affect your ability to focus and taste clearly.

Staying healthy

Your general health can also affect how you experience a honey; for example, a cold or stuffy nose makes it difficult to smell and taste your honey. An achy tooth or certain medications can throw off your senses. Remember, some days you feel great and your senses are as sharp as a pin, and other days are just so-so. Just work the best you can or continue another day — you'll find that over time your senses will recalibrate themselves.

Fasting before tasting

At least one hour before tasting honey, you should avoid eating or drinking anything except water And don't brush your teeth. Strong flavors and generally all foods linger in your mouth and can change your perceptions as you taste.

Avoiding extraneous smells

Hand moisturizers, colognes, and perfumes interfere with your ability to smell correctly. These fragrances linger on the containers and even the spoons you touch with your hands. You may not be aware of these everyday smells the first time you taste honey, but the more sensory work you do and as you focus on fine-tuning your senses, you will become fully aware of these everyday smells around you that you previously ignored.

Think about a time you may have been cooking dinner or just making a pot of coffee when the phone rang or you had to walk the dog — whatever the reason, you had to leave the room. When you came back inside, you smelled that dinner or coffee so distinctly because when you left the room for a few minutes, you gave your nose a break. You see, your nose smells much more than you pay attention to, and once it becomes accustomed to smells around you, it kind of shuts down until you leave the area and then return.

As you practice sensory work, you will smell everything all the time. Now, if someone pops open a pail of goldenrod honey in my honey house, I can smell it from across the room — no kidding!

Setting Up For Honey Tasting

I find nothing more relaxing than kicking back and tasting some newly acquired honey samples. I am constantly asked which honey is the best or which has the best flavor. It's not possible to declare any honeys as having the best flavor because we each have our own personal preferences. It is, however, possible to taste two or more samples of, say, a eucalyptus or mesquite honey and declare one as the best representation of that floral source once you have some experience and become familiar with what qualities make up a good sample of a particular varietal of honey.

Fun fact: As you taste each honey, the honeys you'll memorize the quickest are the ones that are your personal and least favorites. Here is where your taste memories work closely with your emotional reaction to the honey you taste. You'll have to work harder to memorize characteristics of everything in between.

Figure 10-1 shows a tasting session. It's a fun thing to do with friends. You can even make a party out of it (see Chapter 19). You do need a few things before you begin to stage the area where you plan to taste your honey samples. The following sections give you the rundown.

FIGURE 10-1:
A honey tasting session.

Photo by C. Marina Marchese

Picking honeys to sample

You need to choose some honey samples. Whether they're your own or store bought, having a few varietals to taste side by side gives you some references to compare and contrast each honey as you go through the tasting process. I suggest you start by choosing a light-, medium-, and dark-colored sample. The more varied, the better. But start out with no more than three to five samples at each sitting, so you can focus on less and don't overwhelm your palate.

For your first tasting, I guide you through the evaluation process of three common unifloral honeys. I suggest clover, orange blossom, and buckwheat. These honeys are fairly easy to find, and each has very different sensory qualities. Like all honeys, these are produced in very specific regions, so if you are unable to get them in your local area, try a gourmet food shop. Or you find them for sure online. You may also follow along with any honey samples you have handy. For best quality, choose honeys packed in glass containers (not plastic) from a smaller producer rather than a commercial brand.

Gathering your tasting tools

Before you dive into your honey samples, you want to "stage the tasting" with some helpful tools for your first guided tasting session. I suggest the following tasting tools.

Choosing the right spoon

The spoon you use to taste honey is essential and affects how you perceive each sample. Don't use plastic biodegradable spoons. Most biodegradable utensils are corn-based and taste like corn chips or breakfast cereal. And metal spoons are not recommended because they can react with the honey, resulting in "off" tastes. So what do I recommend? Single use plastic mini-tasting spoons. Gather up your clean plastic spoons and put them into a cup labeled "new" or "clean" spoons. Have another empty cup handy labeled "used" or "dirty" spoons. Each time you taste a honey, always use a new clean spoon (even if you are tasting the same sample several times). In other words: No double dipping!

Containers for your tasting samples

You need a separate container to put each honey into for the actual tasting. Here's where you can whip out some of your favorite wine glasses. It's best not to taste or evaluate honey directly from its original jar or bottle because you need to be able to move the molecules and stick your nose into the container to capture the aromas. You'll understand this better as you read later in this chapter about how to smell honey. The container you taste your honey from should be transparent glass and approximately 5–6 ounces. All the containers should be identical for consistency.

Pour a few spoonsful of each honey into each container, don't overfill - leave room to stick your nose inside for the smelling portion of the evaluation. Cover the wine glass with a piece of plastic wrap to hold those delicate aromas inside the glass. Choose a glass with a rounded base similar to a tumbler or a small stemmed red wine glass — these are perfect and will do the trick. Keep a stack of damp paper napkins or towels nearby to wipe drips of honey as you go through the tasting. Wipe fingers and containers as you go along. Sticky makes stickier, and you do not want things to get out of hand. Spice up your tasting and break out cloth napkins to make things fancy.

Getting organized using a tasting mat

Organize all your honeys on a tasting mat (see Figure 10-2). A tasting mat is simply a sheet of paper divided up into a grid, usually with 4, 6 or 8 sections, one box for each honey sample. Our honey tasting mat has 6 hex shapes to place your honey samples on. Honey should be tasted the same as wines — from light to dark. So set up your honey samples in sequential order starting with clover on the left, orange blossom in the middle, and buckwheat on the right. This keeps you organized as you taste each sample in an orderly fashion. Jot down the order in a notebook and on the tasting mat so you don't get mixed up.

FIGURE 10-2: A simple tasting mat like this helps organize your honey samples.

Photo by C. Marina Marchese

TIP

You can download your own tasting mat by visiting the *Honey For Dummies* online Cheat Sheet at dummies.com.

Picking a palette cleanser

Palate cleansers are an important part of the tasting process. They clear your palate between each honey you taste. Some honeys have a long finish or strong flavor that lingers in your mouth, and this is where a palate cleanser comes in handy. I find that nibbling on a tart green apple between tastings is a great way to refresh your palate and prepare it for the next taste of honey. You should also drink plain water (without ice or lemon).

TIP

Did you know that it is difficult to taste foods that are too cold or hot? Cold and hot temperatures decrease the perception of taste and flavors. For this reason, you'll better appreciate tasting honey at room temperature.

Writing Tasting Notes

Grab a notebook, a clipboard, or a personal journal to record your notes as you work your way through tasting each honey. You can also use our handy Honey Tasting Notes sheet (see Figure 10-3) to keep your thoughts organized. These notes will be your guide for all your honey tastings and a keepsake of every honey you've tasted. Write down all your impressions for each step of the evaluation process. Use a separate sheet for each honey sample. You will find out how to use the honey color and aroma and flavor chart in the color section of the book. Also, include your personal notes and scent memories. There is nothing corny or wrong with jotting down that a particular honey reminds you of the smell of the vase of expired lilacs in your living room.

TIP

You can find a copy of this Honey Tasting Notes sheet included with the *Honey For Dummies* online Cheat Sheet at dummies.com.

Starting with a basic look-see

Now that you have gathered your honey samples and tools and settled into a comfortable chair, you are ready to begin tasting honey. Stage your tasting mat, pour your honeys into the glass containers, and have your spoons, green apple, napkins, and glass of water ready. Wipe all the drips up and now you are ready.

Photo by C. Marina Marchese

FIGURE 10-3: Use the Honey Tasting Notes sheet to write down your evaluations for each honey sample.

Begin with the first honey sample, clover or the lightest one you have available. Have your notebook ready or use our Honey Tasting Notes sheet.

Using a clean spoon, drizzle three to four spoonsful of honey into the bottom of the first container or wine glass. Try not to drip the honey onto the sides of the glass — a clean presentation matters.

Determining liquid or solid

First, take note of the physical state of the honey. Is it liquid, crystallized, or a combination of both? Honey is considered liquid when the entire sample is fluid. Crystallized honey has turned completely firm, pasty, or creamy. Some honeys are in between, meaning it may have various sized crystals floating in liquid or semi-liquid. Write your evaluation in the physical state field on the Honey Tasting Notes sheet.

The physical state is not necessarily important in regards to the flavor, but it's more relevant when you begin the texture and flavor evaluations. The visual evaluation of your honey sample continues with examining it for its *aspect*, meaning everything you can describe about the honey except for its color.

Discovering undesirable stuff

Does your honey sample have a foam streak, floating bee parts, pollen granules, beeswax flakes, or other foreign particles that should not be present in honey? Yuck! Take note of any foreign objects in your notes.

The foam that occasionally occurs in a bottle of honey is made up of air bubbles that happen during the process of extracting the honey from the frames. Foam in honey is unavoidable and rises to the top of the honey jar. Sometimes foam will disappear after settling. If not, take note of it. Often foreign particles float to the top of the jar and end up in the foam. Not desirable! These can be noted in the clarity field on the Honey Tasting Notes sheet.

Evaluating clarity

Another visual aspect of honey is its clarity. Is the honey opaque, transparent, or in between? If you hold the honey up to a light source and the light doesn't pass through it, describe the honey as *opaque*. If you are able to read the newspaper through the honey sample, describe it as *transparent*. If it is in between, the honey is *cloudy* or *foggy*. Keep notes on your impressions of the honey's clarity in the clarity field on the Honey Tasting Notes sheet.

Defining the Color of Honey

The first thing you notice when you look at any honey is the color. You quickly realize that all honey is not the typical medium amber color associated with commercially produced honey sold in most stores. A honey's color changes according to its nectar source, its proteins, and the minerals found in the soil where its nectar source grows. It is these same proteins in plants that act as pigments. They are responsible for turning leaves into different colors in the autumn. A few of these plant pigments are *anthocyanin* (which adds red tones to a honey), *carotene* (adding bright orange), and *xanthophyll* (resulting in yellow). Dark-colored honeys have higher concentrations of minerals and antioxidants, one called polyphenol is what gives them their dark color.

Generally, light-colored honeys tend to be delicate in smell and flavor, while darker ones tend to be full-bodied and rich. However, this does not always hold true. Some dark honeys (like tulip poplar or certain honeydews) have lighter flavors. And some light honeys (like lime tree or honeysuckle) can be quite strong.

DESCRIBING COLOR

The international color chart (called the Pfund Scale) is used by industry professionals to describe the color of honey. The color descriptors are water white, extra white, white, extra light amber, light amber, amber, and dark amber. They are based upon an optical reading by matching colors visually on a numerical scale. This technique is limited because in truth honey can be found in a wide range of colors from yellow to orange or red, or black as motor oil. There are even some honeys that are purple, green, and blue. We have created a Honey Color Guide that's easy to use. You'll find it in the color section of this book.

When honey is in its crystallized state, it becomes lighter in color. That's because of the concentration of crystal structure. And when honey ages or has been heat treated, the color becomes much darker. The color of the honey can be noted in the color field on the Honey Tasting Notes sheet.

TIP

Use the honey color guide in the color section of this book to identify the color of each honey as you sample. Add personal notes about each honey's color. Describe the colors using everyday words you are familiar with. There is nothing wrong with describing the color of a honey as cocoa, salmon, or port wine. Note the intensity and tonality of each color. You may describe a honey's color as burnt orange with a greenish tint or golden yellow with brown along the edges. Any adjective to describe a honey that helps you remember it is acceptable for your personal notes.

Here are visual observations you can likely expect from our recommended honey choices for your first tasting:

>> **Clover honey:** Pale ochre in color, foggy aspect

>> **Orange blossom:** Light golden in color, transparent

>> **Buckwheat:** Black-brown, opaque

Smelling Your Honey

Take your glass of honey, and using a new spoon, smear it all around the inside of the bowl. Don't worry about making it look messy. You need to spread those volatile compounds around so you can capture an authoritative smell of the honey.

Now stick your nose deep inside the glass and inhale. Don't be shy when smelling each sample; nobody is watching:

>> Pay attention to the intensity of the odor.

>> Would you describe the smell of the honey as intense, mild, or assertive?

>> Are you able to place the smells into an aroma family using the aroma and flavor wheel? If not, can you describe what you smell? Does it evoke any personal memories for you?

>> Are you able to further describe it in detail using any of the descriptors in the honey aroma and flavor wheel?

You need to smell quite a few honeys to gain some experience and establish a reference point in order to understand the degree of intensity of a honey. Here's what you can expect from the three recommended samples. See if your senses agree. Take note of the intensity of smell for your honey sample in the odor intensity field under the olfactory notes.

>> **Clover:** Delicate to medium intensity

>> **Orange blossom:** Delicate intensity

>> **Buckwheat:** Very intense, pungent

Now you can begin the process of picking out the aromas using the Honey Aroma and Tasting Wheel. You can find a copy of this wheel in the color pages of this book. Use this wheel to describe the smells and flavors in each honey sample. Begin in the middle and try to choose one of the broad flavor family categories. Then, work your way to the outer edges of the wheel to describe the honey in more detail. Every word to describe a honey is not on the wheel, so you should use your own personal scent memories. Fill in your impression in the odor descriptors field under the olfactory notes on the Honey Tasting Notes sheet.

Can you identify the flavor families that these honeys fall into?

>> **Clover:** Vegetal, warm, wood

>> **Orange blossom:** Floral, fruity, warm

>> **Buckwheat:** Animal, warm, malt

TIP

If you are unable to find a flavor family for a honey sample, try to describe it. Does it remind you of anything in particular?

INTERESTING SMELLS

What makes honey smell so interesting? And how is it possible that a honey can smell like a barnyard, ashes, or the peel of a lime? The secret lies in the unique combination of volatile organic compounds (VOCs) found inside the nectar of each plant. These VOCs are also called floral markers and are similar to essential oils extracted from flowers. Because they are made from natural sources, they don't stick around very long. *Volatile* means they dissipate over time, unlike artificial fragrances or perfumes whose scents linger around for longer periods of time. Volatiles are fragile and evaporate quickly; for this reason you should keep the lid on your honey so the molecules don't escape and take the smells and flavors with them. Over time, the VOCs naturally wan even with the lid tightly screwed on, so consume your honey quickly to enjoy its flavors at their peak.

Here are a few VOCs found in various honeys and their corresponding scents:

- **Hexanol:** Aromatic balsamic
- **Phenolic acids:** Fruity, spicy
- **Linalool:** Sweet, citrus, geranium
- **Furfural:** Cherry, soft almond
- **Sinesal:** Sweet orange

Profiling Honey Characteristics

Now you finally get to taste the honey. Scoop up some honey with another clean spoon and put it into your mouth. Move it around, let it melt and coat your entire tongue. Pay attention to its intensity (like you did when you smelled it). A honey's intensity can be described as mild, bland, or assertive. Take note of the intensity of aroma for your honey sample in the aroma intensity field under the gustatory notes.

REMEMBER

Pay attention to the five taste sensations:

>> **Sweetness:** Refers to amount of residual sugar in honeys; sensed by taste buds located toward the tip of your tongue

>> **Sour/tartness:** Degree of acidity in honeys; tasted at the center and sides of your tongue

>> **Saltiness:** Not a significant component in most honeys; tasted at the tip and center of your tongue

>> **Bitterness:** Tasted in many foods including honeys; tasted toward the rear of your tongue

>> **Umami:** Relating to amino acids or glutamate, which creates a sense of "deliciousness" found in many honeys; the sensation is located throughout your palate.

Does the honey taste cloyingly sweet? You would experience this mostly on the tip of your tongue (where the sweet taste buds are located).

Not too many honeys can be described as salty, but believe it or not, some are salty. Eucalyptus is one commonly salty honey, as are some Hawaiian honeys or others produced near the ocean.

It's common to find honeys that are sour, because honey has a low pH and is quite acidic. These honeys make the sides of your tongue water and your eyes squint. Bitter honeys reveal themselves at the back of your throat, right where you would choke. Umami honeys make your whole mouth water, and you feel like you want to suck your own tongue. Think about how savory foods make your mouth feel; umami honeys can be felt all over your entire tongue. Fill in your taste impression in the aroma descriptors field under the gustatory notes on the Honey Tasting Notes sheet.

WARNING

If you frequently consume foods that are overly sweet, salty, sour, or bitter, you'll discover that your ability to identify these sensations will be diminished. A bland diet recalibrates your ability to recognize tastes and flavors. Watch what you eat before tasting sessions.

See if you agree with the following taste assessments of our selected example honeys:

>> **Clover:** Sweet

>> **Orange blossom:** Normally sweet, sour

>> **Buckwheat:** Umami, bitter

Using the Aroma and Flavor Chart

Now you are ready to begin the best part of tasting honey, challenging yourself to tease out the flavors using our Honey Aroma and Tasting Wheel. Building on the scent memories you worked on earlier and understanding the basic flavor families, you now have a solid foundation to work with.

PHOTO BY HOWLAND BLACKISTON

A selection of different honey varietals showing the range of colors that honey can come in. Discover 50 delicious honeys and their characteristics in Chapter 7.

PHOTO BY C. MARINA MARCHESE

Attending a honey show or festival is a fun way to discover different honeys and find out more about them. Do an internet search to find the one nearest you. Chapter 20 highlights ten great honey festivals.

PHOTO BY HOWLAND BLACKISTON

Be sure to try your hand at making
mead (wine made from honey).
This is a picture of Howland's own
mead. Find this and many other
celebratory recipes in Chapter 14.

PHOTO BY C. MARINA MARCHESE

This yummy "grazing board" will inspire your next honey-themed party. See Chapter 18
for yummy food-and-honey pairings and Chapter 19 for tips on planning a memorable
and fun-filled honey tasting party.

PHOTO BY HOWLAND BLACKISTON

This little jar of Howland's own wildflower honey, along with a verse from Victor Hugo, was a guest favor at his daughter's wedding. Honey always makes an appreciated gift.

A frame of natural comb of honey on display at a breakfast buffet at a deluxe hotel in Saudi Arabia. Serving comb honey is a visual guarantee that it's the real deal. After all, it's just as it came from the hive.

Chapter 16 is all about baking
honey. Howland made this
using the chapter's Grandm
Honey Spice Cake recipe an
beehive cake mold (found on
And he couldn't resist addi
swarm of fondant honey b

Honey has been revered for centuries for its healing powers. Head to Chapter 5 for
preparing honey remedies at home. This Honey & Ginger Tea is just what the doctor orde
Try it with a slice of lemon.

ZU KAMAILOV

Chapter 15 has a bunch of wonderful recipes for cooking with honey. Don't miss this one for Honey & Rum Barbeque Sauce. Outstanding!

BRENT HOFACKER/SHUTTERSTOCK

Thirsty? Ready to celebrate? Try out some of the honey-inspired beverage and cocktail recipes found in Chapter 17. This one is Howland's personal favorite: Honey Old-Fashioned.

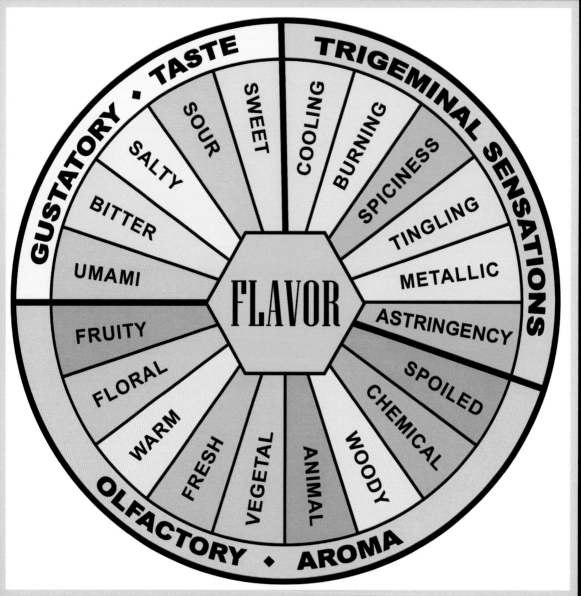

Use this Honey Flavor Wheel to understand the physical process of how we taste honey. There are three separate experiences on the outer edge of this wheel: taste, aroma, and trigeminal sensations. Each has its own list of flavor descriptors. The better you can separate these sensations and describe each one, the better honey taster you will be. See Chapter 9 for how to start thinking like a honey sommelier.

ILLUSTRATION BY C. MARINA MARCHESE AND HOWLAND BLACKISTON

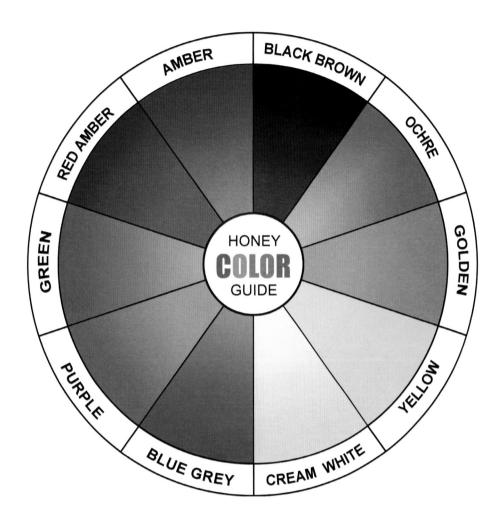

Use this Honey Color Wheel to define your honey color and then describe it matching the colors shown on this wheel. Honey has a wide range of colors. Note that there are different shades within each color category. You can match your honey to a dark, medium, or light shade within a color category. Or you can use your own words to describe the color of your honey. Here are a few of our favorite color descriptors: sunshine, clay pot, mango, and latte. See Chapter 10

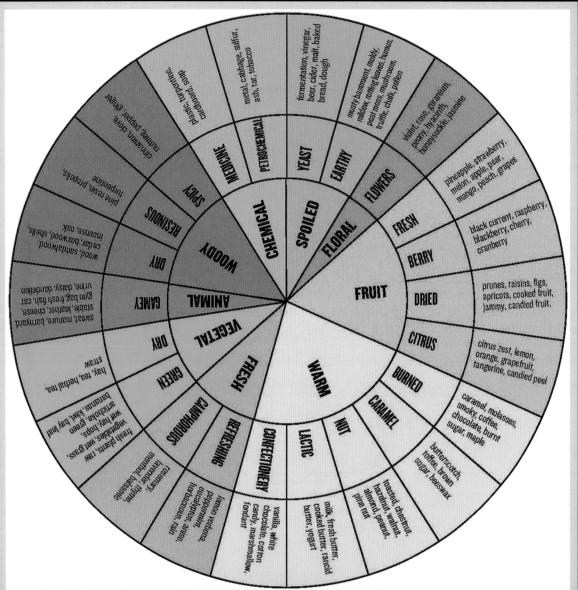

Courtesy of C. Marina Marchese (Excerpted from The Honey Connoisseur, by C. Marina Marchese and Kim Flottum [Black Dog & Leventhal])

Use this Honey Aroma and Tasting Wheel to describe the smells and flavors in each honey sample you taste. Begin in the middle and try to choose one of the broad flavor family categories; then, work your way to the outer edges of the wheel to describe the honey in more detail. Every word to describe a honey is not on the wheel, so you can use your own personal scent memories. See Chapter 10 for more on how to taste honey.

You may be surprised to discover that some of the aromas you smelled in your honey samples may not be present in their flavor when you taste them. In other words, what you smell may not always be what you taste in a honey. This is because the aromas we smell are volatile, and the ones we taste are nonvolatile at room temperature (meaning they do not disperse). Some compounds offer both, which is why some honey flavors are similar to their smell.

As you taste the honey, it mixes with saliva, which dilutes it. Diluting the honey actually enhances the flavors by changing the balance of them. Try to pick out the flavors. Pay attention to when they show up in your mouth during the tasting process (immediately, or over time). Don't forget to cleanse your palette by nibbling on an apple, drinking some water, and waiting between tasting each sample.

You will find that clover honey flavor begins with *dry hay*, then sweet and ends with *cinnamon*. When you taste the clover honey, you'll discover similar flavors that match up with what you smelled. The pleasant vegetal, dry hay notes prevail, and the cinnamon spice from the warm, woody flavor families lingers on.

Orange blossom starts out with fragrant floral notes, changes to warm orange lollipop, and ends sweet. The flavors of orange blossom honey will be greatly enhanced in your mouth in relation to what you smelled. Look for bright, floral notes of jasmine flowers, and fruity and citrus notes (like an orange-flavored lollipop or orange marmalade). A slight milky flavor is also present. It's like tasting a drop of sunshine.

Buckwheat starts out like chocolate, cocoa, and coffee. It ends with dark cherries and is a tad bitter. Buckwheat honey is one of the honeys about which I say, "Its bark is harsher than its bite." By that I mean it smells much stronger than it tastes. Do you detect the warm notes of coffee, cocoa, molasses, and dark ripe red cherries? The animal, barnyard, or cat pee flavor notes do not reveal themselves as strongly as they did in the aroma. Thank goodness. Fill in your aroma impression in the aroma descriptor field under the gustatory notes on the Honey Tasting Notes sheet.

Trigeminals

While the honey is in your mouth, remember to think about those other sensations we describe as trigeminal sensations (see Chapter 9 for more on the role trigeminal nerves play while tasting honey). Does the honey dry out your mouth or make it pucker? Is there a spicy note that stands out to you? There is a difference between spice and spicy. Spice is a flavor with a warm note that is similar to cinnamon, nutmeg, or cardamom. However, *spicy* is a chemical reaction that burns or feels like a hot pepper (but it's not related to temperature). Refreshing and warm sensations are present in many honeys, and they become much more pronounced in crystallized honeys. Fine crystals tend to create a cooling sensation we describe as *refreshing*, similar to putting powdered sugar on your tongue. Warm is described as that feeling you get from tasting maltose sugars or very large crystals in honey.

Clover honey is often crystallized, and you get a refreshing sensation from its superfine crystals. It may remind you of fondant on a wedding cake. The orange blossom honey is somewhat sour, while the buckwheat has a warm, malty, umami sensation and is somewhat astringent. Take note of any trigeminal sensations in your honey sample and mark them in the aroma descriptor field under the gustatory notes on the Honey Tasting Notes sheet.

Determining the Honey's "Finish"

How long can you taste the flavors in each honey? Does it have a long finish or an abrupt finish? Are the flavors evident immediately? After a moment? Or does it take a while for all the flavors to make themselves known? If you pay attention, you'll find flavors show up at different times while the honey is in your mouth. Some honeys start out or end just sweet. For other honeys, additional flavors reveal themselves after your first impression. Another honey may begin with a burst of flavor that quickly vanishes.

Some honeys just die in your mouth, meaning the flavor turns just sweet and is devoid of any aftertaste. Others have flavors that linger forever, such as ailanthus or chestnut honey. This characteristic is described as a honey's *persistence*.

A honey's persistence can be described as absent, short, medium, or long. Pay attention to these final details and take notes for each honey's persistence. Don't get frustrated. This is subtle stuff. After a bit of practice and keen concentration, you'll be a pro at determining the "finish." Fill in your impression about persistence in the field under texture on the Honey Tasting Notes sheet.

Talking About Texture

Be sure to take notes on your impressions of the honey's viscosity or mouthfeel by rolling the wine glass or container around while observing the honey move around the sides. Thin, watery honeys can have a high water content and are likely to ferment quickly. We visit more about evaluating texture later in this chapter.

Does your honey dribble off your tasting spoon? Does it sit on your tongue like a ball? The feel of the honey in your mouth can be described by its weight, or body; viscosity; or texture. Temperature, moisture content, and the sugar composition of a honey are important factors and dramatically change these qualities, as do the floral source and ambient humidity at the time of the harvest.

> Here are some words to describe a crystallized honey's *weight* or *body:* Firm, pasty, or hard.

> Here are some words to describe a liquid honey's *texture or mouthfeel:* Smooth, slippery, velvety, oily, buttery, thick, thin, drippy, or runny.

> Here are some words to describe a crystallized honey's overall *texture:* Gritty, grainy, granular, cat's tongue, creamy, sandpaper or coarse.

> Now describe the actual size of the crystals: Very fine, fine, small, medium, large, or very large.

> Now describe the actual shape and quality of the crystals: Round, angular, soluble, or insoluble.

Fill in all your impressions about the texture of your honey in the mouthfeel field under texture on the Honey Tasting Notes sheet.

Note: A *refractometer* is a tool that accurately measures the water content of honeys. But for initial sensory work we don't use it. Instead we rely 100 percent on our senses and experience. If you have doubts about the water content of a honey sample, by all means break out your refractometer.

Chapter **11**

Taking the Terror Out Of Terroir

The French have a delightful way with words. They call candy *bon-bons* and each other *mon cheri*. But when it comes to wine, they have a word that sounds similar to "terror" to describe a region and the environment that influences its flavors. *Goût de terroir* (taste of a place) or simply *terroir* translates to the English word for soil. Not dirt but glorious, mineral-rich soil.

It tells the story of the ecosystem in a specific region where climate, geography, and geology all harmonize to determine what a wine will look, smell, and taste like. The sensory characteristics of honey change depending upon the type of flower a bee gathers nectar from and also these same environmental variables. Honey production parallels wine production as both are products of nature and their qualities will change according to its terroir.

In this chapter, you discover what makes a quality honey, what standards are used, and why it matters. Quality control and authenticity have been concerns for producers as well as consumers for thousands of years. The quality of some varietal honeys is determined by the floral sources in the region where they were produced while others depend on local terroir and the traditional methods used by those local producers. Dive into the secrets behind a honey and its ever-changing personalities.

Capturing the Flavors of Local Foods

My philosophy is that the honeys with the most authentic flavors clearly echo their floral sources and their native terroir. This is true with some of the best-tasting single origin honeys like yellow sweet clover, which is produced on the prairies of North Dakota; Knotweed in the rocky forest of New England; and orange blossom in the tropical climate of Florida. These honey plants bloom where they are meant to bloom in their native environment and the honey they produce represents the hyper locality.

REMEMBER

Terroir can be thought of as the true meaning of local food where its flavors represent the soil and environment those foods were meant to grow in. If you've tasted the local honey produced in your area, then you have experienced terroir firsthand. Think of terroir as a snapshot of a honey that captures the flavors of the flowers blooming in a specific location at a specific moment in time, with the bees behind the camera. Each honey is unique, and its characteristics are rarely replicated in the same way because Mother Nature's touch is constantly changing.

Ensuring quality standards

The concept of terroir has been around for thousands of years; it is used as a standard of quality control for traditional products associated with a specific region. The ancient Romans monitored agricultural products to ensure quality and deter fraud in the marketplace. Wealthy elites enjoyed the highest quality wine, olive oils, grains, and honey, which were stored in clay pottery vessels called *amphorae*. Each vessel was clearly marked with the name of the producer, the region, and the date it was produced. Every step of the process was supervised by a trustworthy person in each society. These markings were called *Titulus Pictus*, and they made it possible to trace every step of the production line.

The largest depository of discarded clay fragments with these markings was uncovered by an archeologist in Monte Testaccio, Rome. The fragments revealed the history behind each of the products that was stored inside these vessels.

Similar protections were carried out in ancient Egypt — especially regarding honey, which was a valuable commodity and tightly controlled by the state. The government appointed a well-respected individual to observe the harvesting and bottling of each honey harvest to validate authenticity and quality. This individual held the title of *Sealer of the Honey*, or *Divine Sealer*.

Howard Carter, who discovered the tomb of King Tutankhamun, documented each artifact they uncovered. One amphora (shown in Figure 11-1) carried the hieratic script markings that translated to the word for honey bee, which identified the residue in the container as honey.

FIGURE 11-1:
An Egyptian clay amorpha with hieratic script that identifies honey bee.

Photo: Metropolitan Museum of Art, public domain

Today, in the European Union, the concept of terroir has evolved into a seal of approval or trademark on the label of certain regional foods. These seals or *schemes*, as they are called, protect the quality and integrity of these artisan foods. They are regulated by the government, which declares they cannot be produced anywhere else in the world except their designated region using traditional methods.

For example, when you purchase a bottle of Champagne, you expect you are getting the authentic celebratory drink. The label must state that the contents were produced with specific grapes in the Champagne wine region of France. Otherwise, it is just sparkling wine and can't be called Champagne. Why? Because the laws are designed to protect the regional local food values, the producers, and the land from which it was produced, thus ensuring consumers a quality product and not an inferior copy.

You may be familiar with other foods like Gorgonzola cheese, Balsamic vinegar, or Kalamata olives, which are also protected by these laws. These seals stand for *protected designation of origin* (PDO), *protected geographical indication* (PGI), and *traditional specialties guaranteed* (TSG), and they appear on the labels of certain foods with special characteristics related to the specific location in which they were produced. Figure 11-2 shows an example of one of these seals.

FIGURE 11-2:
PDO and
PGI seals.

Certifying and protecting honeys

Certain honeys produced in Italy, France, Spain, and Corsica have earned this highly coveted PDO government seal. Acacia honey produced in Lunigiana, Italy; chestnut honey from Tuscany; and strawberry tree honey from Corsica are just a few honeys that are highly desirable because of the uniqueness of the terroir where they were produced.

In the United States, there are no formal labels to protect foods. However, companies use trademarked names to distinguish their products from the competition. These names do not necessarily represent quality as much as brand recognition. Tupelo and sourwood honeys are uniquely produced in the U. S. and are national treasures that certainly are worthy of protected status.

Slow Food International, an organization dedicated to preserving local food cultures and traditions, has developed a list of foods called the *Ark of Taste*. These foods are in danger due to industrialization, climate change, the abandonment of rural areas, and deforestation. The Ark of Taste names five honeys produced in the United States as endangered. They are sourwood, tupelo, gallberry, guajillo, ōhi'a-lehua, and white kiawe honeys. Think about this: If we do not protect these rare honey plants and the environment in which they are produced, our great grandchildren and future generations may never have the opportunity to taste these unique honeys.

WHAT'S THE BUZZ ABOUT MANUKA?

Touted for its magical qualities, Manuka commands a high price tag for its supernatural healing properties linked to its floral source and its unique New Zealand terroir. The rainforest where Manuka *(Leptospermum scoparium)* trees grow is not duplicated anywhere else in the world. For this reason, a honey labeled "Manuka" can only be produced in this specific region.

The quality of Manuka honey is graded by its Unique Manuka Factor (UMF) system or its amount of *methylglyox*al (MGO) compounds that give it unique properties and antimicrobial strength. The UMF system is comprised of four tests, including authenticity and the amount of MGO compounds, while the MGO system only rates the amount of MGOs present, a unique activity against *E. coli* and *S. aureus* bacterium.

Both ratings assign a numerical value to each batch of Manuka honey. A UMF of 5 or higher is considered a mono-floral Manuka honey, and the equivalent MGO value is 83. The higher the UMF and MGO number, the better the quality. Needless to say, the worldwide demand for authentic Manuka honey has grown, and much of the Manuka honey sold is not true Manuka.

Influencing Nectar

Nectar is the sweet reward for insects and birds in exchange for pollinating the flowers they visit. This is a symbiotic relationship that has evolved over 65 million years of bees sipping up the sweet-smelling liquid nectar for energy and honey-making, and in return, giving each flower the gift of being pollinated.

A flower's nectar glands, or *nectary*, are generally located in the center of the flower at the base of its petals, making it easy for pollinators to access its sweet, liquid nectar. Some flowers also have nectar glands on their petals, leaves, and even their stems; these are called *extrafloral nectaries* and often are where aphids are found feeding.

Each species of flower has its own distinctive type of nectar composed of the sugars sucrose, fructose, and glucose in various proportions as well as proteins, 20 amino acids, salts, and other compounds.

Flowers bloom and produce nectar according to the local conditions they evolve in. The principal factor that influences the quality and quantity of nectar flow of a flower is terroir (soil, moisture levels, temperature, and sunlight) and it varies from day to day and even from hour to hour.

REMEMBER

Some of the compounds in nectar are essential oils, which give each flower its alluring fragrance specifically to attract bees and other pollinators. The combinations of essential oils contribute to the smell of the flower; however, the smell does not necessarily translate to the taste of the honey produced from it. The bees add their own enzymes to the nectar, which also change the characteristics of the honey — most honeys do not resemble the scent of their floral source or even the fruit. Lavender and eucalyptus are two honeys that do not taste anything like the intense aromatic notes we encounter when we smell their flowers or leaves. On the other hand, orange-blossom honey has distinctive notes that recollect the jasmine scent of its flowers.

Getting the Dirt on Honey (Geology)

I've heard wine makers describe soil as a living mixture full of beneficial organisms and minerals, while dirt is something that is stuck on the bottom of your boots. Wine makers in France go as far as to taste their soil before planting a single grapevine to be sure the composition is just right to produce the best wine. In the United States we may not literally taste our soil, but federal regulators designate the pedigree of a wine by where it was produced as its American Viticultural Area (AVA) region. I suggest we institute American Apicultural Areas, or AAAs, to designate regions that produce our rare treasured honeys like tupelo, sourwood, or yellow sweet clover.

The quality and composition of soil greatly varies in the United States and around the world according to the type of rocks that have disintegrated over eons. Soil is composed of a mixture of minerals, organic matter, organisms, air, and water. Every honey plant requires a specific type of soil to grow and thrive. Some plants prefer clay, sandy, silty, or loamy soils or a combination, and the pH and the various minerals and organic materials determine which flowers bloom and when they will produce nectar. Some of these types of soils may hold more water than others or are slower to drain, while others readily absorb heat from the sun or can be too compact for a plant's root system to grow. These irregularities determine whether a plant will adapt to its soil and become a vibrant and prolific nectar producer.

REMEMBER

Because of terroir, plants flourish where they are best adapted. Slight differences in the soil of a region can make huge differences in the flavor of the honeys produced. It's a fact that if we plant the same species of flower in two very different soils, each will produce a honey that will have contrasting sensory qualities and will taste differently. Overall, much work is needed to fully understand how soil affects a honey's sensory characteristics. Take a look at this soil map we have provided to see the wide variety of soil types in the United States. Each soil type supports specific floral sources that honey bees visit to produce honey.

Honey and Geography

Are the bees foraging on a hilltop or in a valley? Along the briny seaside or in an open field where the sun bakes the flowers most of the day?

The earth's surface or typography is varied and covered with vast oceans, mountains, forest, prairies, and deserts. Because plants react to their immediate environment, the local typography of the land determines how long the sun shines or how much moisture a plant receives in a particular area. The slope or altitude of the land can determine whether a flower receives the northern or southern winds, how much rain falls, or whether the temperature is cooler in a valley or on a hilltop.

Flowers that grow in higher altitudes are known to have brighter colors and secrete more nectar than flowers blooming on lowlands. The higher altitudes afford more sunlight and a great fluctuation in day to night temperatures, which facilitates nectar production.

All these geographic factors can result in very distinct differences in a honey's sensory characteristics. It's not always clear how the geology of a specific region alters a honey's flavors, but it has been found that certain honeys produced by the ocean often have a salty note (black mangrove); others produced in the mountains or rainforest (Manuka) have a distinctive evergreen note.

Knowing What Weather Has to Do with It

Honey can be produced nearly anywhere in the world and in a wide range of climates. In fact, anywhere a honey plant can grow and bees are able to forage for its nectar, honey can be found. The weather affects everything from the ability of a flower to secrete nectar to the honey bees' ability to forage for it. This locality can greatly vary throughout a single day and throughout the year. The ideal temperature for a flower to secrete nectar varies among honey plants, but generally, higher temperatures are favorable. The optimal climate for nectar secretion is when temperatures fluctuate between cooler nights and warmer days.

Rain, rain don't go away

All plants need water to survive. But how much is enough? Water influences the growth of every honey plant, its capacity to flower, and most importantly its ability to secrete nectar. The difference between a great honey harvest and a poor one can be the difference of a few inches of rain. Not enough rain causes flowers and leaves to shrivel up and droop. On the other hand, a pounding rain can dilute or wash away the nectar that bees need to make honey. This is especially true for buckwheat and other floral species where the design of the petals exposes an unprotected nectary.

Humidity is the amount of moisture in the air, and it can vary from day to day and year to year. Moist air prevents nectar from drying up and completely evaporating, making it readily available for bees to gather.

Here comes the sun!

Have you ever noticed how a flower will rotate its face and tilt its leaves toward the sun and then continue following its path throughout the day? If you've ever moved a plant from one room to another, you've seen your flowers change directions on their own. This is a flower's basic survival technique, because sunlight is like the electric charge for a plant. Chlorophyll is a light-absorbing pigment that makes plants' leaves and stems green and absorbs the energy from the sun to convert carbon dioxide and water into oxygen and glucose. This process is called *photosynthesis* and produces the sugars found in nectar. Have you ever pulled apart a honeysuckle flower and tasted its sweet nectar? Now you understand why bees are attracted to flowers.

Chapter **12**

Looking at What Can Go Wrong With Honey

Just as a winemaker's touch can affect how his wine will taste, a beekeeper's management of her honey bee colonies and harvesting practices has a role in the quality of the honey produced. Neglecting to follow best practices may show up in the flavor of the honey. This chapter identifies the most common mistakes that result in honey not tasting so good.

In most people's eyes, honey appears to be nature's most perfect and pure food. Flowers, nature, and a bee — what could go wrong? How could the sweet liquid gold produced by an innocent honey bee be anything less than perfect? This magical substance no doubt has amazing qualities, yet its chemical structure makes it quite fragile. And its sensory qualities are vulnerable to what honey sensory experts call *defects:* unwelcomed smells and or flavors that prevent a honey from being exceptional.

Recognizing Defects

Several factors are directly related to how beekeepers manage their colony of honey bees and the methods by which they harvest, bottle, and store their honey, which can influence the quality of the final product. Careless routines can result in off odors and flavors you do not want in your honey jar. Honey sensory experts refer to theses as defects. Many of these defects can only be identified through the skills of a trained taster as they do not show up in laboratory testing. Once a defect has been identified, there are simple changes a beekeeper can make when managing their honey bees to avoid defects in the honey, which results in producing a higher quality product. Following are some common defects found in honey that you can learn to identify through taste.

Burnt honey

When impatient beekeepers rush to bottle their honey quickly or simply want to liquefy it to please their customers' sensibilities, they often apply heat to it. If they happen to miscalculate time and temperature or get distracted and overheat their honey by mistake, the honey can burn. At 104 degrees Fahrenheit (40 degrees Celsius), small crystals in the honey begin to dissolve; beginning at 158 degrees Fahrenheit (70 degrees Celsius), honey begins to caramelize. Burnt honey can be identified by cloyingly sweet and caramelized flavor that turns bitter. It becomes viscous from losing moisture during the process. Burnt honey is clearly evident in lighter- or medium-colored honeys and can be difficult to identify in darker-colored or bolder-flavored honey.

The brood factor

When bees make honey in frames with dark-colored beeswax, the flavor of the honey turns offensive. Beeswax that is more than three years old is considered too old. As bees live and work on the wax, it becomes dark. It should be swapped out by the beekeeper to keep the hive sanitary and make sure the bees have a clean place to store their honey. Inexperienced beekeepers may harvest honey from the nest where the queen lays her eggs and may end up with larvae and pupae in the honey. Yuck! Brood taste can be described as animal, fatty, and bitter.

Medico mayhem

If your honey smells or tastes like a vapor rub or strong aromatic balm, it may be due to the chemical treatments beekeepers used to combat Varroa mites (a tiny pest found inside every bee colony that can cause trouble for the colony). There are many treatments for varroa mites, and some involve highly aromatic plant-based oils like thymol, eucalyptus, menthol, and camphor. If the beekeeper doesn't follow the directions on the Varroa mite treatment or forgets to remove the treatments from the hive, the oils could end up in the beeswax or the honey, making it worthless.

Smoky stuff

Did the beekeeper blow so much smoke inside the hive that the bees choked? If so, they overdid it, and now the honey smells or taste like a BBQ. Honey as well as the beeswax it is stored in is highly porous and absorbs odors easily. An inexperienced or timid beekeeper may use too much smoke out of fear of getting stung, but a little puff is enough to make bees behave. Smoky honey smells and tastes like BBQ sauce, perhaps with a little bit of ash added to it. It's unpleasant but common in countries where beekeepers work with Africanized honey bees that tend to be more defensive than the European species.

Just one word — plastics!

The container that honey is stored in is just as important as how it is harvested. Food-grade glass is always recommended; plastic, not so much. Polyethylene terephthalate or PET bottles and lids may be acceptable as food-grade quality; however, they leave the unpleasant smell and taste of plastic in honey if it's stored more than two years. Then comes the challenge of honey that crystallizes in plastic. It's not a good idea to heat plastic containers with honey or put them in the microwave. Avoid plastic at all cost (though we hope you would finish your honey by then.)

Metal madness

Some equipment used to harvest and extract honey is made of metal, and if not properly cleaned and stored after use, it can develop rusty spots that easily transfer to the honey. Uncapping knives or forks and honey extractors are made of stainless steel, which can develop rusty pit holes that can ruin a perfectly fine-tasting honey. Metallic honey in your mouth can be the most unpleasant experience; it makes the hairs on the back of my neck stand straight up. Metallic taste is commonly found in commercially produced or imported honeys that have traveled in metal drums in shipping containers.

Crossing Crystallization Defects

Bees are masters at chemistry. They create honey, which is a supersaturated solution, meaning it consists of 80 percent sugars (glucose and fructose diluted in 17 percent water). Because glucose is less soluble in water than fructose, it separates from the water molecules by latching onto tiny particles or catalysts inside the honey. These particles may be a minuscule piece of pollen, dust, or even just an air bubble. Crystallization begins at 57–59 degrees Fahrenheit. Although crystallization is a sign of quality, over time the quality of the crystallization structure changes and can eventually lead to fermentation. Here are three examples of defects of honey crystallization to be aware of.

Incomplete crystallization

Honey should crystallize homogenously, meaning the crystal structure should appear evenly throughout the jar. If you see crystals that are separated from the liquid portion of the honey and appear like cotton candy, there is a good chance this honey was exposed to heat or aged poorly, meaning it was exposed to extreme fluctuations in temperature over a period of time.

Crystal striping

Honey that crystallizes evenly and firmly inside the jar occasionally separates from the side of the jar and appears as lighter-colored crystals, which can be mistaken for sugar granules. These lighter-colored crystals become dehydrated and have a higher glucose content than the rest of the honey. This is technically not a sign of poor-quality honey but more of a visual defect.

Separation of honey

Perfectly crystallized honey does not remain stable forever. Over time, all honey is exposed to fluctuating ambient temperatures, simply because the seasons change, or the temperature in your kitchen or in the shop where you bought the honey. Age and fluctuating temperatures will cause crystallized honey to eventually separate into layers. You can see liquid at the top floating above a layer of firmer crystals at the bottom. In this scenario, the glucose has separated from the water and has settled at the bottom of the jar. The fructose has remained diluted in water and becomes the liquid layer at the top.

Storing honey in the refrigerator may accelerate crystallization, but it actually keeps honey stable longer, with less chance of defects.

TIP

Knowing Why a Honey Tastes Like Beer

The sugar-to-water ratio makes honey extremely vulnerable to fermentation. Bees are masters at turning their nectar into a supersaturated sugar honey solution that is 80 percent sugars to 17 percent water. Furthermore, the bees add enzymes to keep it stable, and they store their honey in wax cells with an airtight wax cap on top.

Once harvested, if honey is stored in a moist place where the relative humidity is above 60 degrees Fahrenheit or the lid is not on tight, the honey will grab moisture from the air. Once the honey's water content climbs higher than 17 percent, the naturally occurring yeast is activated, and the honey begins to ferment and smell like beer, ale, or baked bread. Fermented honey often tastes warm and fruity in the early stages of fermentation. It quickly begins to taste like hoppy beer. Some enjoy the early stages of fermented honey when some of the honey flavor remains. But honey that has fermented for more than a year becomes dark and cloyingly sweet. You need some experience to recognize the stages of honey fermenting.

WARNING

You've heard it a million times: Honey never goes bad or spoils. It's true that when kept properly, it can certainly last a long time and remain edible. But in fact, the original quality of honey does not last *forever*. Over time the color gets darker, the flavors dissipate, and the honey loses nutritional and health benefits. Direct sunlight, fluctuating temperatures, high moisture, and time itself are the enemies of honey. It is best eaten fresh (in the same season it was harvested) if you are lucky enough to get your hands on this delicacy.

THE FERMENTED HONEY CRAZE

Fermented foods and beverages have grown in popularity with foodies in recent years. Some, like sourdough bread, yogurt, and sauerkraut, have been around a long time. Others, like kimchi, miso and kombucha, are touted for their contribution to health — specifically, good gut health.

The latest to join these culinary ranks is the use of fermented honey in cooking. A popular recipe on the internet is creating a fermented honey by adding cloves of garlic to unprocessed raw honey. There's just enough water content in the garlic to kick-start the fermentation process. The result is a sweet/savory product that's perfect for pretty much anything (roasted vegetables, cheese boards, marinades, sauces, glazes, and so on).

5

Hey, Honey, Let's Party

IN THIS PART . . .

Gain knowledge about how to shop for honey: where to shop, how to read honey labels, and how to safely store honey.

Find out how to brew honey wine from one or more of the book's six recipes.

Try your hand at whipping up any of the more than 50 fabulous honey-inspired baking, cooking, and beverage recipes.

Maximize your enjoyment by understanding how to pair honey with cheese and other foods.

Take a peek at classic honey and food pairings that are certain to wow your friends and family.

Have some fun and try your hand at hosting a honey-themed party. Just follow our road map for making your party a huge success.

Chapter **13**

Shopping for Your Honey

The best place to buy honey is closest to the source. If you're lucky enough to have an apiary or farm in your local area, I highly suggest that you take a trek out there to get your hands on the freshest honey possible. If it's late summer or autumn (which is typically honey harvest season), you can expect the honey to be fresh off the hive. Maybe even still warm from the bees' bodies.

But if you can't go straight to the beekeeper, there are many other options for purchasing a great jar of honey. In this chapter I cover the pros and cons of buying honey in stores and online and show you how to read labels to make informed choices.

Knowing Where to Shop

With the surging interest in honey, it shouldn't be difficult to find a number of interesting places to purchase it. We always recommend purchasing honey in season directly from the beekeeper. When this isn't possible, there are farmers and green markets where you most likely meet the beekeeper, as well as also fancy food shops that usually have a few unusual honey choices. Make a beeline (pun intended) to explore a few different options. You'll be surprised at the wide selection available, some right in your neighborhood.

Go straight to the source

With the popularity of beekeeping and local honey, it shouldn't be too difficult to find your local beekeeper or apiary. Beekeeping has grown each year into a fashionable hobby and is part of the homesteading trend of keeping chickens, gardening, and canning your own food. Most beekeepers are hobbyists with a few hives in their back yard. They may post a sign in their driveway or in front of their home when honey is available for sale. Some put their honey out on a table and use the honor system. This may be the most exciting way to get fresh honey. And you just may be lucky enough to speak directly with the beekeeper. We suggest that you take full advantage of these random pop-ups and grab the honey before it sells out, as these back yard beekeepers produce small harvests. Their honey is truly local liquid gold.

Farm stands and farmers markets

Farms and farmers' markets (see Figure 13-1) are the next best places to seek out fresh honey. They're scattered around rural and urban areas alike. Most farms welcome visitors, especially at the end of a long summer when you'll find the best bounty of the season. Look for places that offer apple picking, baked and canned goods, maple syrup, handmade pies, eggs, and of course fresh honey. Since beekeeping is seasonal, you'll have better luck getting the good stuff during the summer or autumn harvest season, depending upon the part of the country you live in. Often the honey for sale at these farms and markets is from a local beekeeper who most likely has a relationship with the farm in exchange for pollination services. Check out the label for the beekeeper's location. This will most likely be your local wildflower honey variety. If the bees are pollinating crops at the farm, you may stumble upon a unifloral honey like blueberry, avocado, or orange blossom.

If you are in an urban area, check out the green markets for honey. Since these markets bring in vendors from all around the region, you may find some interesting choices. In fact, most people who keep honey bees in the cities are hobbyists with one to three hives right on the rooftop of the building, and they don't have a place you can stop by to buy their honey. Your city may even have its own honey festival with many beekeepers offering their honey and other products. If you don't see honey samples on the display table to taste, just ask for a taste. You will most likely be greeted with a smile and a spoon. Beekeepers are delighted to offer tastes of their own honey and engage in conversation about their passion for honey bees. A few questions you can ask are

>> Where are your hives located?

>> When was this particular honey harvested?

>> Do you know which floral sources your bees visited to make the honey?

>> Is your honey raw and unheated?

>> How are your bees doing?

FIGURE 13-1:
A farmers' market is a good place to shop for honeys. Chat with the vendor to learn more about the honeys and their nectar sources.

Photo by C. Marina Marchese

Gourmet markets

Fancy food shops or gourmet stores are where you'll find popular honey brands from around the United States and even the world. Since these stores cater to what I call the adventurous eater, you'll find top honey brands alongside specialty products from select producers. Expect to find popular artisanal brands of domestic and imported specialty honeys direct from the producers outside of the United States. A few favorite honeys that always seem to pop up are acacia, chestnut, forest honey (honeydew), and lavender from the European Union. Recently, interesting honeys have been coming in from South America, Madagascar, and Ethiopia. All are well worth a taste. Gourmet shops are also where you can find truffle-infused honey (a huge favorite with some truffle lovers). Be aware that this is not a pure blossom honey. It has been infused with white or black truffles. But it's delicious if you enjoy truffles. Explore the shelves and ask the employees some questions to help you find an interesting new specialty honey you won't find anywhere else. (And be sure to refer to Chapter 7 to help identify some honeys you would like to try.)

Cheese shops

Have you visited your local cheese shop lately? Cheese, like honey, is popping up everywhere. And most cheese lovers understand the tempting combination of pairing cheese with honey. Cheese shops have turned into a gourmet hub where you can find everything under the sun to pair with cheese, including a wide range of local, international, and exotic honeys. This is also a perfect opportunity to pick up any accompaniments for your honey tasting and pairing parties. (See Chapter 18 for more on pairing honey with cheese.) Plan on spending a little extra time to explore the wide range of offerings. There is something for everyone, and more often than not, you'll find the staff knowledgeable and helpful.

Deciphering Labels

Accurate and consistent honey labels are essential for the consumer to navigate the endless sea of honey offerings. Labeling allows customers to make informed choices about the products they purchase. The USDA offers guidance for labeling honey; however, this guidance is not always clearly defined or regulated.

All honey labels must state the name of the product on the front of the honey jar. This may sound ridiculous, because if the label states honey, it's just honey, right? Well, no. In my travels I have seen labels that say honey on the front of the bottle, yet hidden away on the back of the bottle in the fine print under the ingredients are additives like corn syrup or fructose. You may not expect to see this on a honey label, but additives to honey are legal as long as they are listed on the nutritional label and the product is not called honey. It has to be called honey syrup, honey blend, or imitation honey (see Figure 13-2 for a couple examples). If you see this, run the other way as fast as you can to your local beekeeper.

REMEMBER

If other ingredients are added to a jar of honey, the label must clearly identify each one. Some popular additions to yum up your honey are flavors such as raspberry, blueberry, cinnamon, or chocolate. Also, honeys can be infused with lavender or, as mentioned earlier, truffles. These should be labeled as *flavored* or *infused* honeys. There is a huge difference between lavender-infused honey and lavender blossom honey. And truffles neither bloom nor produce nectar — they grow underground.

Next, I highly suggest you look for the country of origin. Domestic honey is usually the safest. Most honey that has been imported comes from honey packers who import huge quantities of honey in big metal drums in shipping containers. Often these honey packers blend honey from various countries, including the United States. For the most part, there is nothing wrong with honey from other countries. But your best bet is to purchase honey in jars from the original producer bearing their label rather than a label from a commercial U.S. importer.

FIGURE 13-2:
The label on these "honeys" are a giveaway that these are not 100 percent the real deal.

Photo by Howland Blackiston

Other required information on the label is the actual product weight in ounces and grams not including the jar, bottle, or lid, so you can decide whether you are getting more for your money. Because honey is heavier than water, 1 ounce of honey in volume is equivalent to 42.5 grams in weight.

Look for the manufacturer's contact info. Small producers may list the name of their farm and their home address for traceability. Larger companies list their corporate offices, and there's no way to know where that honey was actually produced. In recent years, I've seen honeys that avoid stating where the honey was produced and instead the label states where it was packaged.

Now more than ever has it been essential to read the *entire* nutritional facts label. Every few years, the FDA updates the information required on all honey labels, and sellers must comply. Here we demystify each one of the details on the panel.

Nutrition labels

The FDA's guidance for proper labeling of honey and honey products was last updated in March of 2018. The document is intended to advise and recommend best practices; however, it does not establish legally enforceable responsibilities for the firms that manufacture, process, pack, label, or distribute honey and honey products. Again, we recommend purchasing honey from a known source and reading labels carefully.

Honey is a nutritional food; unlike other sweeteners, honey has traces of beneficial minerals, vitamins, and essential amino acids. As part of a balanced diet, honey can be consumed daily in moderation to supply energy and sweeten up a snack or meal. Only you and your doctor can determine whether honey can safely be consumed as part of your diet and health routine. Here, we dissect the valuable information on a honey label (see Figure 13-3).

Simplified Format

Nutrition Facts

Serving Size 1 Tbsp (21g)
Servings Per Container 22

Amount Per Serving

Calories 64

	% Daily Valve
Total Fat 0g	0%
Sodium 0g	0%
Total Carbohydrate 17g	6%
Sugars 16g	
Protein 0g	

*Percent Daily Values (DV) are based on a 2,000 calorie diet.

Simplified Tabular Format

Nutrition Facts
Serving Size 1 Tbsp (21g)
Servings 22
Calories 64
*Percent Daily Values (DV) are based on a 2,000 calorie diet.

Amount serving	%DV*	Amount serving	%DV*
Total Fat 0g	0%	Total Carb. 17 g	6%
Sodium 0 mg	0%	Sugars 16 g	
		Protein 16 g	

Linear Format

Nutrition Facts Serv size: 1 Tbsp (21g), Servings: 22, Amount Per Serving: **Calories** 64, **Total Fat** 0g (0% DV), **Sodium** 0mg (0% DV), **Total carb**, 17g (6% DV), **Sugars** 16g, **Protein** 0g, Percent Daily Values (DV) are based on a 2,000 calorie diet.

FIGURE 13-3: A typical honey nutrition label.

Courtesy of Howland Blackiston

When reading a honey's nutritional label, be sure to look at the serving size or servings per container or, simply put, how many servings are in the jar of honey. Serving sizes are standardized so you can compare similar foods. Serving sizes are based upon how much a person typically consumes — not necessarily how much you *should* consume. They represent the recommended amount or portion size of honey that constitutes one serving. When adding honey to a larger recipe or using it for baking, the serving size does not necessarily apply as the honey is distributed evenly throughout the entire recipe. You can get an idea of how many servings are in your jar of honey by reading the servings per container.

Calories — everyone seems to be obsessed with calories. Calories refer to a measure of how much energy you will get from a serving size of honey. So if there are 60 calories in one serving of honey and you eat a whole jar containing 16 servings, you will have consumed 960 calories! Eating more calories than your body uses is linked to overweight and obesity, so use honey in moderation and consult your doctor to determine the best choice for you. I say sticking to portion control and eating real honey are more important than the number of calories unless you are on a strict diet.

The good news is honey has no saturated or trans fats, cholesterol, or salt. It also contains no fiber or proteins whatsoever. It is basically made up of carbohydrates that break down to sugars, best for energy workouts, long busy days, or just a sweet tooth.

All honey labels must include the following warning for feeding honey to infants because of possible exposure to botulism spores:

"*WARNING*: Do Not Feed *Honey* to *Infants* Under One Year Old"

True Source

True Source is a voluntary certification program to combat illegally shipped honey imports, insuring full traceability of honey from hive to bottle and food safety and purity testing by third parties. The True Source seal (see Figure 13-4) guarantees the honey is indeed from the country named on the label. This may be somewhat misleading: To be clear, True Source regulates honey importers, exporters, packers, and U.S. beekeepers who engage in these activities; however, as stated on their website, "Beekeepers registered with True Source Certified are NOT audited or certified by a third-party audit firm."

FIGURE 13-4:
The True Source seal guarantees the honey comes from where it says it comes from.

Courtesy of Howland Blackiston

Honey washing is a term used to describe the act of marketing honey or honey as an ingredient in certain foods in a way that deliberately misleads the consumer for monetary benefit. For example, companies may use "made with real honey" to tout the health benefits of snack foods or power drinks that are clearly not healthy, thus misleading the consumer. In truth, domestically produced honey is too costly to be added as an ingredient in the food manufacturing process, so most of the honey used is lower quality and less expensive and always imported. Your best bet is to buy or make your own food when possible and use the honey of your choice to sweeten it up.

Gluten-free

Honey is naturally gluten free because it does not have the protein gluten found in wheat grains like spelt, kamut, barley, rye, and oat. And it's not usually produced in the same facility in which these grains are processed or transported. So, if you are sensitive to gluten, you'll be glad to know that honey is gluten free.

Vegan

Although honey is made from the nectar of flowers, it is processed by an insect, which disqualifies it as a vegan food. Honey bees carry honey back to the hive inside their honey stomach and add enzymes to break it down during the transformation to honey. For this reason, honey is not vegan friendly. I have met a few people who follow a strict vegan diet and do consume honey; their reasoning was that other sweetener choices were either artificial, highly processed, or just did not taste good. One thing they all had in common was that they wanted to purchase honey from beekeepers who treated their colonies in a humane way and made sure the bees had enough of their own honey when they needed it.

Raw, natural, organic, all natural — Descriptors that mean nothing

As consumers we are always looking for the best-tasting foods that also are good for us. Honey certainly is thought of as a healthy food, and we rely on the label to help us navigate the oceans of honeys available in the marketplace. Common words we see on the front of a honey's label are "raw," "natural," "organic," and "all natural," but what do these words really mean? Unfortunately, nothing! Technically, the FDA does not regulate or set legal definitions or rules for how these words are used on food labels. It's shocking to think that we may be fooled into making a purchase by assuming that the front of the honey label tells us all we need to know. Most of us are accustomed to trusting these words and rarely think about comparing the front of the label to the actual ingredients on the back label.

GMO

Can honey be genetically modified? Not literally, however, honey bees do visit some flowers of plants that have been genetically modified. The pollen from these floral sources can end up in the honey they produce. *Genetically modified organisms* (GMOs) are living organisms that have their genetic codes artificially altered in the lab using genetic engineering. Primarily, they are maize, soybean, canola, cotton, and papaya crops. In the United States there are no formal GMO labeling requirements. However, some food producers include this statement on their label. In the European Union, Australia, and other countries they have established regulations and thresholds for honey containing GMO pollen. Any honey containing more than 0.9 percent must declare "GMO" on the label, which is rare because the amount of pollen in any sample of honey ranges from about 0.1 percent to 0.4 percent.

STORING HONEY SAFELY

The natural enemies of honey are time, temperature, moisture, and sunlight. Honey is a raw food similar to a tomato or apple. It doesn't last forever. Aged honey may be edible, but after a few years it loses its flavors and health benefits.

Honey is best stored at room temperature in your kitchen or pantry, away from direct heat, sunlight, and high moisture. Honey does not do well with wide fluctuations in temperature over a period of weeks or months, such as warm days with cool nights or warm homes that are then blasted with air conditioning. You won't notice it right away, but the crystal structure may become uneven, or a perfectly even crystallized honey may begin to separate. Keep the lid tight so the honey does not absorb moisture in the air. It is not necessary to store honey in the refrigerator after opening the jar unless you don't plan on consuming it all in the next two years. Also, if the honey is whipped or creamy and you don't want it to separate, cold storage is recommended.

Fair Trade Honey

Look for the Fair Trade seal (Figure 13-5) on honey produced in developing countries to be sure the beekeepers are paid fair market value for their honey, thus insuring a fair living wage, healthcare, education, and community benefits for workers. It also prevents child labor and promotes opportunities for disabled people as well as gender equality. The World Fair Trade Organization (WFTO) sets these principles, and they are upheld.

FIGURE 13-5:
The Fair Trade seal is used on honeys produced in developing countries.

Courtesy of C. Marina Marchese

We recommend keeping it simple and purchasing your honey from a beekeeper to get the best quality out there. Why not buy two and keep one in the refrigerator until you are ready to consume it? Our motto is *you can never have enough honey.*

IS HONEY KOSHER?

According to Chadbad.org, pure, raw honey is considered Kosher because it is not produced by the bee but from the nectar of a flower, which bees then transform. They also advise that you check for the certification seal from a reliable Kosher agency.

Chapter **14**

Brewing Honey Wine (Mead)

've been a beekeeper for decades, and I confess that I simply love my bees. But in the winter I get fidgety when I can't spend time tending to my "girls." And so a number of years ago I looked for a bee-related hobby that would keep me serene until spring. I thought, *Why not make mead?* Mead is an alcoholic beverage made by fermenting honey with water and yeast. It's regarded as the oldest alcoholic beverage, made long before the grape was first used to make wine. Until about 1600, mead was regarded as the national drink in England. Over the years since then, its popularity had dwindled. But today mead is coming back in favor.

When mead is made right, the character is simply delicious! It can be dessert-sweet (like a fine French Sauterne) or bone-dry with little or no perception of sweetness. Mead is naturally gluten free. Some meads are fruity, and some are spicy. It can be still or sparkling. The color of the beverage can range from a very pale golden to a deep dark hue. Like a fine red wine, meads tend to get better with age. Each has an aroma that reflects the distinct honey it was made from. In short, there are endless varieties depending upon the recipe and fermentation process used.

Here in the United States, many commercial "meaderies" are popping up all across the country. So there is no shortage of all kinds of meads to enjoy. The simply wonderful news (in my opinion) is that mead is something that can be easily made at home, and with delicious, celebratory outcomes! And it is perfectly legal to do so for your own consumption, but you need a liquor license to actually sell your mead.

Virtually all suppliers of do-it-yourself beer- and wine-making kits also offer mead-making equipment to hobbyists. All you need is a little space to set up shop and some honey to ferment. The key to success is keeping everything super-sanitary; all your utensils, vessels, and surfaces must be cleaned thoroughly so as not to contaminate the fermentation process.

In this chapter, I cover the basics of mead making and share some great recipes from some of the many fine meaderies here in the United States. And I've included my own favorite recipe that's been the source of many kudos from friends and family members.

REMEMBER

There's more to mead making than can be covered in a single chapter. Think of this as a basic introduction to mead making. I strongly urge you to get hold of an entire book devoted to mead making. There are quite a few out there. I've included a couple of suggestions in Appendix B for online resources that offer books on mead making, as well as the equipment you will need. Read up on the fine details of the craft and then try some of the wonderful recipes included in this chapter. Begin with the basic "traditional mead" recipe. It's the simplest to start out with, and the results are rewarding. A helpful website on mead and mead making is www.gotmead.com.

TIP

Accuracy is critical. Making mead is an exercise in precise chemistry — not just a pinch of this and a dash of that. It's mighty handy to have a kitchen scale that can read grams. Precise measurements by weight are often used in mead recipes, including some in this chapter.

Discovering Mead's Long History

No one really knows where or when the idea of making and drinking mead actually started. But considering it's a product of the natural fermentation of honey when mixed with water, it's reasonable to imagine that our earliest ancestors may have discovered mead by accident. We know as far back as 6000 BC humans collected honey from wild hives to eat (see Chapter 1). It's entirely possible that at some point, the collected honey mixed with rainwater and wild yeast from the environment and fermented naturally. And then was tasted. Holy mastodon — that's some powerful honey water!

Throughout history, mead has been revered as a beverage reserved for special ceremonies and grand occasions. It was enjoyed by royalty and the rich and powerful (keep in mind that honey was a very expensive commodity). The Egyptian pharaoh King Tut loved mead, as did the Norse explorer Erik the Red. Queen Elizabeth (the first) is known to have enjoyed a tipple or two of mead during her rein in the mid to late 1500s. The Greeks regarded Dionysus as the God of Mead long before he was known as the God of Wine. Shakespeare drank mead, and Chaucer frequently refers to mead's seductive powers in *The Canterbury Tales*. And we've all read how Robin Hood and his merry men had a taste for mead. Now we know why they were so merry.

Introducing Seven Types of Mead

Around the world, many different names are given to many different variations of honey-based wines. But traditionally, mead can be classified into one of several basic types. And within each of these there can be countless variations, depending upon the honey used, the *mazer* (person who makes mead), and the specific recipe followed. I focus on these few traditional ones, and later in this chapter I share a recipe for each of the seven mead types listed in the following sections, provided by some seasoned and professional mead makers. It's terrifically fun making mead, and it's something that can be done at home with a rather modest investment in equipment and supplies.

TIP

Depending upon the type of mead, your recipe, and your mead-making finesse, the alcohol content of your mead can range between 6.5 percent and 22 percent alcohol by volume (ABV). The ABV may even be as high as 60 percent or more when the mead is *fortified* by adding distilled spirits.

Traditional mead

Sometimes called "show" mead, traditional mead is a basic mead made solely from honey and water in the proportions of approximately 2½ pounds of honey per 1 gallon of water. There's a recipe for this type of mead in this chapter.

Sack mead

This sweet mead is made just like traditional mead (honey and water), except for the addition of approximately 25 percent more honey. It makes a lovely sweet dessert wine. There's a recipe for this type of mead in this chapter.

Hydromel

Hydromel is quite similar to traditional mead, although it can be dryer and typically has a lower alcohol content. There's a recipe for this type of mead in this chapter.

Bochet mead

Pronounced *BO-shay*, this is a traditional version of mead that involves caramelizing the honey before fermenting it. This process produces some warm, caramel notes that are simply delicious. There's a recipe for this type of mead in this chapter.

Metheglin

Metheglin is a mead made with the addition of various herbs and/or spices. Common spices used are cloves, cinnamon, and ginger, and herbs used include juniper, rosemary, and sage. This was a big hit during the Middle Ages. There's a recipe for this type of mead in this chapter.

Sack metheglin

Sack metheglin is a spiced metheglin style of mead, but it's sweeter as a result of adding more honey. It's great as a digestif after dinner.

Mead made with fruit juices

This style of mead (mixing various fruit juices with honey) results in four different variations of juice-based meads, as follows:

>> **Pyment:** A blend of red or white grape juice and honey. Pyment (also called Clarre) was a very popular drink during the Middle Ages.

>> **Cyser:** A blend of apple cider (juice) and honey. I have read that this was the "strong drink" often referred to in biblical times.

>> **Melomel:** A ferment of honey, water, and fruit juice(s) other than apples or grapes, this drink was popular in Roman times. Hail Caesar! There's a recipe for a cherry melomel in this chapter.

>> **Morat:** A mead made from honey, water, and the addition of fresh mulberries. The result is a lovely, dark, and delicious beverage. It's like summer in a bottle!

MAKING HOOCH

Careful: It's not legal in the United States to make strong spirits at home, unless you get an expensive federal permit. Also, distilling booze, if you don't know what you are doing, can result in a dangerous toxic outcome. So I'm *not* suggesting you try this. But, as a matter of satisfying your intellectual curiosity, here's how brandy is made from mead. It involves a distillation process using a *still* (a device that separates the alcohol content from the mead).

Even though it's illegal to do this without a federal permit, nearly all states in the United States allow you to own a still, and you can even use your still, so long as you're *not* making spirits. You can legally use stills to make essential oils, perfume, or distilled water. But no hooch. A search on the internet will turn up retailers selling distillation equipment.

It's also interesting to note that mead brandy can instantly become *mead liqueur* by merely adding some honey to sweeten the spirit. The liqueurs Drambuie and Irish Mist add spices and honey to the Scotch or Irish whisky that the respective brands use.

Getting the Necessary Mead-Making Equipment

Seriously, making mead at home is a lot of fun. And if you are a beekeeper, now you have something else to do with all that honey you harvest! To make mead you need to invest in some basic equipment and tools. But you don't have to spend a ton of money. Many different basic start-up kits are available online from beer- and wine-making vendors. A kit like the one shown in Figure 14-1 will do the trick just fine. Appendix B includes some of my favorite online resources for mead making. Check 'em out.

REMEMBER

Whether you purchase a kit or assemble the different tools yourself, here's what you need to make a batch of mead:

>> Primary fermentation vessel used to get the fermentation started. The one in Figure 14-1 is the big white pail.

>> Secondary fermentation vessel where the rest of the fermentation process will take place. That's the big glass "carboy" in Figure 14-1.

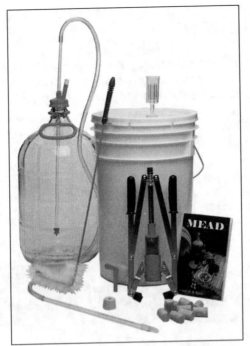

FIGURE 14-1:
Here are the basic elements of a typical kit for mead making at home. Easy-peasy.

Photo by Howland Blackiston

» A fermentation valve fitted in the top opening of the carboy. This allows gasses to escape during fermentation, and prevents oxygen and bacteria from entering the carboy.

» Some food-grade hosing to siphon the mead from one container to another

» A hydrometer to measure specific gravity during mead making. It helps you keep track of the fermentation process.

» And of course the recipe ingredients for making the mead. All mead includes honey!

Figure 14-2 shows the same equipment but on a larger scale at a commercial meadery.

FIGURE 14-2
A mead-making
setup at a
commercial
meadery.

Courtesy of Bergen House Meadery

KNOWING SOME TRICKS FOR SUCCESSFUL MEAD MAKING

Keep the temperature in the room you are making mead between 65 and 68 degrees Fahrenheit (18 and 20 degrees Celsius). I find that my basement is a good place to make mead, as the temperature holds steady within this range. If the temperature is higher than 75 degrees (24 degrees Celsius), the yeast may die; if it's lower than 50 degrees (10 degrees Celsius), fermentation ceases. Note that a portable space heater with a thermostat helps control temperatures during winter.

Keeping everything clean and sterile is critically important. Your equipment and working area must be kept spotless and bacteria free so as not to contaminate your precious mead and spoil the successful outcome. Less than sterile conditions can result in off tastes or gallons of honey vinegar. Keep very sterile laboratory conditions, please! This cannot be overemphasized.

Understanding Useful Mead-Making Terms

There are a whole bunch of terms used during mead making that may not be familiar to you. The recipes that follow make use of some of these terms, so you'll want to become familiar with them. I've listed the ones you'll come across in the recipes.

ABV: This acronym stands for *alcohol by volume*. It's a standard measure of how much alcohol (ethanol) is contained in a given volume of an alcoholic beverage (expressed as a volume percent).

Brix: Degrees Brix is the sugar content in the mead's "must" solution. One degree Brix is 1 gram of sucrose in 100 grams of solution. It can be used to estimate the potential alcohol content. To get an alcohol conversion level, multiply the stated Brix by 0.55.

Carboy: A glass vessel used to ferment and age mead in. Typical sizes are 1, 3, 5, and 6.5 gallons. The glass variety is relatively easy to clean and keep sterile. It's also heavy and breakable. Alternatively, some very nice plastic fermentation vessels are now on the market with built-in fermentation valves. They also come in various sizes. This is the type I've settled on for my mead making.

Clarification: A mead-making process involving the *fining* and *filtration* of mead to remove suspended solids to create a sparkling clarity to the mead.

Fermentation valve: These are one-way airlock devices that enable CO_2 to be released during fermentation but prevent any oxygen, yeast, and bacteria from entering the fermenter and harming your mead.

Final gravity (FG): Using a hydrometer, this is the measurement of the density of finished mead. By knowing this measurement and the "original gravity" measure, you can calculate the alcohol content of your finished mead. See the sidebar "Determining your mead's alcohol content."

Fermentation: A chemical reaction in mead making involving the conversion of sugars to alcohol by yeast.

Fining: A *clarification* process where flocculants, such as bentonite or egg white, are added to the mead to remove suspended solids. Fining is considered a more gentle method of clarifying than filtering.

Fortification: The process of adding pure alcohol or a very strong spirit to a wine to increase its ABV.

Hydrometer: An instrument used for measuring the specific gravity of liquids based on the concept of buoyancy. By measuring the specific gravity of your mead before and after fermentation, you can calculate the ABV (alcohol by volume) of your product. See the sidebar "Determining your mead's alcohol content."

Lees: This is the sediment that occurs during and after fermentation. It consists of dead yeast and other solids. The lees are separated from the mead by *racking*.

Must: The name for a mixture of honey, water, and other ingredients. The *must* is what you start out with. Eventually it ferments into mead.

Original gravity (OG): The initial or "original" gravity reading of the must. It is a measure of density. Water has a gravity of 1. The more honey you put in the must, the higher the original gravity will be. Use a hydrometer before fermentation to record the original gravity. See the sidebar "Determining your mead's alcohol content.

Oxidation: The degradation of mead through exposure to oxygen. In some aspects oxygen plays a vital role in fermentation and the aging process of mead. But excessive exposure to oxygen later in the process can produce faults in the mead.

Pitching: This is the term for adding the yeast to the must. You pitch the yeast into the must. Many recipes call for the yeast to first be mixed with warm water. It's best to follow the instructions that come with the yeast before you pitch it.

Primary fermentation bucket (tank): A bucket or tank that is used to create the initial batch of must. Often it will have a spigot at the bottom so liquid can be drained out. The large top opening makes it easy to mix and stir ingredients. The light-blocking property of a fermentation bucket/tank is good for making mead.

Primary ferment/fermentation: This is the first stage of fermentation once you have combined all the ingredients together. The primary ferment is usually done in a large primary fermentation bucket/tank.

Racking: This is the process of siphoning off the liquid, leaving the dead yeast cells behind. Recipes may specify that you "rack your mead" several times. Each time the product becomes more clear as the dead yeast cells are separated from the mead. Racking also helps the flavor of the mead.

Residual sugar: The amount of sugars remaining in the mead once the ferment has completed.

Secondary ferment: This refers to the fermentation that occurs in the second container (likely a carboy), after you have siphoned the liquid out of the primary fermentation bucket/tank.

Starter: This is a batch of yeast that is prepared to be pitched into the must. Often it is dry yeast mixed with warm water to activate it. Some starters come already in liquid form.

Sulfites: Compounds (such as potassium metabisulfite or sodium metabisulfite) that are added to mead to prevent oxidation, spoilage, or to stop further fermentation by the yeast.

DETERMINING YOUR MEAD'S ALCOHOL CONTENT

Drop a hydrometer into your mead ingredients *before* fermentation. Record where the surface of the liquid crosses the scale. This is your *original gravity measurement* (OG). Say, for example, the OG is 1.06.

When the mead is all done with fermentation, drop a hydrometer into your finished mead and record the specific gravity. This is your *final gravity* measurement (FG). Say the FG is 1.01.

You can estimate the amount of alcohol in the mead by using this formula:

Percentage of alcohol = ((1.05 x (OG – FG)) / FG) / 0.79

For this example, the equation would read:

Percent alcohol = ((1.05 x (1.06 – 1.01)) / 1.01) / 0.79

Therefore, the mead's estimated alcohol percentage is 6.6.

TIP

Some recipes call for *sulfating* your mead (by adding metabisulfite tablets) to hinder the growth of undesirable bacteria. Personally, I no longer do this and I have yet to have any contamination of my mead. It just seems better to me not to add (and drink) chemicals if you can avoid it. But you decide for yourself.

Traditional Mead (Show Mead)

Courtesy of Talon Bergen, Bergen House Meadery. www.bergenhousect.com

When mead makers talk about "traditional" mead, they are referring to the simplest of meads. For a traditional mead, you use only water and yeast in addition to honey. Traditional mead is sometimes referred to as "show mead."

The most important ingredient in any mead recipe is honey. When you are selecting honey, think about the characteristics that come from the honey that you want in your mead. If you use clover, you will have hints of cinnamon just like when you are tasting raw clover honey. Traditional mead in particular highlights the beauty and the quality of the honey. If you taste your honey and think that the flavor would be nice in a glass of wine, then that is the honey you want to use to ferment with!

INGREDIENTS

1 gallon nonchlorinated water

3 pounds honey

2.5 grams GoFerm brand yeast nutrient (6 grams if you use the whole 5 grams of wine yeast)

2 grams wine yeast (Wine yeast typically comes in packets of 5 grams. Don't bother weighing it. Your gallon of mead will come out great even if you use the entire 5-gram packet.)

4 grams Fermaid O brand yeast nutrient

DIRECTIONS

1 Bring your gallon of water just to a simmer and remove from heat.

2 Add the honey and the warm water to a five gallon, food-safe bucket. The warmth helps the thick honey blend with the water. Mix vigorously with a long-handled spoon. Splashing is encouraged to add oxygen into the mixture. Once the water and honey have been mixed, the solution is called a "must."

3 Mix your GoFerm with about one cup of the warm mixture.

4 Place a thermometer into the must. Once it is 104 degrees Fahrenheit, add the yeast. Don't worry if the mixture is a little cooler than that. But don't add the yeast if it's warmer than 104 degrees. Let the mixture rest for ten minutes. This is a great time to clean up.

5 Add ¼ cup of the must to the yeast/GoFerm mixture and let stand for another five minutes. You should notice visible activity at the end of that five minutes.

6 Add the yeast mixture to the must and mix vigorously. If you have a lid for the bucket, put it on and shake it up. You are looking to add lots of oxygen to the must at this point. You can't overdo it!

(continued)

7 Cover with a clean towel and leave it at room temperature.

8 In 24 hours come back to your fermenting must and add 1 gram of Fermaid O. Stir to mix thoroughly.

9 Repeat Step 8 at the 48-, 72-, and 96-hour marks.

10 Let it sit with the towel covering the bucket for a total of four days.

11 Without disturbing the surface, remove a little bit of the liquid with a measuring cup, pour it in a glass, and taste it. If it's too sweet, let it continue to ferment and check it every 24 hours.

12 Once the mead is no longer too sweet, you can carefully rack off the mead into sterilized bottles. Cork and place bottles in the fridge.

13 Leave the mead in the fridge for *at least* a few weeks. The longer you wait, the better the mead will taste.

WARNING: Unless you are certain that your mead is completely dry (that is, no more sugar to ferment) you will want to leave the mead in the fridge. The cold prevents further fermentation. Otherwise, it will continue to ferment and those bottles will become "gushers" that will have to be dumped down the drain.

TIP: When you repeat this recipe, you can start with more or less honey based on how you enjoyed the first batch of mead. Adding more honey will create a sweeter (and more alcoholic) mead (see Sack Mead recipe); removing some honey will create a dryer mead. Scaling up this recipe is as easy as multiplying the ingredients.

Sack Mead

Courtesy of Ben Starr, Starrlight Meadery, www.starrlightmead.com

INGREDIENTS

¾ gallon water

¼ teaspoon tannins

3 pounds honey

½ teaspoon yeast nutrient

5 grams wine yeast

½ teaspoon potassium sorbate (optional)

¼ teaspoon potassium metabisulfite (optional)

EQUIPMENT

Two 1-gallon carboys

Airlock

Rubber stopper

Funnel

Sanitizer

Tubing (siphoning)

DIRECTIONS

1 Sanitize all equipment before starting.

2 Add about 4 cups of the water to a 1-gallon carboy.

3 Add tannins to carboy and swirl to combine.

4 Add honey to the carboy.

5 Fill carboy halfway with water.

6 Shake to combine.

7 Add yeast nutrient and half of the remaining water.

8 Shake to combine and aerate.

9 Rehydrate yeast following manufacturer's instructions.

10 Add yeast and "seal" with rubber stopper and airlock.

11 When the foam on the fermenting mead has died down (approximately two weeks), add remaining water leaving 1–2 inches between the top of the liquid and the bottom of the stopper.

12 When the airlock activity has slowed and a layer of yeast has formed at the bottom of the carboy (approximately two months), rack (siphon) into a sanitized carboy, trying to leave as much dormant yeast as possible in the bottom of the first carboy.

13 Top up to 1–2 inches from the bottom of the stopper with water and "seal" with airlock and stopper.

(continued)

14 When the mead is clear, rack to a sanitized carboy.

15 Taste the mead. (Add potassium metabisulfite and sorbate at this time, if you plan on making it sweeter.)

16 If you want it sweeter, add some honey (diluted in water) to top it up.

17 Once you have it to the sweetness level you like, bottle and cork it.

Bochet Mead

Courtesy of Talon Bergen, Bergen House Meadery. www.bergenhousesect.com

Pronounced *BO-shay*, this is a traditional version of mead that involves cooking the honey before fermenting it. The cooking process causes some burnt caramel notes that are simply delicious in your dry session meads.

WARNING

If you search YouTube for *bochet,* you will find some video how-to's with terrible advice. Please don't cook all the aroma and flavor out of your honey! I describe the easiest and most approachable method. This is the same recipe that I use at Bergen House Meadery for our bochet.

INGREDIENTS

8 pounds honey

5 gallons of nonchlorinated water

5 grams of 71b yeast

12 grams Fermaid O brand yeast nutrient

DIRECTIONS

1 Place honey in a crockpot and turn it to high, leave the lid ajar, and walk away for six hours.

WARNING

Some crockpots set on high can climb above 215 degrees Fahrenheit (101 degrees Celsius) when left on for six hours. If you think this may be the case with yours, check the temperature every hour or so and switch to a lower setting to achieve 215 degrees F (101 degrees C).

2 Bring 1 gallon of water to boil, and pour it into your fermentation bucket.

3 Pour the "cooked" honey onto the boiling water and stir to dissolve.

WARNING

The honey may look cold because as soon as you remove it from the heat, there is no movement to indicate that it's actually the same temperature as boiling water. If it gets on you, it will seriously burn you. Trust me, I've learned the hard way.

4 Add the remaining 4 gallons of water and mix vigorously. It will be too hot to add the yeast. We assume you have sanitized your fermentation vessel well, and we know the must is sterile since you boiled everything. So just cover with a clean towel and binge watch your favorite show until the temperature of the must drops to 104 degrees Fahrenheit (40 degrees Celsius).

(continued)

5 Pitch the yeast and mix vigorously (you want to introduce lots of oxygen).

6 Cover with a clean towel and leave it at room temperature.

7 In 24 hours come back to your fermenting must and add 12 grams of Fermaid O. Stir to mix thoroughly.

8 Repeat Step 7 at the 48-, 72-, and 96-hour marks.

9 Let it sit with the towel covering the bucket for a total of four days.

10 Without disturbing the surface, remove a little bit of the liquid with a measuring cup, pour it in a glass, and taste it. If it's too sweet, let it continue to ferment and check in every 24 hours.

11 Once the mead is no longer too sweet, you can carefully rack off the mead into sterilized bottles. Cork and place bottles in the fridge.

12 Leave the mead in the fridge for *at least* a few weeks. The longer you wait, the better the mead will taste.

WARNING: Unless you are certain that your mead is completely dry (that is, no more sugar to ferment), you will want to leave the mead in the fridge. The cold prevents further fermentation. Otherwise, it will continue to ferment and those bottles will become "gushers" that will have to be dumped down the drain.

TIP: If you don't have a crockpot, you can set your oven to 215 degrees F (101 degrees C), place your honey in a stainless-steel pot, and just place that in the oven with the lid ajar. Either way, walk away for six hours.

NOTE: I prefer wildflower honey for this recipe. This is the only time you will hear me advocate for this specific wildflower honey; buy whatever is cheapest. We are cooking the more delicate flavors out of the honey anyway. We are looking for specific gravity of 1.068 to 1.072 (16.6 Brix to 17.5 Brix). You will want to add honey or water to get the must within that range (all honey has a different specific gravity, so different honey will require different adjustments).

Hydromel Mead with Ginger

Courtesy of Talon Bergen, Bergen House Meadery. www.bergenhousesect.com

This recipe is one of the most refreshing drinks you will ever taste. It's a recipe that I use in the meadery all the time. It's my lawnmower beverage because it is so darn refreshing while I cut the grass. And at 6.5 percent ABV, you can enjoy a little more in quantity than most meads.

For this recipe I recommend investing in a "picnic keg" (available at home brewery supply stores) and a fridge large enough to accommodate the keg. It's what makes this mead a sparkling ginger sensation!

INGREDIENTS

400 grams (14 ounces) fresh ginger

4 gallons of nonchlorinated water

8 pounds honey
5 grams of 71b wine yeast

4 grams GoFerm brand yeast nutrient

12 grams Fermaid O brand yeast nutrient

DIRECTIONS

1 Wash ginger and cut into ¼-inch-thick coins (shape and diameter are irrelevant).

2 Set aside ½ cup of water and bring to a simmer. Remove from heat.

3 Bring 1 gallon of water to a boil.

4 Add ginger to boiling water.

5 Turn off heat and let stand with steeping ginger for 15 minutes.

6 Strain the ginger "tea" into your fermentation vessel.

7 Mix in the honey and add the remaining 3 gallons of water to create the must. Mix vigorously with a long-handled spoon. Splashing is encouraged to add oxygen into the mixture. Once the water and honey have been mixed, the solution is now called a "must."

8 Mix the GoFerm and warm water.

9 Check the temperature of the GoFerm and warm water solution. Do not proceed to the next step until the solution drops to 104 degrees Fahrenheit (40 degrees Celsius).

(continued)

10 Add ¼ cup of must to the yeast and GoFerm solution. Let stand for ten minutes. You should start to see activity in the solution at this time.

11 Use your sanitized thermometer to check the must temp. If it's within 5 to 10 degrees F (3–5 degrees C) of the yeast and GoFerm solution, then you can add it to the must. If it's *not* within that temperature range, then add an additional ⅓ cup of must to the yeast solution and wait another five minutes. Check the temperature again. Why do we do this? Because minimizing the temperature difference between the yeast mixture and the must helps eliminate thermal shock to the yeast, and encourage a healthy fermentation.

12 Mix the must vigorously. Remember, the goal is to get oxygen into the must to create a good fermentation. It is impossible to overoxygenate at this point.

13 Twenty-four hours later, add the nutrients. Check the gravity too while you're at it. Taste and document what you're experiencing. You want to see a movement of about 1 Brix or 0.005 SG. Then take the fermenting must and add 4 grams of Fermaid O. Mix well and blend back into fermenting must. Shake or mix vigorously; you're still looking to add oxygen.

14 Repeat Step 13 at the 48- and 72-hour marks.

15 Monitor gravity daily. When your mead is at a specific gravity of 1.018 (4.6 Brix), the whole fermenter needs to be cooled by placing it in a fridge or some alternative method. This will halt the fermentation process. But if the mead is warmed again, the yeast will wake up and start producing alcohol again. This mead needs a little residual sugar for balance, and for this recipe we are looking for a lower ABV.

16 After a week in the fridge, rack the mead into your picnic keg. Go easy and try not to splash and add oxygen. Pressurize the keg to about 1 bar (10 to 15 pounds per square inch is fine).

17 Once the mead is in the keg and pressurized, shake the keg so that the CO_2 will dissolve faster. Keep the keg in the fridge to avoid additional fermentation.

18 Taste-test your mead frequently. When the carbonation seems just right to you, lower the pressure to a serving pressure of about 4 pounds per square inch and either bottle and cork, or serve right out of the picnic keg.

NOTE: I prefer orange blossom honey for this recipe. We are looking for specific gravity of 1.068 to 1.072 (16.6 Brix to 17.5 Brix), so you will want to add honey or water to get the must within that range. (All honey has a different specific gravity, so different honey will require different adjustments.)

Metheglin Mead

Courtesy of Howland Blackiston

I immodestly state that this is an extraordinary mead. It gets better and better when it's allowed to mature for a few years — if you can hold off that long. This is a *metheglin* style mead, the term given to mead that's spiced. My recipe fills a lot of bottles of finished product (I like to stock up and then let it age — a lot). But you can scale the amounts to better suit your needs. Some of my mead is now over ten years old, and it is simply amazing.

INGREDIENTS

32 pounds of dark wildflower honey

13 gallons of nonchlorinated water

2½ packets white wine yeast or mead yeast

4¼ tablespoons of wine yeast nutrient

5 sticks of cinnamon

1 tablespoon cloves

DIRECTIONS

1 Add the honey and water to a large (20 gallon) initial fermentation tank. Stir vigorously to blend and introduce lots of oxygen (it's important at this early stage of the process to introduce as much oxygen as possible). This initial mixture is called "must."

2 Add 2½ packets of either white wine yeast or mead yeast to the must and stir vigorously to blend (wine yeast is available at wine-making supply stores).

 Do not mistake bread yeast for specialized wine yeast. Bread yeast simply won't do the trick.

WARNING

3 Add wine nutrient and stir vigorously.

4 Cover this initial fermentation tank loosely with a clean towel and allow the fermentation to do its thing.

5 Let the must ferment for approximately 3 weeks (or until the vigorous bubbling has subsided).

6 Now rack the liquid into glass carboys (from this point on, avoid splashing as you do *not* want to add oxygen to the must.) You'll likely need several carboys for this recipe. Fill right up to the neck of the carboy, leaving only 2 inches of head space. Divide the cinnamon and cloves between the glass carboys. Place a fermentation valve on each.

7 Rack a total of two or three more times at one-month intervals. Each racking further clears the mead. I know you're eager to drink your mead, but your patience will pay off in a product that tastes amazing and looks beautiful.

8 After the final racking, transfer the mead to sterilized bottles and cork tightly.

9 Store the bottles on their sides in a cool, dark place. The longer this mead is aged, the more sophisticated the flavor. Salute!

TIP: You can get your mead sparkling clear by using one of the filtering devices that are available from beer- and wine-making suppliers. Filtering would be the last step before bottling. Remember, once that initial fermentation is done early in this process, avoid any splashing that would introduce oxygen.

Cherry Melomel Mead

Courtesy of Talon Bergen, Bergen House Meadery. www.bergenhousesect.com

Okay, so you made traditional meads and they were delicious. Now, you want to get creative and make something far more artisanal. This recipe will do the trick. It's for a big and bold *cherry melomel.*

INGREDIENTS

3 gallons nonchlorinated water

12 pounds honey

4 grams GoFerm brand yeast nutrient

5-gram packet of wine yeast

12 pounds fresh cherries

12 grams Fermaid O brand yeast nutrient

DIRECTIONS

1 Bring your 3 gallons of water just to a simmer and remove from heat.

2 Add the honey and the warm water to a 5-gallon, food-safe bucket. The warmth helps the thick honey blend with the water. Mix vigorously with a long-handled spoon. Splashing is encouraged to add oxygen into the mixture. Once the water and honey have been mixed, the solution is now called a must.

3 Use your hydrometer to check on the must's specific gravity (SG). You are looking for a specific gravity of 1.095 to 1.15 or a Brix reading of 23. You can adjust the reading upward by adding more honey or adjust it downward by adding more water.

4 Mix the GoFerm and warm water.

5 Check the temperature of the GoFerm solution, and add yeast if it's below 104 degrees Fahrenheit (40 degrees Celsius). Let stand for five to ten minutes before proceeding to the next step.

6 Add 50 ml (¼ cup) of must to the yeast and GoFerm solution. Let stand for ten minutes. You should start to see activity in the solution at this time.

7 Use your sanitized thermometer to check the must temperature. If it's within 5 to 10 degrees F (3–5 degrees C) of the yeast and GoFerm solution, then you can add it to the must. If it's *not* within that temperature difference, then add an additional ⅓ cup must to the yeast solution, wait another five minutes, and check the temperature again. Why do we do this? Because minimizing the temperature difference between the yeast mixture and the must helps eliminate thermal shock to the yeast and encourages a healthy fermentation.

8 Shake or mix the must vigorously. Remember, the goal is to get oxygen into the must to create a good fermentation. It is impossible to overoxygenate at this point.

9 Cover the bucket with a clean towel and let it do its thing for 24 hours.

10 If you are using fresh cherries, now is the time to wash and de-stem them. This is a time-consuming process.

11 Technically, the cherries are teeming with bacteria from the farm you bought them from. So I place the washed and de-stemmed cherries in a pot, cover them with water, and bring it to 140 degrees Fahrenheit (60 degrees Celsius) and hold it there for ten minutes.

12 Drain and allow the cherries to cool a bit; then bag and freeze them. When you freeze fruit, the cells rupture and it gives you easy access to the juices inside.

13 In 24 hours come back to your fermenting must and add 1 gram of Fermaid O. Stir to mix thoroughly. It's okay to splash a lot — you want to add lots of oxygen to the must.

14 Repeat Step 13 at the 48- and 72-hour marks.

15 Take your cherries out of the freezer and allow them to thaw.

16 Mash the cherries while they're inside the freezer bags. Make sure the skins have all been broken to give access to the juice inside.

(continued)

17 Add the cherries to the mead.

18 Every day you will need to "punch down the fruit." The fruit that is floating at the top will grow mold if you allow it to. The key to stopping mold spores is to stop them from getting oxygen. By gently pushing the fruit that is floating on top, all the way to the bottom, you can eliminate this issue. Keep in mind, however, you no longer want to add oxygen to your mead as this will cause the mead to be less shelf-stable and can cause off flavors.

19 After a week you can remove the cherries by lifting out the hop bag.

20 Without disturbing the surface, remove a little bit of the liquid with a measuring cup, pour it in a glass, and taste it. If it's too sweet, let it continue to ferment and check it every 24 hours.

21 Once the mead is no longer too sweet, you can carefully rack it off into sterilized bottles. Cork and place bottles in the fridge.

22 Leave the mead there for *at least* a few weeks. The longer you wait, the better the mead will taste.

TIP: I like a wildflower honey in this recipe because the honey should be floral and play a supporting role. If you pick a monovarietal honey, it may be overwhelmed by the cherries if the flavor is very delicate and subtle.

TIP: For the cherries, I use seconds from a local farm.

TIP: Put the cherries in a sanitized hop bag when you add them to the mead. This will make racking much easier.

Chapter **15**

Cooking with Honey

Honey is not only wholesome, delicious, sweet and fat free, it's also an incredibly versatile ingredient in the kitchen. There are all kinds of recipes that benefit from a touch of honey's diverse flavors. In this chapter I include a few of my own family recipes, as well as some truly remarkable recipes generously provided by noted honey-loving chefs from all over the United States. I can promise you they are all worth trying.

TIP

Professional chefs like to use metric measurements for accuracy, so some of these recipes include metric measurements. I suggest getting an inexpensive digital scale with a metric option to measure out the ingredients like a pro.

And just for the fun of it, I start the list with a 2,000-year-old Roman recipe from *Apicius' De Re Coquinaria (Apicius on the Subject of Cooking)*. This is likely the world's oldest surviving cookbook, compiled in the first century AD. The book's namesake was Marcus Gavius Apicius, a Roman of that era famously noted as having a prodigious appetite for fine food and drink, although Apicius was not the author of the book that bears his name.

Ova Spongia ex Lacte (Eggs With Honey)

Here's the full recipe courtesy of Apicius' De Re Coquinaria

When in Rome, do like the Romans. Here's an authentic ancient Roman recipe you can serve at your next toga party. Party on!

PREP TIME: 10 MIN	COOK TIME: 10 MIN	YIELD: 2 SERVINGS

INGREDIENTS

4 eggs

1 cup milk

1 tablespoon olive oil

3 tablespoons honey

Generous pinch of black pepper

DIRECTIONS

1 Beat together the eggs, milk, and half the olive oil.

2 Pour the other half of the olive oil into a frying pan and heat. When this is sizzling, add the omelet mixture.

3 Whisk until the mix starts to solidify (whisking will make a lighter omelet).

4 When thoroughly cooked on one side, turn the omelet over and cook on the other side. Fold in half and turn out onto a plate.

5 Gently warm the honey until runny, and pour it over the omelet.

6 Fold this over once more and cut into thick slices.

7 Sprinkle with black pepper and serve.

Honey Cashews

Courtesy of Chef Colleen Grapes, Executive Pastry Chef, Pastry Chef Instructor at NYU Steinhardt.

PREP TIME: 20 MIN	COOK TIME: 18 MIN	YIELD: 4 TO 6 SERVINGS

INGREDIENTS

3 tablespoons honey

1 tablespoon maple syrup

2 tablespoons unsalted butter

1 pound lightly salted cashews

¼ cup granulated sugar

⅛ teaspoon cinnamon

⅛ teaspoon black pepper

1 teaspoon vanilla extract

¼ teaspoon kosher salt

DIRECTIONS

1 Place the honey, maple syrup, and butter into a medium-size pot and melt. Once melted, whisk in the cinnamon, black pepper, vanilla extract and salt to incorporate.

2 Add the cashews and mix until all are coated. Pour onto a parchment-lined sheet tray and spread to one even layer.

3 Pop in 350-degree oven for three 6-minute intervals, mixing in between for a total of 18 minutes.

4 Once lightly browned, put back into a bowl and, while still hot, put the sugar on top. Mix to coat so the cashews crunch with sugar.

5 Pour back onto a sheet in one layer and let cool. Don't let the mixture sit around once it's cool because it will start to get too much moisture from the air.

6 Store in an airtight container.

VARY IT!: You can also sprinkle this mixture with some curry powder; lemon, lime, or tangerine zest; cayenne pepper, or chili spice for something different.

Honey Vanilla Butter

Courtesy of Joy Blackiston

This decadent honey butter recipe makes an outstanding spread on your favorite baked item or anything you top with butter. You can scale up the quantities listed here, as this Honey Vanilla Butter spread makes a wonderful gift for family, neighbors, and friends.

PREP TIME: 10 MIN	COOK TIME: 0 MIN	YIELD: 1 CUP

INGREDIENTS

¾ cup unsalted butter, softened to room temperature

¼ teaspoon vanilla extract

¼ cup honey

DIRECTIONS

1 Using an electric mixer with whisk attachment, whip softened butter until light and very fluffy.

2 Add vanilla and honey gradually while still whipping. Continue until you reach a desired fluffy consistency.

3 Place in a ramekin or two (depending upon ramekin size) and enjoy.

TIP: I like to use clover or orange blossom honey in this recipe.

Creamy Honey & Gorgonzola Dressing

Courtesy of Joy Blackiston

This dressing goes great with nearly any salad. I particularly love it on a Spinach & Bacon Salad, Cobb Salad, or Waldorf Salad. Mix up a batch and keep at the ready in your fridge. Use within a week.

PREP TIME: 15 MIN	COOK TIME: 0 MIN	YIELD: 4 TO 5 SERVINGS

INGREDIENTS

1 cup Greek-style plain yogurt

3–4 tablespoons mayonnaise

⅓ cup crumbled Gorgonzola cheese

1 tablespoon light honey

DIRECTIONS

1   In a bowl, gently stir together the ingredients.

2   Pour over salad and gently toss.

Curried Honey Veggie Dip

Courtesy of Howland Blackiston

This is a real crowd pleaser at our parties.

PREP TIME: 20 MIN	COOK TIME: 0 MIN	YIELD: APPROXIMATELY 1 CUP

INGREDIENTS

1 cup mayonnaise

¼ cup honey

1 tablespoon curry powder

1 tablespoon white wine vinegar

DIRECTIONS

1 Combine mayonnaise, honey, curry powder, and vinegar; mix well.

2 Cover and set aside in the refrigerator for at least one hour to allow flavors to blend. Serve as a dip with vegetables.

NOTE: Use your favorite varietal of honey in this recipe. I use my own wildflower honey from my apiary.

TIP: For fewer calories, use low-fat mayonnaise.

NOTE: Serve dip with assorted fresh raw vegetables of your choice (sliced peppers, celery, carrots, cauliflower, broccoli, asparagus tips)

Honey & Rum Barbecue Sauce

Courtesy of Joy Blackiston

Honey in a BBQ sauce is a natural. It not only adds a wonderful sweetness to grilled meat and fish, but it also caramelizes beautifully if you brush it on during the last minute or so of grilling. Serve it on the side with your grilled protein.

PREP TIME: 15 MIN	COOK TIME: 20 MIN	YIELD: 1 CUP

INGREDIENTS

1 tablespoon vegetable oil

¼ cup minced onion

2 cloves garlic, minced

One 8-ounce can tomato sauce

⅓ cup buckwheat honey (or any dark honey)

3 tablespoons vinegar

2 tablespoons dark rum

1 teaspoon dry mustard

½ teaspoon salt

¼ teaspoon freshly ground pepper

DIRECTIONS

1 Heat the oil in a saucepan until hot. Add the onion and garlic. Cook until tender.

2 Add the remaining ingredients and bring to a boil. Reduce the heat and simmer for 20 minutes.

3 Use immediately, or bottle and store in fridge.

Smoked Salmon Langstroth

Courtesy of Executive Chef Michael Young, MBE

Here's an eye-popping and delicious recipe from the founder of the Institute of Northern Ireland Beekeepers and an international senior honey judge. And a delicious way to launch a fine dinner.

PREP TIME: 30 MIN (PLUS TIME TO MARINATE)	COOK TIME: 0 MIN	YIELD: 8 SERVINGS

INGREDIENTS

2 pounds (1 kilogram) smoked salmon, filleted, with skin off

2 teaspoons sea salt

1 teaspoon finely crushed black peppercorns

3 tablespoons lime juice

8 teaspoons light honey

50 grams fresh dill, chopped

100 milliliters crème fraiche

3 tablespoons lemon juice

Dill sprigs, red chard, and lime wedges to garnish

Bee pollen, mock caviar, and pink peppercorns as a sprinkle garnish

DIRECTIONS:

1 Take a large slice of the smoked salmon and lay it flat on a chopping board. Cut out 8-x-3-inch round pieces and then place in the refrigerator until later.

2 Prepare the remaining salmon by slicing thin slices along its full length. Put aside one nice slice of salmon and place it to the side.

3 Roll out some plastic cling wrap, roughly 20 inches long and 10 inches wide, on a flat surface.

4 Mix in a bowl the sea salt, finely crushed peppercorns, lime juice, and 3 teaspoons of honey. Then, along with some chopped dill, sprinkle some of the mix on the plastic cling wrap. (Remember to keep some of the mix to the side to be sprinkled between the salmon layers.) Place some of the salmon slices on top of the mix. Repeat the process in layers until all the salmon is used and then completely wrap with plastic cling wrap. Place a flat board on top with a 2-pound weight and refrigerate three days, turning occasionally.

5 Remove the salmon from the refrigerator and remove the cling wrap. Across the width, cut into thin strips and place in a mixing bowl. Add the crème fraiche and 1 teaspoon of honey and bind well.

6 Place a lightly oiled 3-inch presentation ring in the center of a plate and fill to the top with the strips of salmon mixture. Pat down firmly and place the circles of salmon on top. Make sure it is nice and level.

7 Remove the ring and add 1 teaspoon of crème fraiche on the top in the center. Garnish with a fine sprig of dill and red chard and lime wedges. Mix 4 teaspoons of honey with 3 tablespoons of lemon juice and then drizzle on the plate. I sparingly sprinkle the plate with a few pink peppercorns, bee pollen, and mock caviar.

NOTE: Serve with brown or pumpernickel bread. Bon appétit!

Chocolate Honey Chili

Courtesy of Chef Samantha Mauro, Devil's Den Confections

PREP TIME: 40 MIN	COOK TIME: 20 MIN	YIELD: 1 CUP

INGREDIENTS

2 teaspoons olive oil

2 medium-sized onions, chopped

1½ pounds ground beef (85% lean)

4 garlic cloves, minced

1 tablespoon chili powder

1 tablespoon cumin

1 tablespoon sweet paprika

1 teaspoon freshly ground black pepper

1 teaspoon salt

Two 16-ounce cans chopped tomatoes

One 28-ounce can tomato sauce

1 cup beef broth

2 tablespoons unsweetened cocoa powder

3 ounces dark or semisweet chocolate, chopped

2 tablespoons honey

Hot sauce (optional)

1 bay leaf

1 can red kidney beans, rinsed

DIRECTIONS

1 Heat a large saucepan over medium–high heat and add the oil. Add the onions and sauté 1 to 2 minutes.

2 Add the meat and break it up with the edge of a spoon. Add the garlic, chili powder, cumin, paprika, pepper, and salt. Sauté for 6 to 7 minutes or until the onions have softened and the meat starts to brown.

3 Add the tomatoes with their reserved juice, the tomato sauce, and the broth, stirring to combine.

4 Stir in the cocoa, chocolate, honey, hot sauce (if using), and bay leaf. Reduce the heat to low and gently simmer for 1 hour.

5 Add the beans, stirring to combine. Heat for 5 minutes or until the beans are heated through.

6 Remove and discard the bay leaf before serving.

TIP: In a pinch, chocolate chips may be used in place of the chopped dark or semisweet chocolate.

Roasted Chicken Thighs with Honey Mustard Glaze and Onion Gravy

Courtesy of Adam Noren

This recipe comes from a friend and fellow beekeeper who happens to be a seriously amazing cook.

PREP TIME: 15 MIN	COOK TIME: 60 MIN	YIELD: SERVES 4

INGREDIENTS

Honey Mustard Glaze (see the following recipe)

Onion Gravy (see the following recipe)

¼ cup vegetable or other neutral oil

1½ tablespoons turmeric

1 teaspoon kosher salt

½ teaspoon pepper

½ teaspoon coriander

½ teaspoon nutmeg

4 boneless skinless chicken thighs

DIRECTIONS

1 Mix the vegetable oil and the spices in the bottom of a mixing bowl large enough to hold the chicken thighs. Add the chicken thighs to the bowl and mix to coat. This step can be done immediately before cooking, or it may be done up to a day in advance and moved to the refrigerator. More time will allow the salt to brine the chicken. Occasionally mix the chicken to ensure even coating.

2 Preheat your oven to 350 degrees, using convection mode if available.

3 In an oven-safe 10- to 12-inch sauté pan or skillet, brown the chicken thighs on medium heat two at a time so as not to overcrowd the pan. Cook for 3 to 4 minutes per side (chicken will still be raw in the center). Watch the temperature so that the spices do not burn. Because the chicken is in an oil-based marinade, you should not need to add additional oil, especially if using nonstick or cast-iron cookware. It's okay if there is some sticking and browned bits are left behind in the pan.

4 As you finish each batch, return the chicken thighs to the bowl in which you marinaded the chicken.

5 With the chicken out of the pan, add the vegetables to the pan (see the following recipe for Onion Gravy) and toss with the oil left in the pan. As the onions sweat, use a wooden spoon to scrape up the browned bits and toss with the onions. Once this is done, turn off heat (onions will be mostly raw).

(continued)

6 Arrange the chicken thighs in a single layer on top of the vegetables with the bone side (the rough side where the bones were removed) up. Brush a third of the Honey Mustard Glaze on the chicken thighs (see the following recipe).

7 Roast in the oven for 10 minutes.

8 Remove from the oven and flip the chicken thighs over so that the smooth side is facing up. Brush a third of the Honey Mustard Glaze on the chicken thighs, and roast in the oven for 15 minutes.

9 Remove from the oven, brush the remaining Honey Mustard Glaze on the chicken, and roast for 10 minutes more.

10 Remove from the oven and transfer chicken thighs to a cutting board. Stir the vinegar into the gravy, and adjust the amount per taste. Let chicken and gravy rest for 10 minutes before serving.

Honey Mustard Glaze

INGREDIENTS

⅓ cup honey

¼ cup Dijon mustard

2 tablespoons Worcestershire sauce

DIRECTIONS

1 Combine all ingredients in a small pot and heat over low heat. Reduce the glaze slightly until it easily coats the back of a spoon. Turn off heat at this point.

Onion Gravy

INGREDIENTS

3 medium onions, sliced pole to pole

4 cloves garlic cut into large pieces

1 tablespoon chopped fresh sage

½ teaspoon fresh thyme leaves

1 teaspoon vegetable or other neutral oil

1 teaspoon apple cider or other vinegar

DIRECTIONS

1 Combine the onions, garlic, sage, thyme, and oil in a bowl, separating the layers of the onions with your hands and lightly coating the vegetables with the oil.

2 After roasting the chicken, stir the vinegar into the gravy, and adjust the amount to taste (see Step 10 in main recipe).

Grilled Scallops with Citrus Marinade

Courtesy of Howland Blackiston

There's something magical about the briny-sweet flavor of the scallops blended with citrus and honey. It's a family favorite around our house.

PREP TIME: 30 MIN	COOK TIME: 4 TO 7 MIN	YIELD: 2 SERVINGS

INGREDIENTS

2 tablespoons honey

1 tablespoon vegetable oil

4 teaspoons lime juice

¼ teaspoon lime zest

¼ teaspoon lemon zest

¼ teaspoon sea salt

Hot pepper sauce (to taste)

¾ pound large sea scallops

1 lime and 1 lemon (cut into wedges)

DIRECTIONS

1 Combine honey, oil, lime juice, lime and lemon zest, salt, and hot pepper sauce (to taste).

2 Pat scallops dry with paper towel and add scallops to the marinade. Marinate covered in fridge, stirring occasionally for the first hour or two, and then let marinate without stirring overnight.

3 Preheat grill to medium-high heat. Lightly oil grill grate to prevent sticking.

4 Grill scallops about 3 minutes; then turn and grill 3 more minutes (or until scallops are opaque throughout and lightly browned).

5 Serve with lime and lemon wedges and a simple green salad.

Roasted Honey–Mustard Potatoes

Courtesy Howland Blackiston

PREP TIME: 20 MIN	COOK TIME: 35 MIN	YIELD: 4 SERVINGS

INGREDIENTS

4 large baking potatoes (around 2 pounds total)

¼ cup honey

½ cup Dijon mustard

½ teaspoon dried thyme leaves, crushed

½ teaspoon dried rosemary leaves, crushed

Salt and freshly ground pepper (to taste)

DIRECTIONS

1 Peel the potatoes and cut each into 8 pieces.

2 Bring a large saucepan of salted water to a boil and then add the potato wedges. Cook for 12 to 14 minutes, or until just tender. Do not overcook.

3 Combine the honey, mustard, and crushed thyme and rosemary in a bowl. Toss the potatoes with the mixture until evenly coated.

4 Arrange the potatoes on a baking sheet sprayed with nonstick cooking spray.

5 Bake at 375 degrees for 20 minutes or until the potatoes brown around the edges.

6 Season to taste with salt and pepper.

Pork Chops with Honey and Sage

Courtesy of Chef Alex Gunuey, host of the video series, Cultured & Cured

The delicate balance between the honey and the acid pairs perfectly with the sage and apples, turning a simple pork chop classic into a refined dish. This is comfort food at its best. For this recipe, use a basswood honey or sourwood honey; both are native to the United States.

PREP TIME: 40+ MIN (PLUS TIME TO MARINATE 2 HOURS TO OVERNIGHT)	COOK TIME: 60+ MIN	YIELD: 4 SERVINGS

INGREDIENTS

½ cup grapeseed oil

3 tablespoons cracked black peppercorns 1 pork + 2 marinade

Zest of ¼ of an orange

8 to 10 large sage leaves

1 tablespoon hot smoked paprika (picante)

Salt to taste

4 tablespoons honey 3 pork + 1 marinade (1 + 1 + 2)

3 tablespoons apple cider vinegar 2 pork + 1 marinade

4 pork chops

2 or 3 Granny Smith apples

5 tablespoons butter

Juice of ½ lemon

½ cup dry white wine

4 teaspoons pomegranate seed

DIRECTIONS

1 In a heavy-bottomed saucepan, place the ½ cup of grapeseed oil, 2 tablespoons of the cracked black peppercorn, the orange zest, and the sage leaves. Simmer at very low heat.

2 Remove the sage leaves when they are nice and crispy, and drain them on a paper towel; put them aside for later use.

3 Keep simmering the oil for at least 20 more minutes to extract all the flavors. You are creating an "infused oil." It will be the base for all upcoming flavoring.

4 Strain half the infused oil into a small bowl and set aside for your final sauce.

5 To the remaining half of the infused oil, add the hot smoked paprika, salt (to taste), 1 tablespoon of the honey, and 1 tablespoon of the apple cider vinegar and mix well. Allow the mixture to cool.

6 When the spiced oil mixture is fully cooled, put the pork chops in a zip-top plastic bag and add the oil mixture to the bag. Make sure the marinade is well distributed and nicely coating the meat. Let it rest in the refrigerator for at least 2 hours or preferably overnight.

(continued)

7 When you are ready to cook the pork chops, take them out of the marinade, and discard the bag, the marinade, and the spices. Pat dry the chops with paper towels.

8 In a very hot cast-iron frying pan, heat the reserved flavored oil, and brown the meat on medium-high heat, about 3 to 5 minutes on each side.

9 When you have the desired caramelization, set the chops aside on a covered platter. Do not clean your frying pan; you will use it later on for your sauce.

10 Now prepare the apples. Wash and core them and cut each apple into eight wedges

11 In the saucepan you used to infuse the oil, melt 1 tablespoon of butter, 1 tablespoon of honey, and the juice of ½ lemon; then add the apple eighths. Cover and gently simmer for 20 to 30 minutes over very low heat.

12 As the apples are cooking, heat your cast-iron frying pan with the flavored oil, meat juices, and bits, and add the remaining 2 tablespoons of honey and the remaining 2 tablespoons of apple cider vinegar. Dissolve and mix with a wooden spoon over medium-low heat until all ingredients are well blended.

13 Slowly add the white wine to the pan and reduce by a third.

14 When reduced, add 2 tablespoons of butter, turning constantly until melted.

15 When the butter is foaming, add the pork chops back to the frying pan and finish cooking them, constantly basting the meat with the simmering liquid for 5 to 6 minutes on each side or until fully cooked. This is an important stage of the process because this is how you delicately blend all the flavors, keep your meat moist, and achieve a nice coloring and crusting on the chops.

16 Remove the chops from the frying pan and set aside in the covered platter. Now you are left with a flavorful, buttery sauce in your pan, ready for the final touch.

17 To see if your sauce is ready, take a clean spoon, dip it into the reduced liquid, take it out, and turn it over with the back of the spoon facing you. The sauce should coat the back of the spoon rather than just run off. If it doesn't, just add a tablespoon of butter and reduce it some more, constantly turning gently over low heat. Repeat the spoon test.

18 When ready, put 2 or 3 tablespoons of the sauce on each individual serving plate; then add a pork chop on top of the sauce and top the chop with 1 or 2 fried sage leaves. Place a few apple slices next to the meat, and sprinkle a teaspoon of pomegranate seeds on top.

19 Repeat with each serving plate.

TIP: This dish is best served with bitter greens to balance the sweetness of the sauce, and some mashed potatoes for classic comfort. Bon appétit!

NOTE: The French term for a sauce that coats the back of a spoon is "napper"; sauces are said to "nappe" when they leave a glossy coating on the back of a spoon.

Honey Orange Mousse

Courtesy of Celebrity Chef Nick Stellino, author and television personality

Here's a frozen dessert with the texture of light whipped ice cream. It's perfect served with your favorite fresh fruit.

PREP TIME: 20 MINUTES	COOK TIME: 0	YIELD: SERVES 8

INGREDIENTS

6 egg yolks

⅓ cup of orange blossom honey

⅛ teaspoon ground nutmeg

2 teaspoons grated orange zest

1 cup heavy cream

DIRECTIONS

1 With an electric mixer, beat the egg yolks and honey in a large bowl until very thick, about 8 to 10 minutes.

2 Stir in the nutmeg and orange zest.

3 In a separate bowl, beat the cream until soft peaks form.

4 Fold the whipped cream into the honey mixture.

5 Spoon the mousse into 8 small (¾-cup) custard cups.

6 Cover the cups with plastic wrap and freeze for 2 to 3 hours.

7 Remove from the freezer 15 to 20 minutes before serving and let sit at room temperature to soften the texture.

Panna Cotta with Honey Stewed Apricots

Courtesy of Chef Colleen Grapes, Executive Pastry Chef, Pastry Chef Instructor at NYU Steinhardt

PREP TIME: 20 MINUTES | **COOK TIME: 15 MINUTES** | **YIELD: SERVES 4**

INGREDIENTS

½ cup whole milk

1 tablespoon Knox gelatin

3 cups heavy cream

¾ cup powdered sugar

1 teaspoon kosher salt

1 teaspoon vanilla extract

DIRECTIONS

1 Place the milk in a bowl and sprinkle the gelatin on top to "bloom." Make sure the sides are clean and the gelatin is submerged. Let stand for 5 minutes.

2 In a saucepan, bring the heavy cream, sugar, and salt almost to a boil and turn off.

3 Add the bloomed gelatin and stir with a spatula until dissolved.

4 Add the vanilla extract.

5 Pour about ¾ cup of the liquid into a clear glass and place in the refrigerator for 3 to 4 hours until set. If not using that day, cover tops of glasses with plastic wrap.

6 When ready to serve, demold the panna cotta onto a serving plate and spoon the honey stewed apricots on top.

Honey Stewed Apricots

INGREDIENTS

12 ounces dried apricots

5 cups water

1 cup honey

¼ teaspoon kosher salt

½ vanilla bean

1 medium-sized cinnamon stick

1 star anise

2 cardamom pods

DIRECTIONS

1 Slice the apricots lengthwise into 3 or 4 strips and place in a large saucepan.

2 Place the rest of the ingredients in with the apricots and mix together.

3 Cook over medium heat until most of the water has been absorbed. Leave juicy and let cool to room temperature. You can thin by adding some more water or adding liquor such as brandy or Amaro Montenegro.

Honey Crème Brûlée with Passion Fruit and Raspberry and Cherry Coulis

Courtesy of Executive Chef Michael Young, MBE

There are many who say that crème brûlée (French for "burnt cream") is beautiful and perfect as it is and doesn't need to change, but then they haven't tasted honey brûlée, have they? Just remember: For sheer value, just add honey.

This recipe creates a marvelous sweet for which my taste buds have never forgiven me. The inside color has an opaque luster that is a divine manifestation. Once eaten, it will never be forgotten.

PREP TIME: 60+ MIN	COOK TIME: 60+ MIN	YIELD: 8 SERVINGS

INGREDIENTS

Honey Raspberry and Cherry Coulis (see the following recipe)

310 milliliters double cream (or heavy whipping cream if you can't find double cream)

1 vanilla pod

6 egg yolks

2 whole eggs

200 grams honey

3 passion fruits

DIRECTIONS

1 Preheat the oven to 275 degrees.

2 Pour the double cream in a saucepan. Split the vanilla pod and scrape in the seeds; chop up the pod and throw that in.

3 Bring to the boiling point and remove from the stove. Let sit to cool a little and let the vanilla flavor the cream.

4 In a heat-proof bowl, beat the egg yolks, the whole eggs; add the honey.

5 Pour in the cream and slowly bring to a boil, stirring constantly. The mixture should be thickish but not grainy. Remove from the heat as soon as the mixture slightly thickens and strain through a fine sieve into a large jug.

6 Remove the seeds from 3 passion fruits and gently mix into the mixture.

7 Place small ramekins or small honey pots in a deep tray and carefully pour the custard mix into each dish.

8 Gently pour hot water inside the dish (to create a bain-marie) until the water level is two-thirds up to the top of the dish. Cover the tray tightly with cling wrap.

9 Place on the center shelf of the oven and bake at least 50 minutes; if your custard dish is deeper than normal, a few more minutes in the oven are necessary for the temperature to penetrate inside the core. The brûlée should still be slightly wobbly.

10 When cooked, allow to cool slightly; then chill in the refrigerator.

11 When ready to serve, put a teaspoon of honey on top of the crème brûlée and toast with a blowtorch.

Honey Raspberry and Cherry Coulis

INGREDIENTS

147 grams honey

4 tablespoons brandy or cherry liqueur (optional)

300 grams fresh cherries

200 grams fresh raspberries or 350 grams raspberries packed in light syrup

DIRECTIONS

1 Place the fruits into a saucepan. Stir in honey and brandy or liqueur (optional). Bring slowly to a boil, and then simmer 1 minute.

2 Puree the fruit. Use a stick blender to puree and then strain it through a fine strainer to remove the seeds, if preferred.

3 Just before serving, place a spoonful of honey on top of the brûlée.

4 Alternatively, the coulis can be served in a small pouring jug and added to the brûlée at the table.

Chapter **16**

Baking with Honey

H oney works well as a substitute for refined sugar in recipes because the liquid blends easily and quickly with the other ingredients, adding its own sweet, delicate flavor. Baking with honey gives a more delicate texture to scones and biscuits and a chewy consistency to cookies, whereas sugar just adds plain sweetness.

Swapping Out Sugar for Honey

You can substitute honey in your favorite baking recipes, but when you do, be sure to take the following into consideration:

» Because honey contains fructose (and glucose) which is sweeter than sugar, you can use less honey than sugar to achieve the same desired sweetness.

» To substitute honey for sugar in recipes, use 3/4 cup of honey for every 1 cup of granulated sugar the recipe calls for. Refer to Table 16-1 when replacing sugar with honey (depending on the honey you are using and the recipe you are following, you may need to experiment a bit with these ratios).

» If you are measuring honey by weight, 1 cup of honey will weigh 12 ounces.

» Note that a 12-ounce jar of honey by weight equals one cup (8 ounces) of granulated sugar.

» For easy cleanup when measuring honey, coat the measuring cup with nonstick cooking spray or vegetable oil before adding the honey. The honey will slide right out of the cup.

» Honey helps baked goods stay fresh and moist longer. It also gives baked goods a warm, golden color. When substituting honey for sugar in baked goods, follow these guidelines:

   ● Reduce the amount of liquid in the recipe by ¼ cup for each cup of honey used.

   ● Neutralize the acid in the honey by adding ½ teaspoon of baking soda for every cup of honey used. But if your recipe already calls for baking soda, don't add more.

   ● Reduce the oven temperature by 25 degrees to prevent overbrowning. You may have to extend the baking time a bit, so bake your yummies longer at a lower temperature.

TABLE 16-1   ## Honey Replacement Estimator

If the Recipe Calls for This Much Sugar	Replace the Sugar with This Much Honey
1 Tbsp (15mL)	2 tsp (10mL)
2 Tbsp (30 mL)	1 Tbsp 1 tsp (25mL)
1/4 Cup (50mL)	2 Tbsp 2 tsp (40mL)
1/3 Cup (75mL)	4 Tbsp (60mL)
1/2 Cup (125mL)	1/3 Cup (75mL)
2/3 Cup (150mL)	1/2 Cup (125mL)
3/4 Cup (175mL)	2/3 Cup (150mL)
1 Cup (250 mL)	3/4 Cup (175mL)
2 Cups (500mL)	1 1/4 Cup (300mL)

TIP

Be sure to experiment by using different honey varietals in your recipes to produce different flavor profiles in your baked goods. See Chapter 7 to find out about the flavor characteristics of 50 different varieties of honey.

Checking Out Some Recipes

Here are some great recipes from my own kitchen and some friends who are professional artisan bakers. We start, just for the fun of it, with a recipe from the ancient Roman empire, where honey was so revered it was once used by Romans to pay their taxes.

TIP

Professional chefs like to use metric measurements for accuracy, so some of these recipes include metric measurements. I suggest getting an inexpensive digital scale with a metric option to measure out the ingredients like a pro.

Roman Libum Cheese Cake and Honey

Courtesy of Apicius' De Re Coquinaria

Libum was a traditional sweet cheese cake made by ancient Romans. It was often made as a sacred act of worship to household deities. It can be served hot or cold, and should be generously drizzled with honey. This recipe comes from the world's oldest surviving cookbook, compiled in the first century AD.

PREP TIME: 15 MIN	COOK TIME: 40 MIN	YIELD: 4 SERVINGS

INGREDIENTS

1 cup plain, all-purpose flour

8 ounces ricotta cheese

1 egg, beaten

Bay leaves

½ cup light honey

DIRECTIONS

1 Sift the flour into a bowl. Beat the cheese until it's soft and stir it into the flour along with the egg.

2 Form a soft dough and divide into four parts. Mold each one into a bun and place on a greased baking tray with a fresh bay leaf underneath.

3 Heat the oven to 425 degrees. Cover the cakes with your brick* and bake for 35 to 40 minutes until golden brown.

4 Warm the honey and place the warm cakes in the honey so that they absorb it. Allow the cakes to soak in the honey for 30 minutes before serving.

*Keeping the recipe authentic, the Romans often covered their food while it was cooking with a domed earthenware cover called a *testo*. You can use an overturned, shallow clay pot, a metal bowl, or a casserole dish as a testo.

Honey Peanut Butter Cookies

Courtesy of Chef Patty Pulliam

Please be careful with these cookies; they are seriously addictive. No, seriously. You've been warned.

PREP TIME: 20 MIN	COOK TIME: 10 MIN	YIELD: 5 DOZEN COOKIES

INGREDIENTS

½ cup unsalted butter

1 cup creamy peanut butter

½ cup brown sugar

1 cup honey

2 large eggs, room temperature, lightly beaten

3 cups all-purpose flour

1½ teaspoons baking soda

1 teaspoon baking powder

½ teaspoon salt

DIRECTIONS

1 Preheat oven to 350 degrees.

2 In a bowl, mix the butter, peanut butter, brown sugar, and honey.

3 Add eggs; mix well.

4 Combine the flour, baking soda, baking powder, and salt; add to the peanut butter mixture and mix well.

5 Roll into 1- to 1½-inch balls and place on ungreased baking sheets. Flatten with a fork dipped in flour.

6 Bake until set, 8 to 10 minutes.

7 Remove to wire racks to cool.

Cracked Black Pepper Biscuits with Thyme Honey

Courtesy of Cookbook Author Marc J. Sievers

PREP TIME: 30 MIN	COOK TIME: 20 MIN	YIELD: 8 BISCUITS

INGREDIENTS

Thyme Honey (see the following recipe)

2 cups all-purpose flour

1 tablespoon sugar

1 teaspoon kosher salt

2 teaspoons black pepper, freshly cracked (plus more for garnish)

2 teaspoons baking powder

½ teaspoon baking soda

8 tablespoons butter, diced, very cold

1 cup English cheddar, freshly grated

1 cup heavy cream, very cold

Egg wash (1 extra-large egg, lightly beaten with a splash of water)

Fleur de sel, for garnish

DIRECTIONS

1   Line a half sheet pan with parchment paper. Set aside.

2   Start by sifting the dry ingredients into a large mixing bowl, excluding the fleur de sel.

3   Using a pastry cutter, incorporate the butter until the mixture takes on a crumb-like texture

4   Add the cheese and heavy cream. Using your hands, gently mix until combined. The dough will be very sticky.

5   Remove the dough from the bowl and place onto a lightly floured surface

6   Form the dough into a ball. Using a rolling pin, roll out the dough into a ¾-inch-thick rectangle.

7   Evenly cut the dough into 8 pieces and transfer to the prepared half sheet pan.

8   Brush the top of each biscuit with egg wash and sprinkle with more black pepper and fleur de sel.

9 Refrigerate the sheet pan with the dough for 30 minutes.

10 Meanwhile, preheat the oven to 400 degrees.

11 Bake for 15 to 20 minutes, or until the tops of the biscuits are lightly browned.

12 Serve either warm or at room temperature with the Thyme Honey (see the following recipe).

Thyme Honey

INGREDIENTS

½ cup honey

5 sprigs fresh thyme

DIRECTIONS

1 In a small saucepan set over high heat, add the honey and thyme.

2 Allow to come to a boil.

3 Remove from the heat, cover, and allow to sit for 30 minutes.

4 Serve with the biscuits.

Grandma's Honey Spice Cake

Courtesy of Chef Patty Pulliam

This is such an old-fashioned Grandma-style cake. Enjoy it with a nice cup of tea and a loved one.

PREP TIME: 20 MIN	COOK TIME: 60 MIN	YIELD: 1 LOAF (12 SLICES)

INGREDIENTS

2/3 cup packed brown sugar

1/3 cup whole milk

2 cups all-purpose flour

1½ teaspoons baking powder

½ teaspoon ground cinnamon

½ teaspoon ground nutmeg

1/8 teaspoon ground cloves

2 large eggs

½ cup honey

1/3 cup sunflower oil

DIRECTIONS

1 Preheat oven to 325 degrees.

2 Prepare an 8-x-4-inch loaf pan with oil and flour.

3 In a small saucepan, combine brown sugar and milk. Cook and stir over low heat until sugar is dissolved. Remove from heat.

4 In a large bowl, whisk flour, baking powder, cinnamon, nutmeg, and cloves.

5 In another bowl, whisk eggs, honey, oil, and brown sugar mixture until blended. Add to flour mixture; stir just until moistened.

6 Bake 50 to 60 minutes or until a toothpick inserted in the center comes out clean (cover top loosely with foil if needed to prevent overbrowning).

7 Cool in the pan 10 minutes before removing to a wire rack to cool completely.

Glaze

INGREDIENTS

1/3 cup confectioners' sugar

2 teaspoons milk

DIRECTIONS

1 In a small bowl, stir confectioners' sugar and milk until smooth.

2 Drizzle over cake.

Armenian Paklava Dessert

Courtesy of Albert Mikhitarian

I make this dessert for our Christmas Eve feast every year. For years my mother made this for the family. It has been modified to use honey instead of the traditional sugar syrup (after all, we're a beekeeping family).

PREP TIME: 30 MIN	COOK TIME: 75 MIN	YIELD: APPROXIMATELY 12–14 SERVINGS)

INGREDIENTS

2 cups chopped walnuts

2 cups chopped unsalted pistachios

1/3 cup sugar

½ teaspoon nutmeg

1 teaspoon ground cinnamon

1 package phyllo dough, thawed

2½ sticks of unsalted butter, melted

2 tablespoons fresh lemon juice

1½ cups honey

Powdered sugar (optional)

DIRECTIONS

1 Mix nuts, sugar, and spices and set aside.

2 Butter the bottom of a 9-x-13-inch baking dish.

3 Brush 5 to 10 layers of phyllo dough with melted butter and lay in bottom of baking pan.

4 Spread 1 1/3 cups of nut mixture on top of the first layers of dough.

5 Add 5 to 10 more layers of dough, brushed with butter.

6 Sprinkle with 1 1/3 cups of nut mixture.

7 Repeat Steps 5 and 6.

8 Top with 10 layers of buttered phyllo dough.

9 Cut into a diamond pattern, using diagonal cuts and cutting through all the layers.

(continued)

10 Bake 1 hour and 15 minutes at 300 degrees until golden brown. Remove from oven.

11 Gently heat the honey and lemon juice until runny and pour into the grooves in the pattern.

12 Let the honey soak in for 1 to 2 hours at room temperature.

13 Serve at room temperature with a sprinkle of crushed pistachios and powdered sugar (sugar is optional).

TIP: Keep sheets of phyllo dough covered with wet paper towels when you're not working with them to keep them from drying out.

Fennel/Honey Doughnuts

Courtesy of Ethan Pikas, Cellar Door Provisions

PREP TIME: 90 MIN	COOK TIME: 34 MIN	YIELD: 1 DOZEN DOUGHNUTS

INGREDIENTS

Poolish (see the following recipe)

33 grams fennel oil (see the following recipe)

Honey glaze (see the following recipe)

396 grams high-gluten flour

12 grams instant yeast

6.4 grams kosho (Japanese seasoning)

278 grams egg, beaten

210 grams poolish

78 grams raw honey

12.5 grams salt

122 grams butter

DIRECTIONS

1 The night before making the doughnuts, make the poolish. (See the following recipe.) Poolish is a highly fluid, yeast-cultured dough.

2 Place the flour, yeast, kosho, egg, poolish, and honey in the bowl of a stand mixer.

3 Using the dough hook attachment, mix 3 minutes until dough forms a shaggy mass. Allow this mixture to rest 30 minutes before proceeding.

4 Now add in the salt, fennel oil (see the following recipe), and butter. Mix at medium high speed, 10 to 12 minutes, until the dough is very silky and strong.

5 Place in a sealed container large enough for the dough to double in size, and allow the dough to proof at room temperature 2 to 3 hours.

6 Fold the dough over on itself 3 times and place in the fridge overnight.

7 The following day, roll the dough to 12.7 millimeters thick.

8 Place in the freezer for 45 minutes before cutting.

9 Use a 2½-inch doughnut cutter to cut out doughnuts.

10 Allow the doughnuts to proof at room temperature until risen by 1 1/2? times.

(continued)

11 Heat the fennel oil, bringing it to 335 degrees.

12 Fry doughnuts 3 to 4 minutes per side. Check the center using a cake tester to be sure the doughnuts are cooked all the way through.

13 Allow the doughnuts to cool 7 to 10 minutes and finish by dipping in the honey glaze (see the following recipe).

Poolish

INGREDIENTS

62 grams whole-wheat bread flour

62 grams high-gluten bread flour

125 grams milk kefir

2.5 grams instant yeast

POOLISH

1 Combine the instant yeast, both flours, and the milk kefir, mixing thoroughly.

2 Leave to ferment overnight at room temperature in a sealed container that is large enough to allow the poolish to double in size.

Fennel Oil

INGREDIENTS

240 grams sunflower oil

32 grams fennel fronds

8 grams fennel seeds

DIRECTIONS

1 Put the oil and the fennel fronds and seeds in a small pot and infuse over low heat for 25 to 30 minutes or until oil is strongly flavored.

2 Strain and put aside.

Honey Glaze

INGREDIENTS

115 grams honey

30 grams milk kefir

2.2 grams salt

DIRECTIONS

1 Using the whisk attachment on your stand mixer, whip all ingredients at medium speed until thick and glossy.

TIP: Milk kefir is commercially available in the dairy department of many markets. It's a fermented milk similar to thin, drinkable yogurt. It's prepared by inoculating cow, sheep, or goat milk with kefir grains.

Honey Granola Bars

Courtesy of Chef Patty Pulliam

These fabulous granola bars can be mixed up with any nut/seed/dried fruit combo that suits your fancy! It's the perfect, healthy, take-along snack to stave off hunger!

PREP TIME: 20 MIN	COOK TIME: 18 MIN	YIELD: APPROXIMATELY 20 BARS

INGREDIENTS

3 cups old-fashioned oats

2 cups unsweetened puffed wheat cereal

1 cup all-purpose flour

1/3 cup chopped walnuts

1/3 cup raisins

1 teaspoon baking soda

1. teaspoon ground cinnamon

1 cup honey

¼ cup sunflower oil

1 teaspoon vanilla extract

DIRECTIONS

1 Preheat oven to 350 degrees.

2 In a large bowl, combine all dry ingredients. In a small bowl, combine honey, oil, and vanilla; pour over oat mixture and mix well. (Mixture will be sticky.)

3 Press into a 13-x-9-inch sided pan lined with parchment paper. Bake 14 to 18 minutes or until set and edges are lightly browned. Cool on a wire rack. Cut into bars.

Focaccia with Honey, Prosciutto, and Grapes

Courtesy of Chef Zachary Golper, author, owner Bien Cuit Bakery. www.biencuit.com

I met Zachary when I was speaking at a honey summit for the National Honey Board. He is a great fan of including honey in his award-winning bakery and also has an amazing palate for distinguishing flavors in honey varietals. This bread needs no condiments or accompaniments. It is designed to be a rich, salty, sweet, and deeply flavorful afternoon snack, or to serve as its own course with dinner. It's perfect served in advance of any course containing alliums (garlic, scallion, shallot, leek, chive, or onion).

TIP

Have a digital scale that's set for measuring grams for the most accurate results.

PREP TIME: 30 MIN	COOK TIME: 25 MIN	YIELD: 4 SERVINGS

INGREDIENTS

300 grams biga (see the following recipe)

Dressing (see the following recipe)

250 grams semolina flour

6 grams salt

35 grams extra-virgin olive oil

40 grams honey

225 grams warm water

100 grams finely minced prosciutto (set aside at room temperature for at least one hour)

DIRECTIONS

1 Prepare the biga and allow it to mature for 15 to 18 hours before making the dough. (See the following recipe.)

2 Using a wooden spoon, combine all ingredients (except for the minced prosciutto) in a large bowl. There is no need for any kneading, but all ingredients must be thoroughly incorporated together.

3 Cover tightly and allow to ferment at room temperature for 2 hours, undisturbed.

4 On a well-floured surface, using a bowl scraper, gently turn the dough out of the bowl.

5 Lightly stretch the dough into a large square. Fold the right third on top of the middle third and then the left third on top of that. Now fold the top third onto the middle third and the bottom third on top of that. Turn upside down and gently place the dough back in the bowl. Tightly cover.

6 Allow to rest for 1 hour and repeat Step 5, the stretching into a square and folding process.

7 Allow to ferment for an additional hour. When the dough is turned out onto the table and stretched again into a large square, sprinkle the minced prosciutto across the entire surface of the dough. Now fold it as before.

8 Instead of placing the dough back into the bowl, place it instead onto a half sheet tray (lightly coated with extra-virgin olive oil). With oiled hands, massage the oil across the surface of your dough, making sure the entire dough is covered with oil.

9 After 1 hour, massage the dough with a little pressure to coax it in all directions, so that the dough covers the entire interior of the sheet pan. If you are unable to get the dough to stretch that much, wait 20 minutes and massage it out again. Depending on the strength of your flour, it may take 3 massages (an entire hour) to get the dough fully stretched into the sheet pan.

10 Allow the dough to rise to the height of the sides of the sheet pan. This may take up to 3 hours if your kitchen is a cool temperature.

11 Preheat your oven to 415 degrees.

12 Before baking, top the dough with halved Red Malaga, Catawba, Steuben, or Emperor grapes (Emperor are the best) spacing the halves 1 inch apart, cut side up. Gently push them into the dough until they are flush with the dough's surface.

13 Bake focaccia until the entire top is browned and when you thump it with your finger it makes a hollow sound (approximately 25 minutes, rotated 180 degrees once after 15 minutes).

14 While focaccia is baking, make the dressing (see the following recipe).

15 Using a pastry brush, apply the dressing across the top of your focaccia shortly after it comes out of the oven, while the bread is still very hot.

16 Remove the focaccia carefully from its pan using two spatulas from opposing angles and place the bread on a cooling rack to cool off completely before eating.

(continued)

Biga

125 grams milk (It's okay if it's cold. The biga will reach room temperature within an hour of mixing it.)

Pinch of yeast (approximately 0.25 grams)

175 grams semolina flour

1 Mix all ingredients together using a butter knife or small spatula. Place in a 2-quart container with an airtight lid.

2 Allow 15 to 18 hours to ferment at room temperature.

Dressing

50 grams extra-virgin olive oil

20 grams honey (I use milk thistle.)

5 rams rosé vinegar

1 gram finely ground sea salt

Pinch of finely ground fenugreek

Pinch of finely ground white pepper

1 Whisk together the ingredients until fully emulsified.

Honey Banana Oatmeal Pecan Bread

Courtesy of Joy Blackiston

This is a bread that includes all my favorite flavors in each bite. Once you try it, you'll want to scale up this recipe so you have more than one loaf on hand. You can substitute walnuts or hazelnuts for the pecans (but pecans are my fave).

PREP TIME: 20 MIN	COOK TIME: 55 MIN	YIELD: 1 LOAF

INGREDIENTS

½ cup unsalted butter (softened)

¼ cup honey

2 eggs

3 ripe bananas, mashed

¼ cup buttermilk

1 tablespoon vanilla

1 tablespoon baking powder

1 tablespoon baking soda

½ teaspoon salt

2 cups all-purpose, unbleached flour

½ cup regular oats

1 cup coarsely chopped raw pecans

DIRECTIONS

1 Preheat oven to 350 degrees.

2 In a medium bowl, cream together the butter and honey till smooth and creamy.

3 Beat in the eggs (one at a time).

4 Add the bananas, buttermilk, and vanilla. Mix until well blended.

5 Mix in the baking powder, baking soda, and salt

6 Blend in the remaining ingredients and pour into a buttered 9-x-5-x 3-inch loaf pan.

7 Bake for 55 minutes or until your cake tester comes out clean.

8 Cool on a wire rack.

Honey Cornmeal Muffins

Courtesy of Megan Forman, chef/co-owner, Gracious Bakery www.graciousbakery.com

These freshly milled cornmeal muffins use only wildflower honey and crystallized ginger as sweeteners.

TIP

Have a digital scale that's set for measuring grams for the most accurate results.

PREP TIME: 30 MIN	COOK TIME: 15 MIN	YIELD: 10–12 MUFFINS

INGREDIENTS

206 grams all-purpose flour

170 grams freshly milled cornmeal

½ teaspoon baking soda

2 teaspoons baking powder

½ teaspoon salt

235 grams whole milk

120 grams wildflower honey

50 grams egg

60 grams butter, melted and cooled

60 grams canola oil

100 grams diced crystallized ginger

DIRECTIONS

1 Preheat the oven to 375 degrees. Line muffin pans with muffin cups.

2 Whisk together the flour, cornmeal, baking soda, baking powder, and salt in a medium-sized bowl.

3 In another container, whisk together the milk, honey, and egg.

4 Pour the entire container of liquids into the bowl of flour; gently combine halfway. Add the butter and oil; stir until batter is homogenous. Allow batter to rest for 10 minutes.

5 Scoop the batter into the muffin cups, about ¾ full.

6 Bake the muffins for about 15 minutes, until the top is set and a toothpick inserted comes out clean.

7 Remove muffins from oven and when safe to handle, remove from pan and serve warm.

Honey Lavender Shortbread

Courtesy of Megan Forman, chef/co-owner, Gracious Bakery www.graciousbakery.com

This simple, classic cookie with earthy flavors is a best-seller at our stores.

PREP TIME: 20 MIN	COOK TIME: 15 MIN	YIELD: 25 COOKIES

INGREDIENTS

2 teaspoons freshly ground lavender flowers

¾ cup confectioners' sugar

¼ c buckwheat honey

16 ounces butter

4 cups all-purpose flour

1½ teaspoons salt

1 Tablespoon turbinado sugar (for garnish)

DIRECTIONS

1 Preheat the oven to 325 degrees.

2 In the bowl of a stand mixer fitted with the paddle attachment, cream together on speed 2 the ground lavender, confectioners' sugar, honey, and butter until pale yellow, light, and fluffy.

3 Stop the mixer. Scrape down the sides of the bowl. Add in the flour and salt. Combine all on speed 1 until incorporated thoroughly. Do not overmix.

4 Scrape the dough out onto a sheet of parchment paper (sized to fit your sheet pan). Place another sheet of parchment paper on top. Gently roll out the cookie dough to the length and width of the parchment, about ⅛-inch high.

5 Place the sheet of rolled-out dough on the sheet pan. Refrigerate for 1 hour until firm.

6 Remove from refrigerator. Peel off top side of the parchment and cut dough into 3-x-1¾-inch rectangles. Place individual cookies on a fresh sheet of parchment and line the sheet pan. Sprinkle the top with turbinado sugar.

7 Bake for about 15 minutes, or until light golden brown. Remove from oven; allow to cool completely before handling.

Honey Bourbon Pecan Pie

Courtesy of Joy Blackiston

We have served this with every major holiday meal for decades, made of course with dark wildflower honey from our own hives. Serve with a generous dollop of fresh, lightly sweetened whipped cream.

PREP TIME: 15 MIN	COOK TIME: 50 MIN	YIELD: 8 SERVINGS

INGREDIENTS

¼ cup sugar

3 tablespoons all-purpose flour

3 eggs, lightly beaten

1 cup dark wildflower honey

⅓ cup unsalted butter, melted

¼ teaspoon salt

1 teaspoon bourbon whiskey

1 cup pecans (coarsely chopped)

1 unbaked 9-inch pastry shell (typically comes frozen)

½ cup pecan halves (for garnish)

DIRECTIONS

1 In a small bowl, combine the sugar and flour. Stir in the eggs, honey, butter, bourbon, and salt. Add the chopped pecans and mix well.

2 Pour into pastry shell. Arrange pecan halves on top of the pie filling.

3 Cover edges loosely with foil to keep crust from overbrowning.

4 Bake at 350 degrees for 25 minutes. Remove foil and bake another 20 to 25 minutes longer or until a knife inserted in the center comes out clean.

5 Cool on a wire rack. Chill in the refrigerator before cutting and serving.

Chapter 17

Using Honey for Thirst-Quenching and Celebratory Beverages

oney is a wonderful, natural sweetener because it has flavor and sensory interest where refined sugar is just plain boring and sweet. So it's a terrific alternative and can be substituted in recipes of all kinds. In this chapter I include some of my favorite beverage recipes. There are some for both young and old. And there are some for grown-ups who enjoy the celebration of preparing and imbibing in a perfectly crafted cocktail (all made with honey, naturally).

Making Honey-Inspired Beverages

Here are some wonderful recipes to substitute honey as the sweetener. You can choose any varietal of honey; it's fun to experiment using different ones and taste the differences. Each will bring a different flavor profile to the beverage. I like to use lighter honeys (like clover) with light-colored, more delicate beverages (such as the recipe for Brinley's Honey Lemonade), and darker, more robust honeys (like buckwheat) with darker-colored, stronger flavored beverages (such as the recipe for Honey Ice Coffee Slushy).

Brinley's Honey Lemonade

Courtesy of Brinley Bergen

YIELD: MAKES 1 PITCHER

INGREDIENTS

1½ cups lemon juice
(approximately 8–10 lemons)

1½ cups honey syrup (see the
sidebar **"Easy recipe for honey
syrup"** later in this chapter)

3 cups water

Sliced lemons

DIRECTIONS

1 Combine the lemon juice, honey syrup, and water in a pitcher.
Top with lots of ice. Stir well to combine and chill all
ingredients.

2 Serve over fresh ice. Garnish each serving with a slice or two
of lemon.

Hot Chocolate with Peanut Butter and Honey

Courtesy of Howland Blackiston

YIELD: MAKES 4 SERVINGS

INGREDIENTS

4 tablespoons dark honey

4 cups milk

4 tablespoons cocoa powder

4 tablespoons creamy peanut
butter

DIRECTIONS

1 In a saucepan, add the milk and honey and heat over medium-
high heat. When the mixture comes to a boil, add the cocoa
powder.

2 After the cocoa dissolves, turn off the heat and add the peanut
butter. With a whisk, mix all ingredients so that the peanut
butter blends in and the hot chocolate reaches a creamy, thick
consistency. Serve immediately.

Iced Coffee Honey Slush

Courtesy of Howland Blackiston

YIELD: MAKES 4 SERVINGS

INGREDIENTS

2 ½ cups strong, fresh brewed coffee, chilled

1 cup coconut milk

6 tablespoons dark wildflower honey

DIRECTIONS

1 Pour chilled coffee into a 16-cube ice cube tray and freeze into solid cubes. Keep the cubes frozen.

2 Place coconut milk and wildflower honey in a blender. Add the 16 frozen cubes of cold-brew coffee concentrate. Pulse the blender at first; then run on high to turn the ingredients into a slushy (this may take a few minutes of pulsing).

3 Pour evenly into 4 small glasses and enjoy.

Monkey & Oats Smoothie

Courtesy of Howland Blackiston

YIELD: MAKES TWO 16-OUNCE SMOOTHIES

INGREDIENTS

1 cup vanilla yogurt

½ cup Quaker rolled oats

¾ cup milk

¼ teaspoon vanilla extract

¼ cup honey

2 bananas cut in 1-inch slices and frozen

DIRECTIONS

Combine all ingredients in a blender and pulse until the bananas are broken up; then blend on high until all the ingredients are combined into a smooth, creamy consistency. You can add additional milk if needed to blend the smoothie completely.

Mixing Honey-Based Cocktails

Here's a selection of cocktails using honey syrup as a key ingredient (the recipe for honey syrup is listed in the upcoming sidebar). Most of these cocktail recipes involve the ingredients first being shaken with ice and then strained into a glass of your choice filled with fresh ice (I prefer crushed ice). Each of the following recipes yields one serving. I have sorted the recipes by different types of spirits.

Special thanks to John S. Bliss, friend and mixologist, for sharing most of the recipes in this section. (Recipes not from John are noted as such.) Here's to you, John!

Gin

Gin is a favorite summertime spirit of mine. Here are a couple of recipes I like to savor as the warm summer sun sets on the horizon.

EASY RECIPE FOR HONEY SYRUP

Honey *syrup* is used in every one of these cocktail recipes (and in one of the non-boozie recipes in this chapter). It's more flavorful and healthier than the simple syrups that are traditionally made with white granulated sugar. You can make up a batch and store it in the refrigerator until it's 5 p.m. again. You may be wondering why you don't add pure honey to the cocktail. Why a honey syrup? It's because honey syrup dissolves faster and more easily in cold drinks than pure honey does. If you use pure honey, you'll likely wind up with a lumpy, gooey cocktail.

Simmer one part water and two parts honey until the honey dissolves completely (you can experiment with different honeys for different flavor profiles).

Let cool, bottle, cap tightly, and store in the refrigerator for 2-3 weeks.

Bee's Knees

INGREDIENTS

2 ounces gin

¾ ounce lemon juice

½ ounce honey syrup

DIRECTIONS

Shake with ice; strain into a glass with new ice.

Bee Sting

INGREDIENTS

2 ounces gin

¾ ounce lemon juice

¾ ounce honey syrup

½ ounce Ancho chili liqueur

DIRECTIONS

Shake with ice; strain into a glass with new ice.

Tequila

This Mexican distilled beverage, made from the blue agave plant, has become a favorite for many. Here are a few that are a big hit among my guests.

Blackberry Margarita

INGREDIENTS

1 ounce lime juice

1 ounce honey syrup

5 blackberries

5 mint leaves

2 ounces Anejo Tequila

DIRECTIONS

Shake with ice; strain into a margarita glass with new ice.

Honey Bee

INGREDIENTS

2 ounces Reposado Tequila

1 ounce honey syrup

¾ ounce lemon juice

DIRECTIONS

Shake with ice; strain into a glass with new ice.

Jose Wallbanger

INGREDIENTS

1 ounce mezcal

1 ounce Galliano

1 ounce lemon juice

1 ounce honey syrup

DIRECTIONS

Shake with ice; strain into a highball glass with new ice.

Vodka

Martinis these days are way more than gin, vermouth, and an olive. This delicious recipe is a real winner.

Pear Martini

INGREDIENTS

2 ounces vodka

2 ounces pear juice

1 ounce limoncello

½ ounce honey syrup

1 thin twist of lemon rind for garnish

DIRECTIONS

Shake with ice; strain into a traditional martini glass. Garnish with a thin twist of lemon rind.

Scotch whisky

A bar is incomplete without a bottle of Scotch. So put it to more use than just "Scotch on the rocks." These recipes will give you a whole new appreciation of one of the world's most famous spirits.

Beansley

INGREDIENTS

2 ounces Scotch

½ ounce Drambuie

½ ounce sweet vermouth

½ ounce Meyer lemon syrup

½ ounce honey syrup

DIRECTIONS

Shake with ice; strain into a glass with new ice.

Blosh

INGREDIENTS

2 ounces Scotch

½ ounce mezcal

½ ounce Canton ginger liqueur

½ ounce honey syrup

3 drops orange bitters

DIRECTIONS

Shake with ice; strain into glass with new ice

Gold Rush

INGREDIENTS

2 ounces Scotch

1 ounce honey syrup

¾ ounce lemon juice

DIRECTIONS

Shake with ice; strain into a glass with new ice.

NOTE: This cocktail also works with bourbon.

Grapefruit Penicillin

INGREDIENTS

2 ounces Scotch

1 ounce grapefruit juice

¾ ounce honey syrup

¼ ounce ginger liqueur

DIRECTIONS

Shake with ice; strain into a glass with new ice.

Scotch Carpano

INGREDIENTS

1½ ounce Scotch

¾ ounce Drambuie

¾ ounce sweet vermouth

½ ounce lemon juice

¼ ounce honey syrup

DIRECTIONS

Shake with ice; strain into a glass with new ice.

Whiskey (bourbon or rye)

Whiskey is my go-to choice when the days get short and the air is chilled. Any of these recipes will bring a warm glow to your cocktail hour.

Brown Derby

INGREDIENTS

2 ounces bourbon

1 ounce grapefruit juice

¾ ounce honey syrup

DIRECTIONS

Shake with ice; strain into a glass with new ice.

Honey Tangerine Sour

INGREDIENTS

2 ounces bourbon or rye

1½ ounces tangerine juice

½ ounce lemon juice

1 ounce honey syrup

DIRECTIONS

Shake with ice; strain into a glass with new ice.

Bees in the Attic

INGREDIENTS

1½ ounces rye

½ ounce black raspberry liqueur

½ ounce sweet vermouth

1 ounce grapefruit juice

Spoonful of honey (to taste)

DIRECTIONS

Shake with ice; strain into a glass with new ice.

Honey Old-Fashioned

Courtesy of Howland Blackiston

INGREDIENTS

½ ounce honey syrup

2 dashes Angostura bitters

2 dashes orange bitters

2 ounces bourbon or rye

½ slice orange

1 maraschino cherry

DIRECTIONS

1 Gently muddle the fruit, syrup and bitters in the bottom of a lowball glass; then add bourbon or rye.

2 Fill the glass with ice and stir.

Rum

I always associate rum with tropical islands, parties, fun, and vacations. So bring that fun home, anytime, and try these honey-inspired rum cocktails. By the way, that Bermuda recipe is my go-to poolside beverage.

Air Mail

INGREDIENTS

1 ounce light rum

½ ounce lime juice

½ ounce honey syrup

1 ounce champagne (or to taste)

Lime for garnish

DIRECTIONS

1 Shake rum, lime juice, and honey syrup with ice and strain.

2 Top with 1 ounce (or more) of champagne.

3 Serve in a champagne glass with a twist of lime.

Bermuda Honey Bee Punch

Courtesy of Howland Blackiston

INGREDIENTS

1 ounce Goslings Black Seal dark rum

1 ounce light rum

½ ounce honey syrup

2 ounces pineapple juice

2 ounces orange juice

1 dash Angostura bitters

1 teaspoon Drambuie

1 maraschino cherry for garnish

1 orange slice for garnish

DIRECTIONS

1 Shake rums, syrup, fruit juices, and bitters with ice; strain into a highball glass with new ice.

2 Float 1 teaspoon Drambuie on top.

3 Garnish with a cherry and an orange slice.

Chapter **18**

Pairing Honey with Cheese and Other Foods

Honey is hitting the sweet spot in the culinary world, taking its rightful place front and center on the menu in many restaurants across the country. It is being used as an unexpected ingredient to revamp classical dishes; to perk up cocktails; and most exciting, to highlight cheeses. Honey complements all food groups and it simply makes everyday foods taste better. Here we visit the land of milk and honey.

Creating the perfect honey pairings calls for an understanding of intensities, aromas, flavors, textures, and even visual appeal. In this chapter, I share with you the secrets of pairing honey with cheese from my years as a honey instructor at Murray's Cheese Shop in New York City. For those of you who are not familiar with Murray's, they are regarded as a legend in the world of cheese, and everyone who works there is as passionate about cheese as I am about honey. Over the past 15 years, I have worked with their cheese mongers to create the best honey and cheese pairings for classes at their Bleecker Street classroom. During our planning sessions, we would taste a wide variety of cheeses and honeys side by side and pick out flavors to curate interesting and educational tasting flights for attendees. Each pairing featured a mouth-watering combination of colors, aromas, flavors, and textures to tickle each participant's tongue. At the end of this chapter, you'll find some of my favorite pairings you can try at home or your next gathering.

Pairing Honey with Cheese

Move over tea and toast, honey has a new sidekick that will delight your taste buds while engaging your sense of culinary adventure. Have you tried pairing cheese with honey? It's a marriage made in heaven — think of it as a fresh spin on the classic milk and honey. Just imagine the soul-satisfying sweetness of honey drizzled over a creamy, salty cheese, now a bite of crusty bread, and say a fig or walnut for that extra tactile pleasure. If this sounds divine and ignites your curiosity, exploring this mouth-watering duo is for you. As you may expect, there are many styles and flavors of cheeses to complement every single beekeeper's honey. You'll want to stage your tasting session similar to Figure 18-1.

FIGURE 18-1:
A honey and cheese tasting session in progress.

Photo by C. Marina Marchese

Understanding the dynamics of honey and cheese

What would cheese be without honey bees? These pollinators are essential to the plants that livestock dine on to make cheese nutritious and delicious. So how do we begin to choose the best cheese to pair up with honey? It's simply a matter of mixing and matching flavors and textures that please you.

You can refer to Chapter 7 where we profile the 50 best honeys and choose the ones you would like to pair up with cheeses. You can start by understanding the weight or intensity of the honey you have on hand. Concentrate on the smell and flavor. Is it light and delicate (sage, black locust, or fireweed), midrange (linden, clover, or orange blossom), or pungent or intense (eucalyptus, buckwheat, or oilseed rape)?

It's a matter of taste

Once you have pinned down the flavors in your honey, it's time to pick a cheese.

There are no hard and fast rules for creating a magical combination; however, when it comes to pairing these two, it's all about the sensory experience. Like honey, cheese is a terroir-driven food, meaning the environmental variables in its production impart unique characteristics to the final product.

Applied to cheese, we consider the type of animal (cow, sheep, goat, or buffalo) milk from which the cheese was produced, the pasture that particular animal grazed on including the microclimate, seasonality, and the cheese maker's touch that make each cheese unique.

TIP

Check out the cheese counter at your local store and ask to taste a few samples. Taste a variety of cheeses — old, new, stinky, and blue. If this isn't possible, start with what you know or what you like. Taste and the enjoyment of foods are subjective, so experiment to find a combination that is pleasing to your palate.

Engaging all your senses makes your pairings and all food more enjoyable. Visual appeal and presentation is important to how we perceive all food, so express your personal style when creating pairings (see Figure 18-2). Honey should complement the cheese, so a little goes a long way. Cheese, like honey, is best served at room temperature, so remove your cheeses from the fridge 30 minutes before serving.

FIGURE 18-2:
A honey and cheese tasting plate from one of my pairing workshops.

Photo by C. Marina Marchese

SAY CHEESE!

All cheese is made from milk, and when animals are well fed, are able to graze freely, and eat a variety of grasses and grains, the cheese produced will be exceptional. Different animals make different kinds of milk. Here we venture into the sweet world of milk.

- Cows produce the most milk of any animal; they can produce up to 20 gallons a day! Their milk is composed of lactose and water, and it is often described as grassy and sweet.

- Sheep only produce 2 quarts of milk a day. Because the milk is very fatty and sweet, it is possible to make much more cheese with sheep's milk than cow's milk. The milk is generally creamy, yellow, and shiny. The flavors are barnyard, nutty, and oily.

- Goats produce only 2 gallons of milk a day, and their milk is described as goaty (animal), sour, and sometimes minerally and spicy. This milk is also high in nutrients.

- Water buffalos produce about 6 gallons of milk a day, and their milk is characterized as herbal, grassy, sweet, and aromatic, similar to eating flowers. It can be described as what we think traditional fresh milk should taste like. Think mozzarella.

Conjuring Creative Pairings

Are you ready to dive into honey and cheese? Here are my expert tips on what to take into account when mixing and matching this dynamic duo. I also include a few sample pairings for you to begin experimenting with. It won't be long before you find your favorite heavenly combo.

Choosing complementary duos

Pairing honeys with cheeses of equal aroma and flavor intensities creates balance.

Think about delicate honeys with delicate cheeses and rich, strong honeys with bold cheeses. *Note:* Sweet honeys balance out a salty, bitter, or acidic cheese.

Try ricotta cheese with light, delicate honeys, such as acacia, sage, or fireweed honey.

Pair blue or stinky cheeses with bold, dark honeys having animal or woody notes, such as heather, eucalyptus, or goldenrod.

Pair Brie or Gouda with wildflower honeys of medium intensity, such as thyme, macadamia, or gallberry honey.

Considering that opposites attract

Here we try the reverse theory: Opposites attract.

Pair light and sweet honeys with salty or blue cheeses or dark rustic honeys with light, mellow cheeses.

Contrast cheddar with a bold honey that has warm or vegetal notes, such as oil-seed rape or mimosa honey.

Contrast Parmigiano-Reggiano or Manchego with a sweet and mellow honey with vegetal or woody notes, such as rosemary or alfalfa honey.

Taking texture into account

The texture of our food adds to the overall enjoyment and is an important part of the sensory experience.

Who can resist chewing on honey in the comb or the fine granules of a whipped or crystallized honey? These two are all about the mouthfeel which adds another dimension to the overall tasting experience. Try equally textural cheeses that are gooey, crumbly, or firm.

Try honey in the comb with a smooth triple crème cheese.

Try crystallized honey with a crumbly or firm cheese.

Staying local

If it grew together, it goes together. Regional honey is naturally a perfect complement to the cheeses and foods that were produced in the same season or the same region. This is the true meaning of terroir or a taste of a particular place. Try local honeys with the local seasonal fruits, vegetables, meats, and cheese produced in your area.

Just go for it!

If you like it, then it is delicious! There's no right or wrong. Start with cheese and honey pairings that you know and like. When in doubt, choose a mild, soft cheese such as ricotta, cottage cheese, or even plain yogurt. They're light enough to let the honey shine and be the star. Don't be afraid to experiment. You never know what will become a favorite honey pairing!

Considering Classic Pairings of Honey and Food

Enjoying a variety of flavors and textures keeps tasting interesting, and you may just stumble upon your next can't-live-without combination. For added texture and flavor, serve some roasted or salted nuts like pistachios, walnuts, or macadamia. Try dried or fresh fruits — anything goes here, so pick your favorites in a range of tart cherries or apricots, fruity dates or raisins, or freshly sliced green apples or figs. Why not include fresh herbs like rosemary or mint to create some drama? Consider olives, cornichons, cured meats, or sweet peppers. Bread or crackers are a necessity as well as wine, beer, or mead to wash them down. Italians call these types of cold grazing plates *il pranzo del Contadina* or "plowman's lunch."

Choose what you like and experiment often. There are endless choices and combinations, so there's something for everyone. Test your choices on your family and friends by serving a platter of various food and honey pairings at your next holiday gathering. I guarantee lively conversation and loads of good cheer for all.

Read more about planning a honey-themed party in Chapter 19.

TIP

Following are ten classic honey and cheese pairings along with suggested accompaniments to get you started:

>> **Acacia honey and Pecorino Romano cheese**

- **Accompaniments:** Dried apricots, prosciutto, or almonds
- **Why it works:** Acacia honey is super sweet, light, and delicate, contrasting with the salty, waxy texture of Pecorino Romano cheese.

>> **Coriander honey and goat cheese**

- **Accompaniments:** Sesame breadsticks, macadamia nuts, or dried cherries
- **Why it works:** Goat cheese has a spreadable creamy texture and a sour note that is a perfect complement to bring out the coconut, white chocolate, floral, and spice flavors of coriander honey. In its crystallized state, the honey is crunchy and chewy, contrasting with the pasty goat cheese.

>> **Linden honey and Gouda cheese**

- **Accompaniments:** Sliced green apples, mustard pretzels, or Marcona almonds
- **Why it works:** Gouda cheese is creamy with nutty and sweet caramel notes, cutting the acidity of lime tree honey.

>> **Orange blossom honey and Gruyère**

- **Accompaniments:** Cornichons, rosemary sprigs, or Genoa salami
- **Why it works:** Both share similar warm, fruity notes. Gruyère has a super buttery texture and nutty flavors that are a perfect balance for the floral and stewed-fruit notes of orange blossom honey.

>> **Sourwood honey and Manchego cheese**

- **Accompaniments:** Pears, pecans, or wheat crackers
- **Why it works:** The rich, nutty, caramelly, cheesy, and caramelly maple notes of the honey complement sourwood's warm, spice notes of anise.

» **Red bamboo honey and triple cream cheese Brillat-Savarin**

- **Accompaniments:** Dried dates, buttery flatbreads, or Jamon
- **Why it works:** Brillat-Savarin is a buttery, luscious, decadent cheese with sweet, salty, and mushroom notes and is perfect for the warm, caramelly notes of bamboo honey.

» **Goldenrod honey and ricotta**

- **Accompaniments:** Fresh peaches, pine nuts, or mint leaves
- **Why it works:** Ricotta cheese is a neutral cheese that lets goldenrod's bright floral and fruity notes shine.

» **Eucalyptus honey and French mountain cheese Tomme**

- **Accompaniments:** Plums, Prosciutto di Parma or hazelnuts.
- **Why it works:** Both the eucalyptus honey and Tomme style cheese have funky, animal qualities to them. Eucalyptus is described as brothy with licorice and Tomme very minerally.

» **Chestnut honey and Brie cheese**

- **Accompaniments:** Figs, walnuts, olives, or green grapes
- **Why it works:** Chestnut honey is a complex mix of wood and warm fruit with an aromatic note. It can be quite bitter for some, but pairing it with the earthy and mushroom notes of a Brie cheese can balance that out.

» **Buckwheat honey and Stilton or blue cheese**

- **Accompaniments:** Cranberries, dark chocolate, or cashews
- **Why it works:** Buckwheat honey is a very intense-flavored honey with luscious malty notes of coffee beans and chocolate that can stand up to a buttery, stinky blue cheese.

» Deciding what to serve

» Setting up grazing boards and tasting flights

» Playing honey-themed games

Chapter **19**

Honey, Let's Have a Party

Tasting honey is fun, but tasting honey with friends can quickly turn into a yummy party. In this chapter, I share tips on how to serve and plate honey for mouth-watering grazing boards, delectable menus, and blind tasting games to play while indulging. The ways to incorporate honey into a party are endless, so have fun and feel free to use any of the ideas in this chapter.

Planning the Party

Celebrating the holidays or a special event with friends or family can be made sweeter by creating a theme around honey. Sweet sixteen birthdays, Rosh Hasha-nah, and weddings are events that naturally include honey in the theme, but you can add honey to any party to make it more delicious and engaging. Once you decide on your party theme, you are ready to set the date, determine your budget, and create your guest list.

TIP

If you're sending out invitations, why not make them honey themed? There are many websites that have free invitations to download or templates so you can design your own. Here are a few lines you may want to use when designing your own invites:

Buzz on over for a sweet party.

Honey, it's sure to bee a great time.

You're invited to a bee day party.

A honey theme is a nice idea for an anniversary party, an engagement party, or a wedding reception. Honey symbolizes love. For example, honey jars make the perfect party favor at each guest's place setting. Tie them up with a color-coordinated ribbon and a tag displaying your personal message. One favorite message is "Life is the flower for which love is the honey" by Victor Hugo (shown in the color section of this book).

Deciding on the theme

Next, decide what style your party will take on. Will it be a sit-down formal meal or a casual buffet-style party? How about a honey-themed pot luck? Or perhaps you just want to have a few friends over for some drinks, a honey tasting flight, or just to play some interactive honey games. The type of party you have will help you decide what serving items, décor, and menu you need to create.

Setting the mood

Dress up your party space by decorating around your theme to set a festive mood for your guests. Most party shops carry bee- and honey-themed décor, but also think about incorporating honeypots, dippers, and honey bears. Gold and amber are perfect color choices for balloons, napkins, tablecloths, and other festive items. Don't forget flowers and beeswax candles to create an inviting scent to make guests comfortable and relaxed.

CREATING A HONEY OF A PLAYLIST

Set the mood by choosing music that fits the theme and create a party playlist. Here are some of our honey-related favorites. Intersperse these with other tunes so you have a large enough playlist not to loop songs over and over. Here's your starting point:

- "A Taste of Honey" by The Beatles, The Temptations, Peter & Gordon
- "Honey Bee" by Lucinda Williams
- "Honey" by Bobby Goldsboro, Mariah Carey
- "Honey Child" by Bad Company
- "Honey Don't" by Ringo Starr, Carl Perkins
- "Honey for the Bees" by Alison Moyet
- "Honey Pie" by Barbara Streisand
- "Honey to the Bee" by Billie Piper
- "Honey, Honey" by Abba
- "Honey, I'm Home" by Shania Twain
- "Honeybee" by Blake Shelton
- "Honeycomb" by Jimmy Rogers
- "Honeysuckle Rose" by Fats Waller
- "I Always Cook with Honey" by Judy Collins
- "I Love You Honey but I Hate Your Friends" by Cheap Trick
- "I Love You Honey" by John Lee Hooker
- "Slow Like Honey" by Fiona Apple
- "Sugar Pie, Honey Bunch" by The Four Tops, Dolly Parton
- "Sweeter Than Honey" by Jefferson Starship
- "Syrup & Honey" by Duffy
- "Tupelo Honey" by Van Morrison
- "Wild Honey" by Nazareth, The Beach Boys

Assembling the Right Stuff

You'll need some everyday kitchen tools to make serving the various types of honeys with minimal drips and stickiness. Most you may have already like spoons, knives, and spatulas. Here are the best ways to serve up your liquid gold.

Liquid honey is best transferred into small serving bowls with a deep spoon or small ladle. If you need portion control for individual servings, try a measuring spoon. If possible, I suggest hard plastic or silicon. Avoid metal because it reacts with the flavor of the honey. The same goes for the serving bowls — glass or porcelain works well. Crystallized honey can be scooped out of the jar with two utensils — one to scoop and the other to scrape. So depending upon the firmness of the crystals, you can decide whether you need two spoons or a knife and a spoon. Crystallized honey that is firm and thick will need a strong spoon or knife, and pastier honey works best with two spoons.

TIP

Lightly grease your serving spoons with some vegetable or coconut oil so the honey slips easily off the spoon, leaving little waste and helping you to measure correctly. This also makes cleanup less sticky.

Honey in the comb is a beautiful site — perfectly shaped hexes filled with honey ready to ooze out into your mouth with each bite. A small chunk of comb or a slab on a white plate shows off the three-dimensional design that the bees worked so hard to produce. Honeycomb typically comes in a hard or flexible plastic container. The best way to remove it so it stays in one piece is to use a spatula and a fork. First, I use the spatula to gently loosen around the edges and separate the honeycomb from its plastic container. Take care not to force it out of its box; it is quite delicate and soft. With my other hand, I use the fork to stab the sides of the chunk where the cells (not the cappings) are to lift it out of the container. If you are just serving a small chunk, slice the honeycomb into a cube with a small thin knife and lift the piece you want, again stabbing the side with the fork so you don't upset the integrity of the wax cappings. Place the honeycomb on a dish or platter.

Developing Your Menu

Finally, I arrive at the fun part, planning a honey party menu. The number of guests attending determines how much food to prepare. Be sure to ask your guests if they have any food allergies or preferences. It's common for some to have dietary needs or preferences, so do ask and try to accommodate everyone. Generally, a dinner party menu should include multiple courses, and honey can easily fit into each one. You can always begin with light appetizers — hot or cold, simple finger foods work well, as do honey nuts or pretzel mixes with honey cocktails or mead. The main dish can be your favorite meat or fish with a few side dishes. Vegetarian or vegan options can also be delicious and may be necessary for some of your guests. Or you may prefer a bowl of soup and a salad with honey dressing, which can become a complete meal in itself. See Chapters 15 through 19 for recipes to make your party memorable.

REMEMBER

Don't forget dessert! Try a savory cheese and honey grazing board or sweet honey cake, pie, or ice cream.

How do you choose what to serve? Of course, something that is both yummy and easy to prepare. You can always ask guests to bring a little something; everybody has one favorite dish that they love to share.

Remember, we eat with our eyes, so presentation and a variety of colors, textures, and flavors will make your guests' mouths water (see Figure 19-1). Plan foods that can be prepared or bought ahead so you can relax and enjoy your own party. Once you have decided on your menu, stay organized by making a shopping list for all the foods and decorations at least two weeks before your party. You may consider foods that are specifically bee-pollinated, which can serve as an introduction into conversations about the importance of honey bees and their gift of honey.

FIGURE 19-1:
Here's an idea of how to stage a plate of food pairings for each of the honeys in the individual cups.

Photo by C. Marina Marchese

Creating Honey Grazing Boards

Cheese plates are traditionally served after a main meal in France and other European countries. They include a small cup of the local honey to drizzle on the cheese and bread or even an elegant touch of a chunk of honey still in the comb. Today the cheese platter has evolved into a grazing board that includes a wider selection of nibbles that complement both the cheese and the honey. Grazing boards can be served as an appetizer with before-dinner drinks, as a dessert, or as a light snack, or they can be the main meal.

Begin building a honey grazing board by choosing your favorite serving platter or an interesting wooden board; there are so many available, with various handles and embossed designs, in every size and weight. Decide how many people are grazing and whether it is a full meal or just a snack. Choose three to five different cheeses and plan on 4 to 6 ounces of cheese per person. I like to include at least three different varietals and styles of honey. Liquid honey in a small bowl with a small serving spoon or dipper is perfect. Crystallized honey for a unique texture and chunk honey as the headliner make a great conversation statement. Fill up the rest of the board with all sorts of finger foods. Anything goes — the more variety you include, the tastier it will be. Tickle your palate by choosing foods from the five different taste categories I mention in Chapter 9:

>> **Sweet:** Honey, dried fruit, or grapes

>> **Sour:** Cornichons, olives, or green apples

>> **Salty:** Nuts, crackers, or olives

>> **Bitter:** Dark chocolate, peppery crackers, or pickled radishes

>> **Umami:** Cured meat, savory dips, or cheese

Garnish with fresh herbs, edible flowers, or garden greens to make the ultimate presentation and woo your guests. Don't forget serving plates, cheese knives, mini serving spoons, and toothpicks so guests only touch the foods they want to take. There's no limit to the types of foods that you can include to dress up your board.

Piloting Tasting Flights

A tasting flight is simply a group of foods or drinks that share some similarities or differences. It can consist of three to eight honey samples or more if you like. In a nutshell, you will be tasting various honeys and making discoveries about each one through comparison and contrast. Take and compare notes along the way.

Prepare a honey tasting flight by gathering up a few things. You'll need some small plastic spoons, enough so each taster has a clean supply to taste each sample more than once — possibly three or four times. Each taster should have a bowl or plastic cup for clean spoons and another for used ones. Label each clearly so no one gets confused and grabs a used sticky spoon to taste the next honey. Everyone will need a glass of water, or you can mix up some honey cocktails from Chapter 17. Since this is a fun and entertaining tasting and not a formal evaluation of the honey samples, you don't have to be as strict about cleaning your palate. Have some paper or cloth napkins and some light nibbles ready for each guest. Nuts, pretzel sticks, or chips and dip are great to balance the sweetness of all the honeys. Afterwards, you can prepare a meal if you like. All these items can be staged on a tasting mat similar to the one in Figure 19-2.

FIGURE 19-2:
My honey tasting
party setup.

Photo by C. Marina Marchese

You'll have fun creating and staging tasting flights for friends and family members. Follow our photo below to get the sweetness started.

A *vertical tasting flight* is a group of honeys produced from different styles of honey, producers, or regions.

> **Sample vertical tasting flight:** Five types of crystallized honey or three types of orange blossom honey produced in the same region or by the same producer over a three-year period

On the other hand, *a horizontal tasting flight* is comparing honey harvested from similar floral sources, regions, or producers.

> **Sample horizontal tasting flight:** Four types of orange blossom honey, five honeys produced in Wisconsin, or three summer honeys

Here are a few ideas to plan your tasting flight:

>> **Light to dark:** You may simply taste a few honeys you have on hand from lightest to darkest or all light or all dark honeys.

>> **Single apiary:** Try tasting various harvests from the same apiary. These can be by season (spring, summer, or fall) or even by year.

>> **Travelers flight:** Perhaps you or a friend have just returned from a trip abroad or cross-country and brought back some honeys.

>> **Rare and exotic:** Taste honeys that you've never tasted before.

>> **Clover is not just clover:** Gather up a bunch of clover or wildflower honeys from a few stores in your area.

Compare and contrast.

Including Fun Honey Games

Playing games is a sure way to break the ice at a party. You'll connect with friends on a deeper level, and some will come out of their shell when the giggling starts.

Trio tasting game

In this game the host or one guest prepares three samples of honey in three identical dark-colored cups. Two of the honeys are the exact same sample, and the third sample is the odd one. Choose honeys that are similar in color and texture to make this game more challenging. If you don't have dark cups, blindfold each of the tasters and help them with tasting each sample. They must guess which of the three honeys is the odd one. The winner gets to prepare the next trio test and watch the victims squirm.

Honey spelling game

Each guest gets one cup containing the little pieces of paper or a stack of index cards with the individual letters to spell out "honey bee," "honey sommelier," or any other honey and bee-centric words and phrases. Next, have each guest scramble the letters to see how many new words they can come up with using some or all of the letters. The person who can come up with the most words wins!

Show Friends How It Went

I know your honey-themed party is going to be a sweet success! You'll find creative ways to make it special and memorable. Take photos to share, and send everyone home with a honey swag bag. Post your photos on your social media pages and create your own party hashtag. Here are a few good ones you can use: #BeeSweetHoneyParty #HeyHoneyLetsParty or #GetBuzzedHoney.

6

The Part of Tens

IN THIS PART . . .

Celebrate your honey knowledge and attend one of these top-ten honey festivals in the United States.

Find the answers to more than ten frequently asked questions about honey.

Discover the ten most amazing and special honeys you simply must experience.

Chapter **20**

Ten Great Honey Festivals

Bee and honey lovers unite! If you are looking to share your passion for all things honey, you've come to the right place. Honey festivals are popping up everywhere in the United States and around the world. You can celebrate everything about bees and honey and satisfy your sweet tooth while traveling the world. Now that's definitely something to buzz about. Sample local honey, mead, baked goods with honey, and honey-themed foods; check out bee-themed arts and crafts, bee demonstrations, and bee beards; participate in educational games and contests; enjoy parades and music — and maybe even witness the crowning of a Honey Princess and Queen.

This chapter covers ten terrific honey festivals around the United States.

TIP

Be sure to do an internet search for "Honey Festivals Near Me" to find even more.

Oregon Honey Festival, Ashland, Oregon

Get ready for a full weekend dedicated to honey and mead at the Oregon Honey Festival. Taste honey from around the great state of Oregon, find out about beekeeping, and discover how to catch a swarm. This festival hosts live musicians, balloon rides, and workshops on how to make seed bombs.

www.facebook.com/OregonHoneyFestival/

Philadelphia Honey Festival

At the Philadelphia Honey Festival, you can experience a live beehive up-close and personal, participate in a honey extraction, and watch as a crazy beekeeper wears a bee beard of thousands of live honey bees. Sit in on a workshop on how to cook with honey and garner some historical recipes made with honey.

https://phillyhoneyfest.com/

NYC Honey Week, Rockaway Beach

Celebrate the busy bees who pollinate the city that never sleeps during NYC Honey Week. This festival takes place at Rockaway Beach, just a short train ride or drive outside of Manhattan. Beekeepers line up along the shore offering a taste of their honey produced on the rooftops of some of the most famous skyscrapers in Gotham City. Visitors get to pick the best honeys, play bee-themed games, and draw on the boardwalk.

http://nychoneyweek.org/

Honey Bee Fest, New York

Tucked away in upstate New York, the Narrowsburg Honey Bee Fest is a honey festival that has been gaining popularity for its small-town warmth and famous honey parade. Visitors dress up in bee costumes and walk down Main Street while beekeepers offer tastes of their local honeys. There are bee murals on the town buildings, and even honey ice cream is served.

www.facebook.com/HoneyBeeFest/

Sweet Bee's Honey Festival, New York

Step back in time at the Museum Village in upstate Monroe, New York. You'll be delighted by this honey and artisan food festival. Listen to live music, get your face painted — with bees, of course — and even take a ride in a horse-drawn carriage. Mead and honey ciders are available to taste.

www.honeyfestival.com/

Vermont's Golden Honey Festival

Named one of the top ten events in Vermont, the Golden Honey Festival is part of the local farmers' market in Proctorsville. The many vendors all have products that are directly connected to bees and honey. You'll find crafters selling beeswax lip balms and soaps, honey-bee fabrics and t-shirts, and even a honey apple pizza!

www.goldenstageinn.com/vermont-honey-festival

Arizona Honeybee Festival, Phoenix

Find out about beekeeping, see how to cook with honey, and listen to live music with the entire family at the Arizona Honeybee Festival. Phoenix is where it all happens, with plenty of activities for youngsters. There's even a bee rescue and relocation class for those who want to save swarms or wild bees.

www.facebook.com/AZHoneybeeFest/

Michigan Honey Festival

The Michigan Honey Festival is hosted by a nonprofit organization dedicated to educating the public about honey bees. There are hands-on activities and bee demonstrations. Visitors can taste local honeys and enjoy live music. Vendors offer samples of their own honey, and bee-friendly plants are available for purchase. This event takes place each year in the famous town of Frankenmuth, which is decorated for Christmas year-round.

www.michiganhoneyfestival.com/

Tennessee Honey Festival

Experience the sweet taste of honey at this fun-filled festival in Nashville. Find out about the importance of bees and other pollinators. The event includes a full day of interactive bee classes in a mobile bee yard, food trucks, fun crafts for kids including hive painting, and lots of vendors offering honey. They even have a VIBee experience for guests who are interested.

https://tennesseehoneyfestival.com/

Uvalde Honey Festival, Texas

Located in historical Uvalde County, this festival celebrates its heritage and promotes honey-bee conservation. There's a magical street dance, great food, music, and crafts for everyone. There is also another honey festival in Austin where you can get a bee-themed henna tattoo and customize your own bee t-shirts at a printing station.

www.facebook.com/uvaldehoneyfestival/

Chapter **21**

More Than Ten Frequently Asked Questions about Honey

When I give a talk about honey, it seems that the same questions come up time and time again. I suspect the audience must think how clever I am to immediately come up with such a thoughtful answer. But what they don't know is that I've had tons of practice answering these same questions over and over.

So here are the top questions, some of which may be on your mind!

By the way, if you're thinking about hosting a honey-themed party, you can draw from these questions to create your own honey quiz ("Jeoparbee") with the winner getting a honey-inspired gift basket. (See Chapter 19 if you're considering a honey-themed soiree).

What's the best way to store honey once the jar has been opened?

Most people keep their honey in the original container with the lid on tight at room temperature. As long as the lid is secured, the honey's delicate balance of sugar and water qualities keep it fresh and stable. But keep in mind that over time honey naturally crystallizes, and in later stages, the color darkens and subtle flavor qualities fade. Honey is best enjoyed in the same year it was harvested. And if you are serious about retaining its original flavor profile a little longer, keep your honey in the refrigerator. That practice helps extend the honey's original flavor qualities.

Does honey ever spoil or go bad?

There's a yes-and-no answer to this question. Honey stored in sealed containers can remain edible for years, even centuries, but it may not taste very good. Or offer the full benefits. Even when kept securely in a jar, honey is susceptible to physical and chemical changes over time. It tends to darken and lose its aroma, flavor, and nutritional qualities. But it can remain edible for a few years. (See Chapter 22 to read about the 150-year-old honey we recently sampled and enjoyed.) Keep in mind that honey *will* spoil quicker when it's not kept in a sealed jar. Being hygroscopic, honey draws in moisture from the air when it's very humid. That raises the water content, causing it to ferment — and that spoils it.

Why does my honey look like it has two different layers?

Most honeys crystallize, some quicker than others. Crystallization is normal and a sign of quality. But the honey should crystallize evenly throughout the jar, not in layers. This separation is a defect that sometimes occurs following full crystallization. Over time, the crystal structure breaks down because the glucose is not as water soluble as the fructose. The glucose separates from the water and falls to the bottom of the jar as sugary crystals. The water and fructose rise to the top in a watery layer. The honey is now separated into two layers, and the water content at the top is quite high. As a result, the honey is on its way to fermenting. You can stir it or warm it to bring the honey back to liquid, but it will eventually return to the separation phase.

My honey has crystallized; can I get the honey liquid again?

Yes, you can, but why not enjoy the creamy or crunchy texture? If you must liquefy your honey for a specific recipe, warm some water and place your sealed glass jar in the warm water "bath." Stir it or shake it so it melts evenly and quickly. To preserve the original flavor profile of the honey, keep the water at 95 degrees Fahrenheit or lower, which is roughly the highest temperature that would occur inside a beehive. Overheating honey changes the flavor profile and can scorch your precious honey.

What's organic honey?

Some honey jars in stores are labeled as *organic*. It's a great marketing idea, but the claim of being organic is not necessarily an accurate representation for honeys produced in the United States. If you look carefully at such labels, you will likely find that the so-called "organic" honey is from outside the United States, where some organic certifications are regulated by the USDA. In fact, as of this writing, the USDA has not adopted any standards for certifying *honey* as organic in the United States. Therefore, no beekeepers in the United States can truthfully label or tell consumers that their honey is certified organic. Beekeepers may manage their bees without chemical treatment, but who can control where the bees forage? Given that bees forage nectar and pollen at will from flowers that are three to five miles in any direction from the hive (that's around 6,000 acres), there's no practical way to guarantee that none of the flowering plants in this huge area are subjected to chemical treatments or have not been genetically modified. For now, I suggest you read the label to determine the country of origin and decide for yourself whether you want organic or domestic honey, because you can't have both.

What's the difference between Grade A and Grade B honey?

Grade A honey must be very light in color; free of any visible crystals, foreign particles, or defects; and the moisture content must not be higher than 18.6 percent. This honey looks sparkling and flawless on the shelf and has visual appeal to many consumers. This grading system for honey is typically used by commercial honey producers and importers, so be aware that honeys that carry the grading system can also be heated and filtered. As a result, Grade A is what most people buy at the big grocery chains.

Grade B honey is one step below Grade A and must be reasonably free of visible crystals, foreign particles, and defects, and the moisture content must meet the 18.6 percent standard. Generally, this honey is as good as Grade A, but as you can see this system is based upon a rating system and is optional for sellers.

There are also grades C and D. They must be sold as baker's honey and not for direct human consumption.

What accounts for the different colors and flavors of honey?

The color, smell, and flavor characteristics of honey are a direct result of the floral sources the bees visit to collect nectar. Its terroir is also a factor: the soil, climate, and geography where it was produced. (To find out more about why honey looks, smells, and taste unique, see Chapter 11. And to discover how to appreciate the different flavors and tastes of honey, see Chapter 10.).

Why do honey bees make honey?

It is true that honey bees are the only bee species that produce honey. This is because the colony lives year-round spending the winter inside their hive. They produce and hoard honey to feed the colony during the winter, when there are no natural sources of nectar available and the colony is unable to forage during colder temperatures.

Honey is made from the nectar that the bees collect. Honey is the primary source of carbohydrates for the bees, and they use it to feed their young brood and themselves. The bees get their protein from the pollen they collect.

Is it true that eating local honey will relieve pollen-related allergies?

This is certainly a very popular belief; however, I am not aware of any scientific evidence to support these claims. One study, published by the American College of Allergy, Asthma & Immunology, *showed no difference among allergy sufferers who ate local honey, commercially processed honey, or a honey-flavored placebo.* However, rest assured that honey is a very healthy, fully digestible food with many nutritional benefits. (For more information on the healthful goodness of honey, see Chapters 4 and 5.)

Each drop of honey contains less than 1 percent of pollen, so you would have to consume a whole lot of honey regularly to build up your immunity to pollen allergies. Some people consume granules of fresh bee pollen orally. Bee pollen is sometimes sold at farmers' markets, health food stores, and may be available from your local beekeeper (if you're lucky enough to have one).

What does "raw" honey mean?

There is no legal definition of *raw*. I define raw honey as one that is untouched by humans, meaning not altered, heat treated or filtered in any way. It's just as it came from the hive.

How can I test my honey for authenticity?

You may have heard that not all honeys are what they say they are. You want your honey to be pure and natural, particularly when you read stories of honey fraud (see Chapter 8 for more on this topic). You can find lots of homegrown honey testing methods demonstrated online. Poppycock! Honey has to be tested in a lab for authenticity, which costs money. What's a consumer to do? Purchase your honey from local beekeepers and trusted retailers. (Find out how to shop smartly for honey in Chapter 13.)

Why does honey from the same local beekeeper taste different sometimes?

Maybe you purchased honey from a local beekeeper last year, and this year the same beekeeper's honey looks and tastes completely different. What's up with that? The colors and flavors of a honey are a result of the nectar sources bees visit to make the honey. It's possible that the beekeeper has hives in different locations, and the floral sources are quite different from one area to another. Or the beekeeper may have harvested the honey at different times of year when different flowers were in bloom, or it could be that because of changing environmental conditions from one year to the next, different nectar flows were stronger this year from last year.

Why shouldn't you feed honey to a baby?

Medical professionals advise that children should be at least 18 months old before honey is introduced into their diets. Spores of botulism are all around us and naturally find their way into all raw foods and may settle inside a honey jar. Mature digestive and immune systems can normally handle this type of bacteria; however, children under 18 months of age should not consume raw honey. Every individual responds uniquely to ingesting honey, so seek advice from a qualified medical care provider.

How many flowers must honey bees visit to make one pound of honey?

One single honey bee visits between 50 to 100 flowers during one foraging trip. So, to produce 1 pound of honey, she must fly 55,000 miles and visit 2 million flowers! Every drop of honey is precious, so lick your spoon.

How much honey does a worker honey bee make in her lifetime?

On average, a female worker bee produces only 1/12 teaspoon of honey in her short lifetime of approximately 45 days.

What famous Scottish liqueur is made with honey?

Drambuie. The Irish also make a good one branded as "Irish Mist." Delicious!

What's the U.S. per capita consumption of honey?

According to the National Honey Board, on average, each person in the United States consumes about 1.51 pounds of honey per year.

How many honey-producing colonies of bees are there in the United States?

The USDA estimates that there are approximately 2.68 million honey-producing colonies. This estimate is based on beekeepers who managed five or more colonies in 2010.

Do all bees make honey?

No, not all bees. There are 20,000 species of bees on earth, and only a small fraction of them make honey. The species of honey bee used for commercial beekeeping in the United States is known as *Apis mellifera.* And if you want to get technical, even in a colony of honey bees, it's only the female worker bees that collect nectar and actually make honey. The male drone bees don't collect nectar or make honey, nor does the female queen bee.

Chapter **22**

Ten Honeys for your Bucket List

H ere's my top-ten list for some of the most interesting, rarest, and most surprising honeys in the world. If you love honeys as much as I do, these simply must be on your bucket list. Oh, and if you're wondering, as of this writing, I've tasted all but one of these.

The Most Expensive Honey in the World: Elvish

Rock stars may rule the stage, but the king of all honey is called *Elvish*. This super-rare honey is produced deep inside a 1,800-meter cave in the Saricayir Dagi mountains of northeastern Turkey. Professional climbers are needed to scale the dangerous cavern in order to harvest it. The secret to this honey lies in the mineral-rich cave environment and the surrounding floral sources, which enhance the honey's flavor and medicinal qualities.

How pricey is this crazy rare honey? Elvish honey is on the market for $1,511 an ounce. Yep, and I'll do the math for you . . . that's $24,176 for a 1-pound jar of Elvish, more expensive than gold. And that's not counting the few bucks for the jar. By the way, the next time you are at the spice market in Istanbul, impress the locals and ask for Elvish honey by its Turkish name, *Peri Bali* meaning fairy honey.

Now, I bet you're wondering what it tastes like. Since I was unable to buck up enough dough to buy a jar, I have no idea. It looks like I'll have to sell quite a few of these books before I can let you know. Elvish has officially left the building.

Most Sacred Honey: Sidr

The Sidr tree, also known as the Jujube tree, produces one of the most coveted honeys. And it's produced in only one place in the entire world: the mountains of Hadramaut, Yemen. It is believed that the branches of this ancient evergreen tree were used to weave the crown of thorns that Jesus wore at his crucifixion. For this reason, sidr honey is also called *Christ's Thorns*. Sidr trees are uncultivated and are largely untouched by chemicals or pesticides. This ensures a pure honey as required by Muslim religious laws. Yemen's beekeepers further ensure the purity of their honey by harvesting it by hand, without the use of machinery of any kind. They're strict in their colony management. And they are willing to let their bees die rather than feed them sugar syrup during seasons with poor nectar flows.

Locals insist on purchasing their honey still in the comb, as this is a symbol of quality untouched by humans. Sidr honey is very viscous, buttery, and dark amber, like motor oil with an unusually high level of antioxidants.

Most-Difficult-to-Get Honey: Pitcairn Island

If you need your honey in a hurry, you better not order this luscious, creamy, white honey from the remote Pitcairn Island in the South Pacific. Settled in 1790 by mutineers from the HMS Bounty, Pitcairn Island has around 50 residents and 30 beehives, which produce all the honey. This island's bee population has been certified as disease free, and Pitcairn honey is one of the island's main economic resources. If you are inclined to hunt down this rare delicacy, it will take two to five months to receive approval from the government to export this booty, partly because vessels arrive and depart the island very infrequently, so cargo is unpredictable. The island is also pristine in that the bees are disease free, and the locals keep it that way by protecting their borders.

The color of this honey has an attractive pearlescent shimmer, and the fine crystals result in a creamy, dreamy explosion of tropical fruit flavors. Think mango, guava with passion flower, and rose hips wrapped up in one. It's well worth waiting for this spreadable cream bomb.

Most International Awards: Sourwood

If your love of honey has you starstruck, then it's time you got a taste of the internationally celebrated sourwood honey. Sourwood is a sorrel tree that has white bell-shaped, droopy flowers that resemble the fragrant lily of the valley but with sour smelling leaves. But don't let that put you off on its flavor. Sourwood honey has won so many awards it is equivalent to winning the Oscars for best honey. Just for starters, sourwood has won four gold medals at the National Honey Show in London for Best Honey in the World. Then again, it won at judging competitions in 2005 in Dublin, Ireland; 2009 in Montpellier, France; 2013 in Kiev, Ukraine; and 2015 in Deajeon, South Korea.

It's no secret sourwood is a worldwide favorite because of its unique flavor notes of baking spices, anise, gingerbread, and licorice, ending with a warm finish. It's delicate with just a touch of sour cutting the sweet taste. An all-time favorite, it's also slow to crystallize with an unusual green and gray color. No good reason to sour on sourwood honey, folks!

Most Bitter Honey: Strawberry Tree Honey

If you thought buckwheat and chestnut honeys were a bitter pill to swallow, there's a honey produced on the island of Sardinia, in parts of Greece, and in Portugal called strawberry tree honey. It will change everything you thought you knew about honey. It's not the typical strawberry plant that bares the edible berries we enjoy on shortcake with whipped cream. *Arbutus unedo* is the botanical name of Sardinia's most coveted honey, which they call *corbezzolo*. It's the kind of bitter that your tongue and brain need a few minutes to recover from.

I'll try to describe corbezzolo honey for you. But first, are you sitting down? Imagine licking an ash tray and chewing on a crispy green pepper with a bite of bitterness and a touch of fruitiness. At first the taste is quite shocking and unexpected. But this honey can grow on you quickly. Italians drizzle this honey on huge fried raviolis, called *seadas,* filled with their local mountain goat cheese as a warm dessert.

I promise you, corbezzolo is a honey you will never forget. It's produced only a few months out of the year on the windy mountains of the island. It will leave you with a lasting memory and, at $30.00 for a 4-ounce jar, a lighter pocketbook.

Psychedelic Mad Honey: Deli Bal

Would you believe that honey was used by ancient armies as a weapon to get sweet revenge on their enemies? But not just any honey would do the trick — it must specifically be Deli Bal, known throughout the world as the mad honey of Turkey. Historical documents reveal that in 65 BC during a war against King Mithradates of Pontu, the troops of Roman General Pompey happily ate the honey left by their enemies. The soldiers became paralyzed and incapacitated, and 1,000 were ambushed and killed from consuming this toxic honey.

Mad honey is only produced by honey bees who feed off of the nectar produced by certain rhododendron shrubs that grow on mountaintops surrounding the Black Sea. It has been well documented throughout history that if you eat a few teaspoons of Deli Bal honey, it can make you hallucinate, become dizzy and disoriented, and even lose consciousness. These crazy-making properties are because the nectar contains a compound called *grayanotoxins.* In fact, the locals consider Deli Bal's properties as medicinal (in small quantities). This honey is pretty easy to find on the internet, but we strongly recommend caution if you decide to consume it. What does it taste like, you ask? Let me try to remember.

Most Unique Texture: Ling Heather Honey

Ling heather honey has a unique quality called *thixotropism.* In its still state, this honey is firm and jellylike. However, when it is agitated or stirred, Ling becomes temporarily liquid and then returns back to a viscous jelly state. Because Ling honey is so thick, it is impossible to extract it using centrifugal force of a typical honey extractor. It must be hand-pressed out of the combs, which leaves permanent air bubbles suspended in its jellylike texture.

One of the true measures of the purity of Ling heather honey is determined by its ability to remain still when the jar is tilted. Another is the presence of small air bubbles that do not disappear. The color is reddish orange, and it has an unusually high water content measuring about 19–23 percent. Yet it remains stable.

Look for warm, smoky, woody, floral notes and a long finish. Honey-bee hives are loaded onto trucks to get to the boglands and moorland to access the tiny purple bell-shaped flower of the Calluna vulgaris. The locals call the Ling heather bloom *purple haze* because of the breathtaking views of the flowers in bloom covering the moors.

Volcanic Honey: Wenchi

About two hours west of Addis Ababa, Ethiopia, at 3,380 meters above sea level, lies the famous extinct Wenchi volcano. This crater has steep green sides and a crystal blue lake with therapeutic thermal waters at the bottom. Bees are kept by the locals in traditional bamboo cylinders woven together and covered with banana leaves. Their bees feed on the nectar of African redwood trees (Kosso) and tree heath (Hasta), producing a rich, unique-flavored honey influenced by the volcanic rock. The honey is hand harvested and pressed by a group of 40 beekeepers. They are part of a network created by Slow Food International to produce and preserve the best honeys of Ethiopia.

Wenchi honey is amber yellow in color with notes of floral and roasted caramel (most likely from the excess smoke the beekeepers use to harvest this honey).

Silkiest Honey: Ulmo Honey

Hailing from a pristine rainforest in Chile, it cannot be disputed that Ulmo honey is one of the silkiest and creamiest honeys on the planet. It's rich in nutrients with similar antimicrobial active properties rivaling New Zealand's famous Manuka. The South American bees visit the evergreen Ulmo trees because of their pretty and highly fragrant flowers that resemble a camelia flower. During the ulmo bloom, these white flowers cover the Patagonia hillsides, turning them snowy white, resembling a fresh dusting of winter snow.

The honey is nothing less than spectacular. It's amber colored with an unmatched silky, smooth texture with flavors that are a result of the surrounding rainforest. You'll taste buttery vanilla, caramel toffee, jasmine, aromatic cloves, and aniseed.

Most Buttery Honey: Kāmahi

New Zealand may be well known for its magical Manuka honey, but its other secret is Kāmahi honey. This evergreen tree is native to the island and grows in the most impressive forest in the pristine West Coast of the South Island. The flowers resemble long bottle brushes and produce nectar in the summer, which is November/December below the equator, and are a bee magnet.

This pale, lemon-yellow-colored honey has a rich, sticky texture, and the flavor is reminiscent of toffee, vanilla, and buttered popcorn. So grab a jar of Kāmachi honey from the internet, some popcorn, and a good movie, and this may be the honey for your next date night.

7 Appendixes

IN THIS PART . . .

Browse a helpful glossary of honey-related terms.

Discover resources for all things honey, including suppliers, organizations, where to get certified as a tasting expert, and more.

Appendix A

Glossary

ABV: This acronym stands for "alcohol by volume." It's a standard measure of how much alcohol (ethanol) is contained in a given volume of an alcoholic beverage (expressed as a volume percent).

Adulteration: Decreasing or compromising the quality of honey by the addition of other ingredients, heating, or ultrafiltering for maximum profits, thereby deceiving the consumer.

Aftertaste: The finish or remaining flavors in your mouth when tasting honey.

American Apicultural Areas (AAA): Regions of the United States where there is optimum bee forage and terroir.

American Apitherapy Society (AAS): An organization dedicated to educating the public and healthcare community about the use of *apitherapy*.

Amino acids: A collection of organic compounds, the key elements of which are carbon, hydrogen, oxygen, and nitrogen. Proline is the main amino acid found in honey. Proline is added by the honey bee. If the honey has a value of proline below 180 milligrams per kilogram, this can indicate an adulteration of the honey, by sugar addition.

Animal: One of the nine flavor families which describes a gamey smell or flavor of a honey.

Apiary: This is the specific location where a hive(s) is kept (sometimes referred to as a beeyard).

Apicius: A collection of Roman cookery recipes, thought to have been compiled in the first century AD.

Apis mellifera: The scientific name for the European honey bee.

Apitherapy: The use of bee venom and products of beehives to promote health and healing.

Aroma: Odors or smells experienced through the nose when honey is in your mouth.

Artisan honey: Honey that is hand harvested using traditional methods in limited batches.

Astringent: The dry, puckering, trigeminal feeling in your mouth from tannins when you are tasting honey.

Beebread: Is a mixture of pollen and nectar or honey. Honey bees add other secretions and micro-organisms, which causes the pollen to ferment and release amino acids as a main source of nutrition for workers and larvae. Also called *ambrosia*.

Bee pollen: Flower pollen that is collected by honey bees, mixed with honey and enzymes, combed into tiny balls or granules, and carried back to the hive. Rich in B vitamins, enzymes, and minerals.

Bee venom: Bee venom is a chemical substance excreted by a bee's stinger. It's the venom that makes bee stings painful. But honey bee venom is also used in the practice of apitherapy.

Beehive: The "house" where a colony (family) of honey bees lives. In nature, it may be the hollow of an old tree. For the beekeeper, it usually is a boxlike structure containing frames of honeycomb.

Beeswax: The substance secreted by glands in the worker bee's abdomen that is used by the bees to build comb and cap cells. It can be harvested by the beekeeper and used to make candles, cosmetics, and other beeswax products.

Blending honey: The practice of mixing honey by humans from various botanical sources to create a distinctive color, odor, or flavor profile for the marketplace.

Bochet mead: A mead that involves caramelizing the honey before fermenting it into mead wine.

Brix: A measurement of the sugar content in the mead's "must" solution. It can be used to estimate the potential alcohol of the mead by multiplying the stated Brix by 0.55.

Brood: A term that refers to immature bees in the various stages of development before they have emerged from their cells as an adult bee (eggs, larvae, and pupae).

Burnt: A descriptor regarding the smell or flavor of a honey that has been overheated by the beekeeper.

Capped honey: The wax cap bees produce to cover cells containing honey, whereby the beekeeper knows the honey has completely cured and is ready to be harvested. The wax cap serves like a cork on a wine bottle, protecting the honey from spoilage.

Carboy: A glass vessel used to ferment and age mead in.

Chemical: One of the nine flavor families which describes a medicinal smell or flavor of a honey.

Chemical and pollen analyses: Tests performed in the laboratory to identify the chemical composition or pollen profile of a honey sample.

Citrus: A descriptor in the fruity flavor family to describe the sour fruity smell or flavor of a honey.

Clarification: A mead-making process involving the *fining* and *filtration* of mead to remove suspended solids from the mead and give it sparkling clarity.

Clarity: The evaluation of honey that describes everything visual about the honey excluding its color.

Codex Alimentarius: A collection of internationally recognized voluntary guidelines, standards, and codes of practice and other recommendations relating to foods, food production, and food safety.

Colony: A family of bees (worker bees, drones, and a queen) living together as a single social unit.

Color: The visual perception of a honey by our eyes in the way it reflects light.

Comb: A structure of hexagonal cells of wax; made by bees to store honey and also to raise brood.

Connoisseur: An expert in appreciation of aesthetics.

Crystallization: The natural process by which honey granulates and becomes a solid.

Cutting honey: The practice of adding various substances to honey, mainly sweet liquids, to increase bulk for monetary gain.

Cyser: This mead blends apple cider (juice) and honey. Thought to be the "strong drink" often referred to in biblical times.

Defects: Odors or flavors that should not be found in honey; often a result of the beekeeper's mismanagement.

Delicate: A descriptor to describe the lowest intensity in the smell or flavor of a honey.

Dyce method: The most common method to force honey to crystallize in order to create a fine and desirable texture. Developed by Elton Dyce in the mid-1930s.

Elixir: A potion with medicinal or healing qualities intended to be consumed.

Evaluation: An objective assessment of a honey and its sensory qualities.

Extractor: A round, stainless-steel machine that spins frames of honeycomb and separates the liquid honey from the beeswax via centrifugal force.

Fair Trade Certified Honey: A certification that verifies authentically sourced honey which pays fair wages directly to the beekeepers and their families who produce it.

Fermentation (process): A chemical reaction when making mead that results in the conversion of sugars to alcohol.

Fermentation valves: These are one-way airlock devices that enable CO_2 to be released during fermentation but prevent any oxygen, yeast, and bacteria from entering the fermenter and harming your mead.

Fermented honey: The breakdown of sugars in honey when the live yeast is activated when the honey's water content is more than 17 percent (for unifloral honeys) or over 24 percent (for calluna honey or other thixotrophic honeys). Fermentation is considered a defect, and fermented honey can't be legally sold for direct human consumption. Fermented honey is often sold as baker's quality honey.

Final gravity (FG): Using a hydrometer, this is the measurement of the density of finished mead. It's a useful measure because knowing this measurement and the *original gravity* measure, you can calculate the alcohol content of your finished mead.

Fining: A *clarification* process where flocculants, such as bentonite or egg white, are added to the mead to remove suspended solids.

Flavor: The combined experience of odor, taste, and *trigeminal sensations* in your mouth.

Flavor families: The nine general or broad categories of words to describe the smell and flavor of honey.

Floral: One of the nine flavor families which describes the various types of flowers in the smell or flavor of a honey.

Fortification: The process of adding pure alcohol or very strong spirit to a wine to increase its ABV.

Fructose: One of the simple sugars naturally found in honey and fruit, also called levulose.

Fruity: One of the nine flavor families which describes the various types of fruits in the smell or flavor of a honey.

Fume board: A special type of hive cover that can be sprayed with a repellant that forces the bees away from a honey super so that it can be removed from the hive and harvested by the beekeeper.

Gamey: A descriptor to describe the animal or funky smell or flavor of a honey.

Glucose oxidase: An enzyme that is added to nectar by the honey bee and catalyzes the oxidation of glucose into hydrogen peroxide.

Gluten free: Food containing no gluten, which is a mixture of two proteins. Gluten can cause celiac disease for anyone who is sensitive.

GMO: Genetically modified organisms, or living organisms whose genetic material has been artificially manipulated in the laboratory. Pollen from GMO plants can end up in honey.

Grazing board: An informal spread of mostly finger foods presented on a tray or platter that complement various styles of honey.

Gustatory: Concerned with tasting or the sense of taste.

Hive: Any structure where a colony of bees makes their home. A hive can be provided by a beekeeper or the hive can be a nest in the wild.

Honey fraud: Any act of adulterating honey for monetary gain or to avoid tariffs and often unknown to the consumer.

Honey grading system: International system to rate honey by quality from A to D. A is the highest quality, and D is the lowest.

Honey laundering: The act of manipulating the quality of honey to deceive the consumer for financial gain.

Honey sommelier: A person formally trained in the sensory analysis of honey. Coined by C. Marina Marchese in her first book, *Honeybee Lessons from an Accidental Beekeeper*.

Honey super: A component of a manmade beehive that is a box without a top or bottom which holds the frames of honey that the beekeeper will harvest.

Honeycomb: The beeswax hexagonal comb structure that has been filled with honey.

Honeygate: A term used by the environmental watchdog CSE (Center for Science and Environment) for their investigation into a "well-organized" honey adulterating business (such as surreptitiously adding sugar syrup to honey).

Hydromel: Similar to traditional mead, although it can be drier and typically has a lower alcohol content.

Hydrometer: An instrument used for measuring the specific gravity of liquids based on the concept of buoyancy. By measuring the specific gravity of mead before and after fermentation, you can calculate the ABV (alcohol by volume) of the product.

Hydroxymethylfurfural: An organic compound formed by the deterioration of fructose. HMF can form in sugar-containing food (such as honey), particularly as a result of heating or cooking.

Hygroscopic: A substance that will absorb moisture from the air when the relative humidity is high.

Intensity: The initial level of concentration of an odor or flavor.

Invertase: An enzyme produced by yeast that catalyzes the hydrolysis of sucrose, forming invert sugar. Also an enzyme produced by honey bees to break down the sucrose of nectar into glucose and fructose.

Kosher: Food prepared according to Jewish laws of food regulation.

Lees: This is the sediment that occurs during and after fermentation, and consists of dead yeast and other solids. The lees are separated from the mead by *racking*.

Mead: An alcoholic beverage made from the fermentation of honey.

Melissopalynology: The scientific study of pollen in honey.

Mellification: Refers to the making of honey. But the same word can also refer to the legendary process of steeping a human cadaver in honey (mellified man) to make a healing confection.

Melomel: A type of mead made with fruit juice(s) other than apples or grapes.

Metheglin: A mead made with the addition of various herbs and/or spices.

Morat: A mead made from honey, water, and the addition of fresh mulberries.

Must: The name for a mixture of honey, water and other ingredients. The *must* is what you start out with. Eventually it ferments into mead.

Nectar: A sugary liquid secreted by plants, especially within flowers, to encourage pollination by insects and other animals. It is collected by honey bees to make into honey.

Odor: A scent or smell experienced directly through the nose.

Olfactory: Relating to our sense of smell.

Olfactory bulb: A neural structure behind your nose that translates smells into information and memories.

Original gravity (OG): The initial or "original" gravity reading of the must. It is a measure of density. Water has a gravity of 1. The more honey you put in the must, the higher the original gravity will be. Use a hydrometer before fermentation to record the original gravity.

Oxidation: The degradation of mead through exposure to oxygen. In some aspects, oxygen plays a vital role in fermentation and the aging process of mead. But excessive exposure to oxygen later in the process can produce faults in the mead.

Oxymel: From the Latin "acid and honey," oxymel is a mixture of honey and vinegar, used as a medicine.

Pairing: Matching honey with foods or beverages to create a unique tasting experience.

Palette cleanser: Water and green apples to clear or neutralize your mouth in between tasting various honeys.

Papillae: Tiny bumps or taste buds on our tongue and in our mouth and throat where we experience the five taste sensations: sweet, sour, bitter, salty, and umami.

Persistence: The length of time a honey smell or flavor remains perceivable while in our mouth.

Pfund scale: A system used by the honey industry to analyze the color of honey by using measurements in millimeters.

Pitching: This is the term for adding the yeast to the must. You pitch the yeast into the must. Many recipes call for the yeast to first be mixed with warm water. It's best to follow the instructions that come with the yeast before you pitch it.

Pollen: The fine powdery granules that are the male reproductive cell of flowers. When bees, wind, or other pollinators move these grains of pollen to the female stamens inside a flower, it causes pollination, which fertilizes the flower. (Bees collect pollen as a protein food source.)

Primary ferment/fermentation: This is the first stage of fermentation once the wine ingredients have been combined.

Primary fermentation bucket (tank): A bucket or tank that is used to create the initial batch of must.

Propolis: A sticky resinous substance produced by honey bees from the sap of coniferous trees and their own enzymes. It has antiviral properties.

Pyment: This mead is a blend of red or white grape juice and honey.

Queen bee: A female bee, with fully developed ovaries, who is the only bee in a colony that produces male and female offspring — under normal circumstances. (There is usually only one queen to a colony.)

Racking: In making wine (mead), this is the process of siphoning off the liquid, leaving the dead yeast cells behind.

Refreshing: A descriptor to describe the *trigeminal sensation* of cooling in your mouth when tasting honey.

Residual sugar: The amount of sugars remaining in the mead once a wine (mead) ferment has completed.

Resinous: A descriptor to describe a woody smell or flavor of a honey.

Sack mead: A sweeter version of traditional mead.

Sack metheglin: This is a spiced metheglin style of mead, but sweeter as a result of adding more honey.

Scent memories: Personal memories directly related to the odors we experience from people, places, objects, and experiences.

Secondary ferment: This refers to the fermentation that occurs in the second container (likely a carboy), after you have siphoned the liquid out of the primary fermentation bucket/tank.

Sensory analysis: A method and tool originally developed to taste and evaluate wine, it's now being applied to honey.

Spicy: A descriptor to describe the *trigeminal sensation* of piquant in your mouth when tasting honey.

Spoiled: One of the nine flavor families which describes the various types of yeast or earthiness in the smell or flavor of a honey.

Starter: A batch of yeast that is prepared to be pitched into the wine (mead) must.

Sulfites: Compounds (such as potassium metabisulfite or sodium metabisulfite) which are sometimes added to mead to prevent oxidation, spoilage, or to stop further fermentation by the yeast.

Supertaster: Anyone with a sensitivity to the bitter sensation, which is attributed to the gene TAS2R38.

Surplus honey: Refers to the honey that is above and beyond what a colony needs for its own use. It is this "extra" honey that beekeepers harvest.

Tariff: A tax or duty paid on honey that is imported to a particular country to curb competition between domestic producers.

Taste: Referring to the five basic sensations humans can detect on their tongue: sweet, sour, salty, bitter, and umami.

Tasting flight: A selection or menu of various honeys tasted together in one sitting for evaluation or entertainment.

Tasting mat: A placemat to stage or organize your honey samples for a tasting.

Tasting notes: An organized list or journal of an evaluation of a honey.

Terroir: The French term to describe the various environmental conditions that affect the sensory characteristics of honey. They are geography, geology, climate, and bee foraging behavior.

Texture: The feel of a honey sample in your mouth.

Transshipping: The act of transporting honey cargo to various countries specifically to conceal the true origin of the honey and avoid tariffs.

Trigeminal sensations: A group of sensory experiences in your mouth triggered by your trigeminal nerves.

True Source honey: A voluntary system for anyone involved in international honey sourcing to demonstrate compliance by The True Source organization.

Ultrafiltering: The practice of applying high temperatures to honey in order to remove pollen, to conceal the region it was produced in and/or its botanical source.

Varietal honey: Also called unifloral, single origin, or mono-floral. Honey that is primarily produced from a single nectar source and conforms to the sensory characteristics of that varietal.

Varietals: Refers to a type of honey primarily from a single floral source, such as acacia or buckwheat.

Vegan: A philosophy and way of life that excludes the use of animal products.

Vegetal: One of the nine flavor families which describes the smell or flavor of green or dry plants in a honey.

Volatile organic compounds (VOCs): Any chemical that evaporates from honey that is responsible for its smell and taste.

Warm: One of the nine flavor families which describes the smell or flavor of confection-ary, lactic, or nut in a honey.

Warming: A descriptor to describe the *trigeminal sensation* of heat in your mouth when tasting honey.

Woody: One of the nine flavor families which describes a resinous or spicy smell or flavor in a honey.

Worker bee: A female honey bee that constitutes the majority of the colony's population. Worker bees perform all the chores to maintain the hive and colony, including honey production (except egg laying, which is done by the queen).

Appendix B

Helpful Honey Resources

As a new honey connoisseur, you'll welcome all the information that you can get your hands on. In this section I present some online resources that you will find mighty useful in your enjoyment and continuing education in the wonderful world of honey.

Craft Suppliers

After you read Chapter 5, you may want to try your hand at making some honey remedies at home. It's fun, and the resulting products are so good for you, friends, and family. They also make terrific gifts. Here are some of my favorite places to get the supplies and ingredients mentioned in the recipes.

Betterbee

In addition to offering beekeeping supplies, Betterbee has a great selection for candle making and soap making, and even a learning center with relevant articles and how-to information.

8 Meader Rd.
Greenwich, NY 12834
Phone 800-632-3379 or 518-314-0575
Email support@betterbee.com
Website www.betterbee.com

From Nature With Love

Offers an inspiring range of premium-quality, certified organic, conventional and complementary personal care ingredients for use within skin care, hair care, aromatherapy, massage, spa, herbalism, and soap-making applications.

Natural Sourcing, LLC
341 Christian St.
Oxford, CT 06478
Phone 800-520-2060 or 203-702-2500
Website www.fromnaturewithlove.com

Majestic Mountain Sage

A family-owned and operated, full-service supplier of raw materials to the hand-crafted soap and cosmetics industry.

Phone 435-755-0863
Website www.thesage.com

SKS Bottle & Packaging Inc.

Here's an inspiring site for selecting just the right tins, bottles, jars, tubes, and pump containers for your homemade, honey-inspired personal care products. Be sure to check out Chapter 5 for recipes.

10 Skyward Dr.
Saratoga Springs, NY 12866
Phone 518-880-6980, ext. 1
Website www.sks-bottle.com

Organizations and Conferences

Here are my favorite national and international beekeeping and honey associations. Joining one or two of these is a great idea because their publications alone are worth the price of membership (dues are usually modest). Most of these organizations sponsor meetings and conferences. Some have honey shows. Attending one of these meetings is a fantastic way to find out more about honey-related topics and meet some mighty nice people with similar interests.

The American Apitherapy Society Inc.

This nonprofit organization researches and promotes the benefits of using honey-bee products for medical use. Apitherapy encompasses the use of beehive products including honey, pollen, propolis, royal jelly, and bee venom. A journal is published by the society four times a year. Once a year, AAS organizes an apitherapy certification program.

Website www.apitherapy.org

American Beekeeping Federation

This nonprofit organization plays host to a large beekeeping conference and trade show each year. The meetings at these conferences are worth attending because they include a plethora of interesting presentations on honey bees, and of course honey-specific topics. There's always a large honey show as part of the conference. They have an excellent journal for their members. The organization's primary mission is to benefit commercial beekeepers and promote the benefits of beekeeping and bee-related products to the general public.

500 Discovery Parkway, Suite 125
Superior, CO 80027
Phone 404-760-2875
Email info@abfnet.org
Website www.abfnet.org

American Honey Producers

The American Honey Producers Association is an organization dedicated to promoting the common interest and general welfare of the American honey producer. The website provides the public and beekeepers with industry news, membership information, convention schedules, cooking tips, and other information.

P.O. Box 435
Mendon, UT 84325
Phone 281-900-9740
Website www.ahpanet.com

Apimondia: International Federation of Beekeepers' Associations

Apimondia is a huge international organization composed of national beekeeping associations from all over the world, representing more than 5 million members. The organization plays host to a large international conference and trade shows every other year. They host a great international honey show and competition.

Corso Vittorio Emanuele 101
I-00186 Roma
Italy
Phone +39 066852286
Fax +39 066852287
Website www.apimondia.org

The Bee Conservatory

An organization dedicated to protecting all bees and securing environmental and food justice through education, research, habitat creation, and advocacy.

Website https://thebeeconservancy.org/

International Honey Commission

A world network of honey and bee product science. Formed in 1990 in order to create a world honey standard. Objectives include creating new methods and criteria of honey and bee products.

Website www.ihc-platform.net/

National Honey Board

This agency, operating under the USDA, is an industry-funded agriculture promotion group that educates consumers about the benefits and uses of honey and honey products. The well-designed site is a great source for all kinds of information about honey. You'll find articles, facts, honey recipes, and plenty of beautiful images.

P.O. Box 2189
Longmont, CO 80502
Phone 303-776-2337
Website www.honey.com

National Honey Show, London

The National Honey Show is the United Kingdom's premier honey show with international classes, lectures, and workshops. Their annual honey show is held at the end of October in and around the London area. It boasts nearly 250 competitive classes to test your honey knowledge and evaluation skills. The show attracts beekeepers from all over the world to compete for the much-coveted trophies and prize cards.

Website www.honeyshow.co.uk/

True Source Honey

A nonprofit organization with more than 750 members comprised of beekeepers, honey importers and exporters, and packers to call attention to the problem of illegally sourced honey from China.

Website truesourcehoney.com/

Retail Honey-Related Sites

These retail sites sell some wonderful honeys that you simply can't find in most supermarkets. So when you are ready to taste some truly delicious honeys, give these folks a try.

Ames Farm, Minnesota

Unique single-source honey directly from a beekeeper made from hives and floral sources that are fully traceable.

Website www.amesfarm.com/

Apoidea, Pennsylvania

Nectar crafted in Pittsburgh and winner of the Good Food Award for their honey. Visit their new honey shop and café.

Website apoidea-apiary.com/

Asheville Bee Charmer, North Carolina

A honey destination offering 100 percent pure, raw, mono-floral honeys in the heart of North Carolina. Gifts, personal care, and home products including their own honey cookbook.

Website ashevillebeecharmer.com/

Astor Honey Company, NYC

An urban bee farm and shop producing honey from Queens and Brooklyn, New York.

Website astorapiaries.com/

Bee Seasonal Honey, Arizona

A great selection of organic honeys from Brazil by beekeepers.

Website beeseasonal.com/collections/organic-honey

Big Island Bees, Hawaii

Located on the big island of Hawaii, this site offers a selection of rare and exotic honeys and gift boxes.

Website www.bigislandbees.com

Deli Bal, Mad Honey, Turkey

If you are looking for the authentic mad honey from Turkey, here you are. Their website has some interesting history and FAQs to educate and guide your choices.

Website www.delibal.net/

Follow the Honey, Massachusetts

An artsy honey shop that carries everything bee and honey under the sun. Online ordering is available while they are temporarily closed.

Website www.followthehoney.com/

The French Farm

A wide selection of French honey sources — some rare, and all high-quality products.

Website https://thefrenchfarm.com/products/jams-honeys/honey/

Hani Honey, Florida

A full-service beekeeping family offering honey, body care products, and beeswax plus bee rescues, nucs, queens, and educational beekeeping classes.

Visit their new café and shop.

Website hanihoneycompany.com/

Honey New Zealand

Their 100 percent Manuka honey is certified to meet the New Zealand Government's incredibly high export standard. It's packed at the source in New Zealand and then tested twice by independent laboratories to ensure its authenticity and UMF level. Guaranteed and independently audited — their honey is true to label.

Website www.honeynz.com/

The London Honey Company

Purveyors of fine British and exotic honeys from the United Kingdom and beyond. Gift boxes and recipes can be found on their website.

Website thelondonhoneycompany.co.uk/

Manukora, New Zealand

Based in New Zealand, this site sells authentic New Zealand Manuka honey. This honey contains the highest amount of polyphenols and flavonoid compounds. The honey is packed with antioxidants that are responsible for some amazing health properties.

Website www.manukora.com

Maryiza Honey, Ethiopia

Raw, single-origin tree honey produced from traditional hives with a mission to combat deforestation, conserve biodiversity, and increase incomes for forest farmers invested in regenerative agroforestry.

Website www.maryiza.com/

Mieli Manias, Sardinia

Home of the award-winning bitter strawberry tree honey known as corbezzolo in Italian, made by a third-generation beekeeper.

Website www.mielimanias.it/

Mieli Thun, Italy

Pure mono-floral honeys directly from a beekeeper and honey sensory expert in Italy. You'll find mead, vinegar, and gift boxes.

Website www.mielithun.it/en

Miels d' Anicet, Canada

A diverse range of unifloral honeys produced in Quebec and the surrounding region. Visit their shop where you can taste samples of their honeys and shop their other bee-inspired products.

Website mielsdanicet.com/

Mountain Honey, Georgia

Known as the best honey in the world, this apiary produces awarding-winning sourwood in Northern Georgia and North Carolina.

Website mtnhoney.com/

Red Bee Honey, Connecticut

Founded by C. Marina Marchese (co-author of this book), this site offers a variety of 24 different single-origin honeys and gifts.

Website www.redbee.com

SerraMel, Portugal

A family business now in its fifth generation, they produce a nice selection of mono-floral honeys and fruit-infused honeys.

Website fr.serramel.com/produits/le-miel/

Mead-Making Sites

Ready to try your hand at making mead (wine made from honey)? Here are some resources for the equipment and ingredients you will need, plus all kinds of helpful information. Chapter 14 has great recipes for you to try.

Adventures in Homebrewing

A comprehensive site for mead, wine, and beer making. You will find equipment, tools, and supplies, as well as plenty of helpful information. Add this one to your favorites list.

Website: www.homebrewing.org

American Mead Makers Association

The AMMA is a professional, scientific, and educational nonprofit corporation and an industry voice for meaderies within, or doing business in, the United States, as well as a resource for home-based mead makers.

Website mead-makers.org/?v=7516fd43adaa

DIY Mead

Offers basic supplies and equipment for the hobbyist mead maker.

Website diymead.com/mead-making-equipment/

Got Mead?

Got Mead? has been around since 1996. It's the go-to online resource for those interested in drinking or making mead. The site produces podcasts and has all kinds of helpful information and recipes for making mead, drinking mead, shopping for mead, and mead-related events. It's a winner.

Website www.gotmead.com

Homebrewtalk.com

An online forum serving the interests of home brewers of all kinds. There's a good sub-forum for mead makers. Worth a visit.

Website www.homebrewtalk.com

Maltose Express

This wine- and beer-making supply business also sells honey, books, and equipment for mead making. And if you are ever near Monroe, Connecticut, their large retail store and the next-door brewery are terrific fun to visit. They offer free samples (if you are over 21).

Website www.maltosecart.com/

Places to Get Trained/Certified as a Honey Sensory Expert

There is currently only one place in the world to become truly certified as a honey sensory expert, and that's The Italian National Register of Experts in the Sensory Analysis of Honey (see below). But there are other places where you can learn the same skills used by the certified experts, and they too are listed below. Best of all, Chapters 9–12 of this book share these same skills.

Ambasciatori dei Mieli (AMI) (Honey Ambassadors)

Founded by one of the leading honey sensory experts and palynologists in Italy, this organization offers full training and certification in the sensory analysis of honey. Courses are held around Italy and only in Italian. The AMI runs the largest honey competition in Italy called *Concorso Tre Gocce d'Oro* or *Three Drops of Honey* every September.

Website www.ambasciatorimieli.it/

American Honey Tasting Society

This organization was founded in 2013 by Carla Marina Marchese, a co-author of this book and the first U.S. citizen to become a honey sensory expert. AHTS is the only organization in the United States granted accreditation by The Italian National Register of the Experts in the Sensory Analysis of Honey. The AHTS teaches the same four-day introductory course in Sensory Analysis of Honey, and students are awarded a certificate of completion that is recognized by the Register and is valid to continue your studies in Italy. Both online workshops and in-person courses are given throughout the year.

Website www.americanhoneytastingsociety.com

Honey Sensory Education

Founded by leading honey sensory experts in Bologna, Italy, this organization offers the same courses as the Italian National Register. The courses are in English and online, and in-person courses are held in Italy, the United Kingdom, and around the world.

Website www.beesources.com/en/honey-tasting-course-3/

The Italian National Register of Experts in the Sensory Analysis of Honey

Based in Bologna, Italy, this organization is the founder and world leader in honey sensory education and the only organization that offers the full training and certification for those who are interested in becoming a honey sensory expert. Their training courses are offered in Italian and now English. The entire program includes three courses of in-classroom training. Those who complete all three levels and pass the final exam can apply to become a member of the "Albo," the register of honey sensory experts. Members must maintain their membership and skills by attending refresher courses (in Bologna) and submitting a list of their participation in activities relating to honey education. Fewer than 500 people in the world are members.

Website www.albomiele.it/

London Honey Awards

A London-based honey and olive oil competition for quality and package design is now offering honey sensory education.

Website www.londonhoneyawards.com/london-honey-expert-sommelier-certification/

UC Davis Honey and Pollination Center

The University of California at Davis offers classes in beekeeping, mead making, nutrition, cooking, and honey education. Their honey sensory classes use standard sensory techniques and are offered online and in person.

Website honey.ucdavis.edu/

Index

About the Authors

C. Marina Marchese is a beekeeper, author, and founder of The American Honey Tasting Society and the brand Red Bee Honey. She is a member of the Italian National Register of Experts in the Sensory Analysis of Honey. Her books include *The Honey Connoisseur: Selecting, Tasting, and Pairing Honey* with Kim Flottum and *Honeybee: Lessons from an Accidental Beekeeper*, along with numerous articles. An avid world traveler, Marina has had the unique opportunity to taste hundreds of new and old world honeys maintaining an impressive private library of honey samples. She has appeared on numerous TV shows — *Dr. Oz*, *The Chew*, *The Untitled Action Bronson Show*, *Edible Nutmeg on the Road*, and *Weekends With Yankee* on PBS — and featured in Mastercard's small business ad. James Beard Award-winning author Rowan Jacobsen dubbed Marina the "Red Queen" in his book *American Terroir*. Marina is a proud graduate of The School of Visual Arts in New York City.

Howland Blackiston has been a backyard beekeeper since 1984. He's the author of the best-selling book, *Beekeeping For Dummies* (now in its fifth edition) and *Building Beehives For Dummies*. Howland has written many articles on bees, beekeeping, and honey, and appeared on dozens of television and radio programs (including The Discovery Channel, CNBC, CNN, NPR, Sirius Satellite Radio, and scores of regional shows). He has been a featured speaker at conferences and events in more than 40 countries. Howland is a past president of Connecticut's Back Yard Beekeepers Association, one of the nation's largest regional clubs for the hobbyist beekeeper.

Photo by Howland Blackiston

Dedication

We dedicate this book to you, the reader. Because by selecting *Honey For Dummies*, we see that you are no dummy for wanting to expand your understanding, knowledge, and sensory appreciation of this unique, healthy food that has no equal.

Authors' Acknowledgments

Our collaboration on this book was the result of one of those wonderful "just by chance" meetings that took place a couple of decades ago. Howland Blackiston, a hobbyist beekeeper, invited his neighbor Marina Marchese to visit the beehives he kept on his property. Marina watched mesmerized as Howland opened the hive with his bare hands, revealing tens of thousands of docile honey bees, and row after row of newly capped honey. Marina gingerly dipped her finger into a sticky cell and had her first taste of the freshest, most delicious honey. Marina was hooked. In fact, that experience changed her life. She put aside her career as an illustrator and designer to become a full-time beekeeper, with Howland as her mentor. It wasn't long before Marina launched her own brand, Red Bee Honey, and traveled to Italy to become certified as a honey sensory expert. Her enthusiasm and depth of knowledge regarding honey was infectious. Howland just had to learn more about honey. And so, Howland became the student, and Marina became his honey mentor. This is why our first acknowledgment goes to each other. We each thank the other for having expanded our knowledge and appreciation of honey bees and the amazing and delicious honey the bees produce.

Thanks also to our beekeeping and culinary friends who contributed their know-how. Many thanks to Patty Pulliam for her help with the chapter on making honey health remedies and personal care products. Also thanks to those culinary wizards contributing yummy honey-inspired recipes to the chapters on cooking, baking, beverages, and mead making: Brinley Bergen, Talon Bergen (Bergen House Meadery), John Bliss, Joy Blackiston, Chef Megan Forman, Chef Colleen Grapes, Chef Zachary Golper, Chef Alex Gunuey, Samantha Mauro, Albert Mikhitarian, Adam Noren, Chef Ethan Pikas, Chef Patty Pulliam, Chef Haralampus "Bobby" Saritsoglou, Chef Debra Ponzek, Ben Starr (Starrlight Mead Company), Marc J. Sievers, Chef Nick Stellino, and Chef and Honey Judge Michael Young, MBA.

Generous thanks to each of the following companies, individuals, and organizations that contributed to the book's visual content: Cook & Beals Inc., Glorybee, Bergen House Meadery, Sam Droege, Maltose Express, Professor Amihai Mazar (Institute of Archaeology at the Hebrew University of Jerusalem), Charles Mraz Jr., George Poiner, Jr. (OSU College of Science), the U.S. Department of Agriculture, and Dr. Bryant Vaughn.

And thanks to Brenda Renfoe for her valued assistance in keeping track of all kinds of details during the writing of this book.

Marina would like to acknowledge her partner in crime, V-Bee, who has not only put up with years of stings but also has embraced our sticky lifestyle yet never once acted like a drone. I am grateful that he does all the heavy lifting — in fact, he can lift more than 120 pounds of honey, and he keeps everything around our honey house buzzing while I chase this sweet passion. Also to my mentors in Italy, Gian Luigi Maracazzan and Raffaele Dall' Olio, who opened my eyes to the world of honey and have supported the work of the AHTS.

Howland would like to specifically acknowledge his loving wife, Joy, who is the queen bee of my universe. She has always been supportive of my unconventional whims and hobbies (and there are a lot of them), and never once did she make me feel like a dummy for asking her to share our lives with zillions of honey bees.

Writing this book was a labor of love, thanks to the busy bees at Wiley Publishing: Chrissy Guthrie, our development editor, who kept the project flowing; Tracy Boggier, our senior acquisitions editor; and copy editor Christine Pingleton, who made our written words sound very sweet. What a honey of a team!

— C. Marina Marchese & Howland Blackiston

Publisher's Acknowledgments

Senior Acquisitions Editor: Tracy Boggier

Managing Editor: Kristie Pyles

Editorial Project Manager and Development Editor: Christina N. Guthrie

Copy Editor: Christine Pingleton

Production Editor: Mohammed Zafar Ali

Cover Image: © Billion Photos/Shutterstock

Take dummies with you everywhere you go!

Whether you are excited about e-books, want more from the web, must have your mobile apps, or are swept up in social media, dummies makes everything easier.

Find us online!

dummies.com

Dummies is the global leader in the reference category and one of the most trusted and highly regarded brands in the world. No longer just focused on books, customers now have access to the dummies content they need in the format they want. Together we'll craft a solution that engages your customers, stands out from the competition, and helps you meet your goals.

Advertising & Sponsorships

Connect with an engaged audience on a powerful multimedia site, and position your message alongside expert how-to content. Dummies.com is a one-stop shop for free, online information and know-how curated by a team of experts.

- Targeted ads
- Video
- Email Marketing
- Microsites
- Sweepstakes sponsorship

20 MILLION PAGE VIEWS **EVERY SINGLE MONTH**

15 MILLION UNIQUE VISITORS PER MONTH

43% OF ALL VISITORS ACCESS THE SITE **VIA THEIR MOBILE DEVICES**

700,000 NEWSLETTER SUBSCRIPTIONS **TO THE INBOXES OF**

300,000 UNIQUE **INDIVIDUALS EVERY WEEK**

# of dummies

Custom Publishing

Reach a global audience in any language by creating a solution that will differentiate you from competitors, amplify your message, and encourage customers to make a buying decision.

- Apps
- Books
- eBooks
- Video
- Audio
- Webinars

Brand Licensing & Content

Leverage the strength of the world's most popular reference brand to reach new audiences and channels of distribution.

For more information, visit dummies.com/biz

dummies®
A Wiley Brand

PERSONAL ENRICHMENT

Staying Sharp
9781119187790
USA $26.00
CAN $31.99
UK £19.99

Facebook
9781119179030
USA $21.99
CAN $25.99
UK £16.99

Guitar
9781119293354
USA $24.99
CAN $29.99
UK £17.99

Investing
9781119293347
USA $22.99
CAN $27.99
UK £16.99

Beekeeping
9781119310068
USA $22.99
CAN $27.99
UK £16.99

Digital Photography
9781119235606
USA $24.99
CAN $29.99
UK £17.99

Meditation
9781119251163
USA $24.99
CAN $29.99
UK £17.99

Pregnancy
9781119235491
USA $26.99
CAN $31.99
UK £19.99

Samsung Galaxy S7
9781119279952
USA $24.99
CAN $29.99
UK £17.99

iPhone
9781119283133
USA $24.99
CAN $29.99
UK £17.99

Crocheting
9781119287117
USA $24.99
CAN $29.99
UK £16.99

Nutrition
9781119130246
USA $22.99
CAN $27.99
UK £16.99

PROFESSIONAL DEVELOPMENT

Windows 10
9781119311041
USA $24.99
CAN $29.99
UK £17.99

AutoCAD
9781119255796
USA $39.99
CAN $47.99
UK £27.99

Excel 2016
9781119293439
USA $26.99
CAN $31.99
UK £19.99

QuickBooks 2017
9781119281467
USA $26.99
CAN $31.99
UK £19.99

macOS Sierra
9781119280651
USA $29.99
CAN $35.99
UK £21.99

LinkedIn
9781119251132
USA $24.99
CAN $29.99
UK £17.99

Windows 10
9781119310563
USA $34.00
CAN $41.99
UK £24.99

SharePoint 2016
9781119181705
USA $24.99
CAN $35.99
UK £21.99

Fundamental Analysis
9781119263593
USA $26.99
CAN $31.99
UK £19.99

Networking
9781119257769
USA $29.99
CAN $35.99
UK £21.99

Office 2016
9781119293477
USA $26.99
CAN $31.99
UK £19.99

Office 365
9781119265313
USA $24.99
CAN $29.99
UK £17.99

Salesforce.com
9781119239314
USA $29.99
CAN $35.99
UK £21.99

Coding
9781119293323
USA $29.99
CAN $35.99
UK £21.99

dummies.com

dummies®
A Wiley Brand